Modern Movement Heritage

In the twentieth century, architecture, urban planning and landscape during a brief, exhilarating and unique period were transformed in parallel with the theory of relativity, cubism and abstraction in art, twelve tone music, scientific method, rational philosophy, economic and social theory, medical science and industrialism. Modern architecture was a cultural imperative which expressed innovative ideas, the early buildings retaining their potency to this day. It is as much the spirit which generated these forms as the forms themselves which represent a crucial ingredient of our intellectual heritage.

The built inheritance, which epitomises the dynamic spirit of this century, employed advanced technology which has succumbed to long term stresses, and the functional requirements which the buildings originally met have changed substantially. The preservation of significant buildings presents a demanding economic and physical problem. The continued life of both icon and ordinary in an economically driven world depends first upon a shared recognition of their cultural and social value and second, upon their continuing economic viability. Reconciliation of these two key factors lies at the heart of an international movement launched in Eindhoven in 1990 known as DOCOMOMO, an acronym standing for DOcumentation and COnservation of buildings, sites and neighbourhoods of the MOdern MOvement.

Modern Movement Heritage consists of nineteen chapters emanating from authors in eleven countries divided into three parts, Conjectures and Refutations, Strategies and Policies, and Case Studies; these are illustrated with 160 images. The Preface and Introduction by Robert Maxwell and Allen Cunningham provide an overview of the Modern Movement, its intellectual shortcomings, and its cultural significance.

**Dedicated
to
Christopher Dean
who
knew
for
certain
that
modernism
constituted
the
only
hope
for
the
future**

Modern Movement Heritage

Edited by

Allen Cunningham

E & FN SPON
An imprint of Routledge
London and New York

First published 1998
by E & FN SPON
An imprint of Routledge
11 New Fetter Lane, London EC4P 4EE

© 1998 Allen Cunningham
© 1998 John Allan, Chapter 2
© 1998 Neil Jackson, Chapter 16
© 1998 Stefan Hecker and Christian Müller, Chapter 19

Typeset in Frutiger by Solidus (Bristol) Limited

Printed and bound in Great Britain by the Bath Press

British Library Cataloguing in Publication Data
A catalogue record for this book is available from the British Library

Library of Congress Cataloguing in Publication Data
A catalogue record for this book has been requested

ISBN 0-419-23230-3

Contents

Stefan Hecker and Christian F. Müller

Figures

Contributors

John Allan is Principal in Avanti Architects Limited, London.

Cécile Briolle is a partner in Briolle-Marro-Repiquet Architectes, Hyères, France.

Agnès Cailliau is Architecte des Bâtiments de France, Nancy, France.

Maristella Casciato is an architectural historian and Professor at the Università di Roma, Tor Vergata, Italy.

Allen Cunningham is Visiting Professor at the University of Westminster, London, Editor of *The Journal of Architecture*, Chair of DOCOMOMO International Specialist Committee on Education and Secretary of the ISC Publications.

Marco D'Agostini is the Heritage Planning Analyst for the City of Vancouver and a founding member of DOCOMOMO BC.

Cristiana Marcosano Dell'Erba is an architect, Ph.D. in design in Rome, Italy.

Patrick Devanthéry is a partner in P. Devanthéry and I. Lamunière Architectes EPFL in Lausanne and Geneva, Switzerland.

András Ferkai is Professor of Architecture in Budapest, Hungary.

Stefan Hecker is an architect in Lucerne, Switzerland.

Hubert-Jan Henket is Principal of Architectenbureau Henket, Chairman and Founder of DOCOMOCO International and Professor at the Delft University of Technology, The Netherlands.

Hilde Heynen is an architectural theoretician at the Katholieke Universiteit, Leuven, Belgium.

Neil Jackson is Reader in Architectural History at the University of Nottingham, UK.

Dennis K. Johnson is Engineer at Wiss, Janney, Elstner Associates Inc., Chicago, USA.

Wessel de Jonge is the Secretary of DOCOMOMO International and an architect with Leodejongearchitecten in Rotterdam, The Netherlands.

Stephen J. Kelly is Architect and Engineer with Wiss, Janny, Elstner Associates Inc., Chicago, USA, and a founding member of the US chapter of DOCOMOMO.

Marieke Kuipers is an architectural historian at the Netherlands Department for Conservation in Zeist, and is secretary of DOCOMOMO International Specialist Committee on Registers.

Inès Lamunière is a partner in P. Devanthéry and I. Lamunière Architectes EPFL, Lausanne and Geneva, Switzerland.

Robert G. Lemon is an architect and the former Senior Heritage Planner for the city of Vancouver.

He is also Chair of the DOCOMOMO BC Working Party.

Aline Leroy is a journalist in Milan, Italy.

Robert Maxwell is Emeritus Professor of Architecture at Princeton University, USA.

John McAslan is Principal of John McAslan & Partners, London, UK.

Christian F. Müller is an architect with OMA in Rotterdam, The Netherlands.

Tapani Mustonen is an advisory architect with the Alvar Aalto Foundation, Tiilimäki, Finland.

Theodore H.M. Prudon is Professor of Historic Preservation at Columbia University and is the US co-ordinator for DOCOMOMO.

Nina Rappaport is an architectural historian, curator, architectural correspondent and New York co-ordinator for DOCOMOMO.

Jacques Repiquet is a partner in Briolle-Marro-Repiquet Architectes DPLG, Hyères, France.

Hugo Segawa is Professor of Architecture at the University of Sâo Paolo, Brazil.

Preface

Robert Maxwell

The documentation and conservation of historical artifacts produced during the high noon of the modern movement in architecture has something paradoxical about it, since the modern movement proclaimed the rejection of tradition and the end of history. The moment that celebrates the new while rejecting the old does not envisage the moment when the new itself becomes the old, still less that it may then be in need of support.

For the traditional progression of history, Modernism in architecture had substituted a progression of unlimited technological improvement, as if technology were truly outside of human culture, and could become the authentic measure. Abstraction – the method of science – was also seen as a means of generating new form independent from human foibles, and the act of abstraction was seen as the objective uncovering of a latent potency in nature, not as an exercise in personal caprice. The dichotomy between subjective and objective remained invisible. Modernism in literature and in the arts generally, did not produce a similar dichotomy, and no eyebrows are raised when attention is drawn to the way that such accepted Modernists as Joyce and Eliot, or Picasso and Braque, made abundant use from the beginning of allusion and innuendo, along with the unlimited possibilities provided through the new resource of abstraction. By claiming ontological purity, architecture claimed to be in possession of objective knowledge. Within architecture, the uses of allusion and innuendo became immediately suspect and in the 1970s, scandalous, by which time the ideology of Modernism as a technological progression had to be

reasserted in order to preserve the purity of its originating principles in engineering, an attitude that briefly resulted in the style we call 'high-tech', which is already succumbing to the expressive impulse.

The paradox was fed by the polemical ideology of such protagonists of the modern movement in architecture as J.J.P. Oud and Le Corbusier, who led the way in identifying architecture with engineering, thereby seeing it as a subject that develops through research and discovery, where the interest will always be in the new and not in the already known. Decisions in architectural design would now result from rational analysis of the functions, replacing the traditional practice of starting from precedent, which was suffused by convention and custom. That alone would avoid old 'mistakes' and allow the emergence of new things. The irony of supposing that innovation could be cumulative, and the radical become the norm, was not appreciated.

In particular, buildings were to be regarded as experimental, that is, as individual experiments, no longer of interest once conclusions had been drawn. The lessons learned would be fed into a new mode of practice to be available to all, a practical fund of information always changing, always improving, an accumulation of technological know-how which would take its due place as a part of the march of science, confirming the goal of material progress, and creating an undeniable progression in which, just as steam power for automobiles would be utterly replaced by internal combustion, and the telegraph would be replaced by the telephone, so all current building materials would be replaced by reinforced concrete.

This creed was reintroduced into architectural education in Britain by Richard Llewelyn Davies at the end of the 1950s, a period when there was a widespread attempt to rescue the dogma of a scientific architecture and build up an objective body of research. Such an outcome would fulfil the promises that had first been made in 1910, the fateful year when Le Corbusier worked for a time in the office of Peter Behrens and came under the spell of engineering. There was a feeling that World War Two had interrupted the theoretical development of modern architecture, which should now resume its course. During the 1960s the short-lived Hochschule für Gestaltung at Ulm attempted to revive the radical approach of the pre-war Bauhaus. The redemptive force of the new was further revitalised in this period by critics like Marshall McLuhan, who saw each invention in communication technology as super-seding the previous one, so that only the latest device had value. Under these impulses modernism itself took on a new face, the look of raw nature, the *vérité* of Brutalism. The Modernism of the 1920s was now seen as crypto-classicism, a revolution imperfectly realised, not sufficiently new. The New spoke of the future, and this voice was to remain a powerful influence which continues to exert its special appeal today.

Although in the heroic period of the 1920s there was artistic interest in new architecture, in the sense that it was discovering the form of the future, and so was innovative just as new art was innovative, there was a problem in deciding where the new-ness originated. If it resulted from an always improving field of objective knowledge, it could not exactly be a matter of the self-expression of the individual architect. In the Bauhaus, Walter Gropius maintained an ambiguous approach, praising individual artistic invention while encouraging group work as the true source of discovery and the means of achieving equality with industrial methods. At the Bauhaus there had always been from its Expressionist beginnings a place for art within architecture, but this place was rendered ambiguous by the desire to appeal to abstract principles, and by the use of abstract forms, which were regarded both as a gauge of good intentions and as a means of penetrating surface appearance and arriving at fundamental structure. The aim was to achieve objectivity. The great sin was *formalism,* which implied that personal expression had run away with objective research.

But this was a position that was difficult to maintain. A doubt arose as to whether an architecture that developed out of scientific analysis was properly to be regarded as art. This doubt was most clearly expressed by Hannes Meyer, when he claimed that architecture was simply *function times economy*; that is, it constituted a discipline where the outcome was determined by purely material considerations. It is worth noting that Meyer maintained his extreme point of view for only a limited interval, before softening it by allowing that *all art is organisation*, in the way that natural forms already demonstrate a principle of organisation, thus restoring a version of the Renaissance theory which saw all art as following Nature.

This point of view was widely dispersed among artists and architects. Sir Leslie Martin once told me that for his generation, trying to bring abstract art to Britain in the 1930s, the model of fundamental design was taken from nature, in its patterns of growth, its structures of organisation, the geometry of its organisms. D'Arcy Thompson's book *On Growth and Form*, of 1917, was given oracular status in drawing attention to the way that nature, consulting no principle but natural law, produced such aesthetic miracles as the spider's web, the snail shell, the logarithmic growth of leaves on a stem, the 'crown' formed by one drop in falling into the bowl of milk, and so on (see Figures P1–P3). Since engineering design follows natural law, and architecture was now a branch of engineering, there was no longer room for personal expression. Personal expression would lead to the exercise of a personal judgement, in an act of selecting and composing. As Hannes Meyer said, the idea of *composing* a dockyard installation was enough to make a cat laugh. Composition was essentially arbitrary, a sign of human weakness; it did not have the authority of natural selection.

But while a quasi-scientific status was claimed for architecture in theory, the practice of architecture remained in the hands of gifted individuals, and their individual judgements fell short of the theoretical model, and at the same time exceeded it. This ensured that architecture, in following the laws of nature, did not converge into a single objective mode of operation, but diverged into a wide range of possibilities. The methodology called for the rational analysis of function, and this is exactly what each architect of note set out to do. But, while engaged in doing this, each one continued to look for support to what other architects were doing, and without their realising it, their innovative efforts took on a group ideology. The results reflected group values more than they conformed to a single principle taken from nature. So although Modernism became established as a radical methodology, we have no difficulty now in distinguishing the different characters of Scandinavian design, of Italian design, of Greek design, in a historical sequence. We can now be grateful for a theoretical inadequacy that allowed inconsistencies to develop and different characters to emerge, and ensured that individual buildings of the modern movement, while sharing a common purpose, ended up as a highly diverse and differentiated set of artifacts.

The stated aim of functionalism was to free architecture from traditional forms (like Corinthian columns) and allow it to attend to functional imperatives and to social reality. It saw itself as part of a revolution, both scientific and political, and politics was an essential sub-text that linked it to the artist's criticism of society and made it part of the avant-garde. The new arose as much in art as it did in science. In practice, working necessarily in isolation, each individual architect found it *easier* to be an artist than to be a scientist. So the model of the artist as innovator remained powerful within the profession, even if the status was often denied.

However, since the figure of the artist as redefined during the Romantic Movement had been endowed with redemptive status, he could not be seen as simply a craftsman, still less as a propagandist, but must be a visionary, seeking a new reality, a new truth. The newness he revealed had to be investigated for its unexpectedness, for the strangeness it brought to life. Only in this way could it renew the spirit. From this link with art, the new functionalism quickly became part of a formal language, a question of style: the sin of formalism became the norm of revisionism. By 1932 Johnson and Hitchcock could speak of the International Style, and praise the Villa Savoye as a work of art. Attention switches to the indirect qualities of the thing-in-itself. The object, in its very strangeness, attracts a gaze that is avid for meaning. So the meaning of a modern building was not to be restricted to its incidental place in an unfolding body of knowledge, but was to be interpreted as a step in creative endeavour. It has taken half a century for the

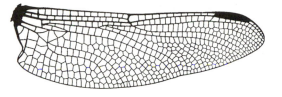

Figure P1 A dragonfly's wing
Source: On Growth and Form (D'Arcy Thompson 1917)

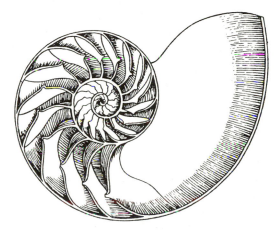

Figure P2 The shell of *Nautilus pompilius*
Source: On Growth and Form (D'Arcy Thompson 1917)

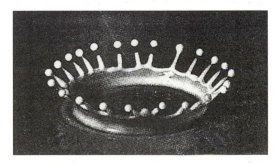

Figure P3 An instantaneous photograph of a 'splash' of milk
Source: On Growth and Form (D'Arcy Thompson 1917)

art of interpretation to turn back within architectural criticism, and explain the motives of Functionalism, the illusions it fostered, and the failures it engendered.

And ironically, many of these failures were technical. A ten-centimetre thick wall of reinforced concrete is a perfectly strong component of a two-storey house: fine as regards structure, but inadequate as soon as we factor in the requirements for sound insulation, surface decoration, energy conservation, weather protection. Yet it is amazing how many examples of modern construction are now at risk of falling down or being demolished because of inadequate construction. The conviction that reinforced concrete was the material of the future far outweighed the rational analysis of its physical properties. If we feel now that buildings showing these kinds of defects are worth preserving, it is not to economise on their replacement, but to recognise their value as a record of a quest, as part of a historical and cultural development that is crucial to our own identity; and in some instances, as an embodiment of values that make them part of an artistic and spiritual heritage.

Now we can ask a question that in the 1920s was not considered. Is Nature truly the model of the beautiful? Is it the basis of the aesthetic? Are the spider's web, the snail shell, the regular patterns of natural growth *aesthetic*? We see them as beautiful, but are they produced with the intention of being beautiful?

We are continually attracted by the beauty of Nature: the glory of sunsets, the sheen of still water, the blue of the summer sky, the colourful riot of the fall season, the majesty of the mountain range, the perpetual motion of the waterfall and its rainbow, and so on, without asking, as we do about human art: what does it mean? Such attributes are all part of Wordsworth's *pathetic fallacy,* an assumption that there exists a feeling *out there* analogous to our feeling *in here*. The natural world that we characterise as good is part of the biosphere we inhabit, only within which is human life possible, and those terms of life cannot be anything but ours, and cannot be anything but good. Our good automatically becomes our beautiful. Our aesthetic derives from an ethic.

So then we feel a strange fascination when we see a snake swallowing a lizard live, or a bird swallowing a struggling fish, or a lion devouring an antelope, and we definitely feel a frisson when we note how the lion goes for the isolated calf or the injured animal, thus following natural law and the statistics of probabilities, but ignoring our sense of fair play. From this comes our cynicism, since the Nature that produces the good also produces the heartless play of chance. Cynicism is the failure to draw together the loose ends. The very existence of a Nature red in tooth and claw then becomes the justification for capitalism, where, to exercise just a little hyperbole, only the fittest survive and only the rich make money.

Chance is heartless, and innocence is not a property recognised by Nature. If today we review the list of the dead resulting from a plane crash we say, *what bad luck, how about suing the airline*, but we no longer see it as the result of a higher moral judgement, an act of retribution for sins not sufficiently acknowledged. The religious spirit that sees God as providence faces a problem every time populations are overwhelmed by earthquake or flood, resulting in the destruction of the innocent along with the guilty, and making impossible a theory of religion as retribution and reward. Voltaire exposed this problem in his discussion of the Lisbon earthquake, and insisted that chance is chance and not destiny. That, in a way, sums up modernity. Chance and complexity together destroy the narrative, along with the values that entered it. We are on our own now. In our materialistic system, we are by now almost incapable of distinguishing ethic from aesthetic. Yet we are discontent with the loss of meaning, meaning is what we desire to recuperate.

The search for an aesthetic that follows natural law and is not the result of arbitrary human intervention continues today in the fascination with more complex natural patterns, the appeal of *chaos theory*, the allure of *fractals*, the charisma of accident in principle as the escape from the *voulu*. It would seem that the same hunger for certainty that created architecture in the image of engineering is now at work re-creating architecture in the image of landscape, that is, as accident. Natural accident. To be within Nature is still an essential aspect that saves us from arbitrariness, and raises our work to the level of principle. We seem unable to free ourselves from the domination of the past except by inventing new myths with the power to exorcise.

The critic's hope of building into our assessment of the new a correction factor that would regularly allow for our illusion, seems over-optimistic. All that we produce today shines with an aura, entices us into the future. In a scientific age, the future takes on the redemptive role that was previously supplied by theology. To this extent our moral universe is greatly curtailed. But instead of certainty, we now work within credibility, and the credibility of our value system is always on the wane, and has always to be renewed. The problem for our ethics today is how to re-establish moral principles in a relativistic framework, how to maintain human value in a universe of heartless chance, and without the sanction of eternal punishment.

To return to the artifact half a century later is to visit the site of a loss, of a dereliction. But it is also to recover the site of a spiritual impulse that renders us back our humanity.

Robert Maxwell
London, November 1997

Introduction

Allen Cunningham

Architecture throughout history may be described in terms of the myths and technologies which influence its making. Classical architecture was evolved by, and served, the most successful empire in Western history for over six hundred years. The myths which surround and maintain this architecture through its origins, include the tabernacle in the desert and wood construction which dictated overall form and abstracted detail, proportional systems derived from the intervals of musical harmony, urban arrangements supporting ritual observances around an assembly of allegorical gods all dictating forms manifested in materials which carry Nature's imprint. Such characteristics are invoked by some to perpetuate for eternity an architecture supposedly dictated by rules divinely given and therefore an expression of Nature's order. This is a weighty, mythical inheritance which Modernism challenged. There is, however, no reasonable adjustment to these myths or the craft technology which supported them which might enable classical rubric to be transposed *in toto* to a period dominated by intellectual invention and technical developments unprecedented in history.

Semper and Viollet-le-Duc made possible a tradition of the new, and by the end of the nineteenth century a confluence of cerebral activity and industrial sophistication created conditions to which every nuance of human activity responded. Bertrand Russell summarised the inheritance:

Western Europe and America have a practically homogeneous life which I should trace to three sources: (1) Greek culture; (2) Jewish religion and ethics; (3) Modern industrialism which itself is an outcome of modern science.[1]

From this the modern world and with it the modern movement evolved. However, as Aalto stated 'We cannot create new form where there is no new content'.[2] New forms were invented, inspired by new myths, to accompany the theory of relativity and the big bang theory of the origin of the universe, cubism, twelve tone music, psychology and sociology, the fourth dimension concept, industrialisation, scientific method, economic theory, rational philosophy and, not least, modern technology. A new architecture inspired by secular needs became the inevitable product of the prevailing intellectual, social and technical conditions.

Whereas the architecture which enriched past civilisations was evolved over periods ranging from hundreds to thousands of years, for that was the pace of history, the twentieth century has been in a hurry. When dynamic change, equated with progress, replaced the security of a perceived, static order, the expectations of a society in whose name traditional values appeared to have been abandoned were challenged and sometimes supplanted. Modern architecture evolved as a recognisable, fully fledged cultural phenomenon in less than one tenth the average time taken to conceive and construct a Gothic cathedral. Such pace has not only created perceptual anachronisms (suburban existence everywhere echoes popular 'taste' untouched by the value systems of modernism), but also encouraged specious declarations of its ephemeral and shallow intentions, its alien presence, and its death. Picasso expressed the difficulties with which the twentieth century artist must grapple when normative expectations are abandoned:

> Painters no longer live within a tradition and so each one of us must re-create an entire language. . . . No criterion can be applied to [us] a priori, since we don't believe in rigid standards any longer. In a certain sense, that's a liberation but at the same time it's an enormous limitation, because when the individuality of the artist begins to express itself, what the artist gains in the way of liberty he loses in the way of order . . .[3]

The myths and technologies surrounding the Modern Movement have provoked approbation and aversion, which dialectic is due for reappraisal.

Five conditions may be selected to illustrate the operative beliefs which signalled the transformation of architecture from the nineteenth century to versions of this productive art which continue to evolve around the world:

- proto-scientific methods were to be applied to architecture, thereby suppressing subjective licence in favour of objectivity – the implication being, if the right question is posed and rational procedures adopted, then the right answer will result;
- a belief in architectural determinism implied a causal link between architectural form and social behaviour, the integrity of the former leading to balance in the latter;
- technology was to be harnessed as a civilising force such that modern building would become, in Colin Rowe's words *a ritual celebration of the humane potential in a mechanised society'*;
- synthetic cubism and abstraction[4] in fine art were transposed thereby introducing transparency and layering to replace perspectival space as a conceptual device, and surface devoid of symbolism;
- consequent upon the science of medicine and the identification of tuberculosis as the price paid for overcrowded, polluted nineteenth century cities, prescriptions for 'ideal cities' were sought which would unify architecture and planning into urban forms to create environments with sunlight, space and fresh air, expressive of human aspirations served by mechanised transport.

Style, dogma and reliance upon tradition were, therefore, replaced with the description of a *modus operandi*.

Such priorities represented a displacement of static values with dynamic imperatives, paradigm shifts insinuating connections between the efficiency associated with Nature, and timeless beauty. The tradition from which the pioneers of the Modern Movement sprang reflected the truth, purity and lucidity of the Enlightenment. In his *'Entretien sur l'architecture'*, Viollet le Duc had stated: 'In architecture there are two necessary ways of being true. It must be true according to the programme and true according to the methods of construction'. The dictum of Frank Lloyd Wright in America was 'Truth to Materials', a monograph on this architect being titled 'In the Nature of Materials' a moral imperative evolved in the wake of Ruskin's Seven Lamps of Architecture XVI in which he states: 'Touching the false representation of material, the question is infinitely more simple [than structural dishonesty], and the law more sweeping; all such imitations are utterly base and inadmissible.' In Vienna, Adolph Loos declared ornament a crime being wasteful, deceptive and primitive. In defining the house as a machine for living, Le Corbusier was asserting that architecture could no longer continue as the response to subjective stylistic preferences but must evolve as the outcome of analytical procedure borrowed from science, emulating Nature as revealed and analysed by D'Arcy Thompson, and exploiting technical advances. The adoption of rational methodology implied any deviation akin to falsification and this, combined with economy of means as an ambition, reactivated the Utilitarian maxim, the greatest good for the greatest number, an ethical dimension new to architecture. Duiker called this process 'spiritual economy'; beauty no longer lay in the eye of the beholder but in the integrity of the process. Hannes Meyer, who succeeded Gropius at the Bauhaus, adopted an extreme position repudiating architecture as art: 'All things in this world are a product of the formula "Function x Economics"; so none of these things are works of art.' The 1937 prospectus for the Chicago Bauhaus offered a more palatable value basis: 'Art as the presentation of the significant and Science as the quest for reliable knowledge are mutually supporting. Each applies material for the other and each humanely enriches the other . . .' John Summerson identified the programme as the catalyst for a humanitarian agenda: '. . . the source of unity in modern architecture is in the social sphere, in other words in the architect's programme . . . [this being] the one new principle involved in modern architecture'. The programme has become 'a description of the spatial dimensions, spatial relationships and other physical conditions required for the convenient performance of specific functions . . . the resultant unity . . . is the unity of a process'.[5]

The extravagant ambitions for modern architecture have been questioned not only by traditionalists but also from within the cultural confines which it occupies. The modernist mind-set has, for example, been described by its detractors as combining physics envy, zeitgeist worship, object fixation and stradaphobia[6] which, if justified, would at best temper, and at worst remove the ethical dimension bestowed upon any version of formative ideologies. On this characterisation Modernism has continued along the traditional evolutionary path it claims so emphatically to eschew, and replaced a nineteenth century, eclectic, historically style-based inheritance with twentieth century, equally eclectic, pseudo-scientific method and imagery. The justification for this view is derived not from the heroic period of Modernism but from those who aped the imagery without regard for its agenda. An attempted escape from this bind has been the resort to the random expressionism of Postmodernism, hung off steel frames, contrived by culturally impoverished architects:

> Contemporary architecture bathes in the Pantheistic limbo of eclecticism. Torn between the dilemma for a frenetic search for novelty and an inherited social mission for a popular language, architecture leafs through history caricaturing remembrances. . . . Collective myth is systematically fractured into countless individualistic trivia, into fastidious and uncompassionate evasions of the human situation.[7]

The motives for a virtual abandonment of Modernist ideals stem from two sources, first the failure of much postwar architecture to meet political, social and technical expectations and second, the intellectual perception that Modernism had been too narrowly prescribed to serve diversified cultural interests. Political realities have deflected the role of architecture linked to social purpose and it is now dominated by commercial patronage. Image conscious corporations worldwide promote rampant eclecticism devoid of any ideological, let alone ethical, substance. Architects are now perceived as the hired guns of consumerism. Heidegger stated the danger: 'What is constant in objects produced merely for consumption is their false surface.' Modernism has, of course, survived such distractions and Martin Pawley's 'technology transfer', resulting in the 'tendency towards a virtuoso preoccupation with the tools of architecture rather than with its goals'[8] merely indicates the swing of the pendulum between myth and technology by architects liberated from the straightjacket of dogma.

Where there continues an assault on the Modern Movement, it may be divided between professional criticism, the propaganda leeched from this source which feeds public prejudice and the more direct response of a visually uneducated public to an admittedly unfamiliar, experiential world. Criticism has fed on misunderstanding of its intentions derived from the very propaganda issued to publicise the cause. A revisit to *The International Style* of 1932 discloses why, from the start, misreadings have taken root, the first of which is implicit in the title, deceptive in two fundamental respects. First is the false inference that a monolithic, co-ordinated, international movement existed and second, that it could be adequately described in terms of its outward, contingent appearance. The compositional rubric as summarised is indicative of the superficial interpretation:

> The principles are few and broad. . . . There is, first, a new conception of architecture as volume rather than mass. Secondly, regularity rather than axial symmetry serves as the chief means of ordering design. These two principles, with a third proscribing arbitrary applied decoration, mark the productions of the international style.[9]

This early attempt to establish Modernism as a new orthodoxy belied its true intentions. Among other myths which have perverted much of the discourse around Modernism and been presented as imperatives may be included functionalism and economy of means as ends in themselves, total detachment from precedent and exclusive resort to modern technologies. Modern architecture was even blamed for social breakdown.[10] John Entenza's commentary on the Eames' house is closer to expressing Modernism's intentions: 'This house presents an attempt to state an idea rather than a fixed architectural pattern, and it is as an attitude towards living that we wish to present it ... a natural and unaffected development of a modern building idiom.'[11] Modernism is dependent upon clear methodology but open ended, an intellectual condition described by Whitehead as 'an adventure in the clarification of thought, progressive and never final. But it is an advantage in which even partial success has importance.'

The critical appetite has been fed by technical inadequacies matched against modern expectations and dogged a cause which has been misrepresented as a finite project. What has become ever more certain is the necessity for a patient, revisionist dialogue to define and demonstrate a humanist Modernism, the optimistic cultural seeds of which were planted during a decade of unparalleled, dynamic, creative, intellectual activity which proliferated flawed masterpieces and left public comprehension far behind. Anachronistic divides have opened up between technical and visual expectations, fibreglass temple fronts lead to well-tempered environments, high-rise, neoclassical gobbledegook symbolises computerised corporations, veneered Tudor façades and leaded float-glass windows shelter micro-chip households, state of the art electronics are slung between fibrous plaster Corinthian, televisions glow from period cocktail cabinets, video cassettes and compact discs are stacked in Rococo repro side tables, mobile phone conversations emanate from period, four-poster beds, infrared operated rustic garage doors protect state of the art automobiles. A comment relating to modern art is equally apposite to architecture: 'We simply cannot afford another century in which the tastes of the public and those of its aesthetic commentators are as dramatically divergent as they have been during the years of modernism.'[12] Central to inculcating comprehension of the Modernist ethos in order to bridge this palpable cultural divide are innovative educational programmes[13] and first-hand experience of its remaining physical manifestations.

The conservation of our Modernist inheritance as an international movement was launched in 1990 (See Appendix A). At the heart of the enterprise lies a paradox, how can the conservation of buildings dedicated to the future and to change, be intellectually justified?

Architects of the Modern Movement were intent on building permeable borders: transparent walls, mobile installations and transportable houses. They even designed buildings which did not resist the wear and tear of time, but rather incorporated this inevitability into their structure.... The architects of the Modern Movement did not build fortresses or bunkers.... This makes the conservation of their permeable structures so difficult.[14]

The chairman of the Arts Council of Great Britain, Lord Gowrie, declared in 1994: 'If a building becomes redundant for the business it was originally built for it should be knocked down and replaced',[15] a sentiment the Futurists, Hannes Meyer or Mart Stam would have emphatically endorsed. In defiance of the sometimes ephemeral intentions however, the preservation of the object is, in our less certain times, crucial to the memory of the ideologies which spawned its making.

The salient word is 'redundant', for there are two contending interests. A building might become economically redundant, a matter of calculation, or be considered culturally redundant, a matter of qualitative judgement. We must acquire skills in the former in order to sustain arguments around the latter, which require a critical and evaluative repertoire to establish a degree of precision to match the fiscal equation. In conservation, priorities must be clearly defined in order to temper such dictats as that of the noble lord who, if taken literally, would have promoted the demolition of the Maison de Verre, Villa Savoye and La Tourette, Casa del Fascio, Einstein Tower, Van Nelle factory and Zonnestraal Sanatorium, the Schroeder and Robie houses, and so on. Only hardened cultural philistines would have applauded such vandalism.

For a building owner, the economic life of the investment is paramount. Buildings have to pay their way by serving human economic activities. Owners may be unaware, or uninterested, in the historic importance of their property and given the need to adapt it to new requirements may readily sacrifice a unique architectural inheritance in the interests of economic viability; perhaps, in common with Wilde's cynic, too many 'know the cost of everything and the value of nothing', indication of an educational void. The equation is complex and requires value judgements. Any attempt to place cultural values, which are eternal, on an ephemeral economic scale is essentially problematic, but such paradoxes must be addressed.

How may we equate our inheritance in qualitative terms? How is it possible to establish what place in our culture a work occupies? Arthur Koestler in 'The Art of Creation' describes the evaluations applied to the work of artists for as long as critical judgements have been consciously expressed:

'The measure of an artist's originality, put in the simplest terms, is the extent to which his selective emphasis deviates from the conventional norm and establishes new standards of relevance. All great innovations which inaugurate a new era, movement or school, consist in sudden shifts of a previously neglected aspect of experience, some blacked-out range of the existing spectrum. The decisive turning points in the history of every art form are discoveries which show the characteristic features already discussed: they uncover what has already been there: they are 'revolutionary', that is destructive and constructive: they compel us to revalue our values and impose a new set of rules on the eternal game.'

To that may be added Walter Benjamin's observation, which belies the myth that Modernism erupted from a fresh spring, because tradition is whatever claims an affinity with us: 'The uniqueness of a work of art is inseparable from its being embedded in the fabric of tradition.'

A critical aspect in the evaluative process centres upon authenticity. There is on-going debate among historians, critics and philosophers concerning the tampering with paintings by restorers. On the one hand are the London National Gallery restorers who will re-create missing or deteriorated areas of paint, (Figure 0.1) and on the other are those who maintain the only authentic brush strokes are those of the original artist, and these alone should represent any art work regardless of the extent of deterioration. The questions concerning authenticity in architecture are equally apposite, and equally problematic but they lie at the heart of any activity under a conservation banner.

The *Oxford English Dictionary* defines:

Figure 0.1 'The Ambassadors' by Hans Holbein (1497–1543). Significant areas of this painting have been reconstructed (e.g. the skull) by the National Gallery restorers

'Authentic' – original, first-hand , real, actual, genuine [as opposed to counterfeit, forged etc.]

'Authenticity' – as being true in substance, as being genuine.

'Genuine' – natural, pertaining to the original stock, pure-bred, not spurious, being as represented, real, true, not counterfeit, unadulterated.

'Author' – the person who originates or gives existence to anything.

Suppose we divide 'art' works into three categories according to their making. First are those that result from the conception of an author who manipulates material with his own hands, (clay, for example) or employing tools (as with painting or carving). The action from head to hand to material is immediate and contiguous. The second category is again conceived by an author, but who has in mind its replication, either through casting or printing, the final product resulting from a semi-industrial process but not immediately resulting from hands-on manipulation. The object may be scrutinised and signed. The action from head to hand is direct but the final product is at one remove.

Let us assume that the third category of object is also conceived by one author but is constructed, remote in time and distance, from instructions conveyed through drawings or other means, by individuals who played no part in the conceptual process. Most buildings and some fine art objects are thus fabricated. In this third category it is possible that the author never even confronts the object at all let alone intervenes physically in its making. Moholy Nagy 'painted' pictures by telephone when teaching at the Bauhaus, a polemical demonstration separating production from creativity. The action from head to hand is direct in formulating instructions but the fabrication is totally displaced,[16] a process which distinguishes (e.g.) architecture as idea from architecture as instrument.

The *Oxford English Dictionary* would concur that objects made by these three means are all 'authentic' when made. The question to address is which would retain its authenticity if damaged and repaired by other than the author or, in the more extreme case, if destroyed and reconstructed? What are the attributes which might cause different value judgements to be applied according to the means of making and the methods of restoration? Are there clear distinctions between the act of conceiving and the act of making which might affect subsequent value judgements and the attitude to succeeding intervention? How may the value of 'authorship' be scaled, and do our three categories of making imply three grades of authorship and, consequently, three grades of authenticity? How crucial to questions of authenticity is the extent to which an object expresses an 'idea' or 'ideology' in its form, its means of production, its materials? Marcel Duchamp's urinal, signed 'R. Mutt', the bottle rack and bicycle wheel mounted on a stool have been reproduced many times, Schwitters added whiskers to the upper lip of the iconic Mona Lisa and Yoko Ono signed blank sheets of paper with the injunction 'Add Color', each instance of which reinforce the message challenging conventional assumptions associated with 'Art'. If Duchamp, the Dadaists, Ono and hosts of others have failed to deflect our privileging of much creative output as 'Art', how may 'aura' be measured?

Much of the structure and virtually all visible surfaces of Mendelsohn's Pavilion at Bexhill (Figure 0.2) have been modified; the effect is wonderful, but is it authentic? The Carpenter Center in Cambridge, Massachusetts (Figure 0.3), the Curruchet House in La Plata, Argentina (Figure 0.4) and Heidi Weber Pavilion in Switzerland (Figure 0.5) were never seen

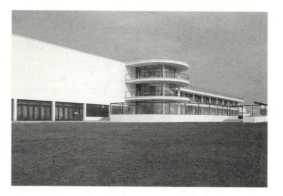

Figure 0.2 De La Warr Pavilion, (Eric Mendelsohn 1933–35) Bexhill-on-Sea, UK. Restored by John McAslan & Partners. Photograph by the author

Figure 0.3 The Carpenter Center, (Le Corbusier 1960–63) Cambridge, Massachusetts, USA, never seen by the architect. Photograph by the author

by the architect Le Corbusier but no one challenges their authenticity. Is Mies van der Rohe spinning in his grave at the reconstruction of his temporary pavilion in Barcelona (Figure 0.6) which has enabled

Figure 0.4 Curruchet House, (Le Corbusier 1949) La Plata, Argentina, never seen by the architect

Figure 0.5 Heidi Weber Pavilion, (Le Corbusier 1963–67) Switzerland, never seen by the architect

Figure 0.6 Barcelona Pavilion, (Mies van der Rohe 1929) Barcelona, Spain. Total reconstruction by Ignasi de Sola Morales. Photograph by the author

new insights and evaluation of an undisputed masterpiece to be conducted at levels which far exceed what a handful of black and white photographs might have generated? Is the second version any less authentic than the first, is it robbed of its aura and have its intrinsic qualities been compromised?

Just as it may, therefore, be conceded that the attitude towards restoring craft-based productions such as, Gaudí's Casa Mila or the Watts Towers of Simon Rodia, would pose distinctly different problems from those directed towards the Villa Savoye or Pessac houses which arise from their making, so the judgement would distinguish between buildings conceived as finite entities by, for example, Aalto, Loos, Wright or Scarpa which are composed of spaces having unique phenomenological attributes, and those conceived as universal space to serve ephemeral needs as indeterminate 'support structures' devised specifically to accommodate the free plan, external extension and internal modification in a permanently transitional state, Marc Piccard's Bains de Bellerive-Plage being a living example (Figure 0.7).

The operative imperative is to search for and conserve the specific ideologies which generated the physical realisation in tune with Wittgenstein's assertion: 'Architecture immortalises and glorifies something. Hence there can be no architecture where there is nothing to glorify.' Authenticity, thus, resides as much in the generating principles and functions to be fulfilled as in the fabric, factors which distinguish architecture as a productive art.

Architecture is not a discipline in the traditional academic sense for there is no clearly defined body of knowledge, no single organising principle, no central intellectual paradigm which serves it. While it is a truism that most theorising by architects is *post hoc*, it may nevertheless be cause for concern that conservation is being conducted by practitioners obliged to invent theories and methods on the hoof,

Figure 0.7 Bellerive-Plage, (Marc Piccard 1936–37) Lausanne, Switzerland. Photograph by Sergio Cavero

sometimes in exemplary fashion but often leaving much to be desired. The seductive vortex of technology in our obsessed times frequently diverts attention away from its proper role as servant rather than master of the conservation cause, in part because its palpable presence provides comfort in a theoretical vacuum, and in part because it serves immediately measurable levels of human need, a prerequisite of the architect's brief.

No single volume is able to encapsulate, let alone encompass, the complexities encountered in documenting and conserving modern architecture. The attempts to portray Modernism as a failed, new orthodoxy have been ill-founded, a critical deception. The chapters included here demonstrate Modernism as a heterogeneous intellectual search (Habermas described it 'an unfinished project'), sharing ideological territory but without any normative aspirations. The motive in conserving selected manifestations of Modernism is not generated by nostalgia, rather the significance rests on their success as manifestations of worthy principle; the presence of the object must not obscure the motive for its making, for that is where the cultural investment lies.

The purpose of conservation is not an end in itself, but a means of evaluating our inheritance and providing a platform for the future. In this respect modern architecture is not a special case for it shares common ground with every other area of our culture which retains examples spanning thousands of years from ships, aeroplanes, automobiles, canals and bridges, to settlements, houses, palaces, temples, cathedrals and monuments. In each category the grounds of justification must be established, the public persuaded and relevant conservation techniques evolved. Such are the causes around the Modern Movement Heritage this publication aspires to serve.

Notes

1 Bertrand Russell, '*The Problem of China*' (London, George Allen & Unwin, 1922) p. 96.
2 G. Schildt, *The Decisive Years*: Volume 3, p. 226.
3 Andrew Graham Dixon, '*A History of British Art*' (London, BBC Books, 1996). Pablo Picasso in conversation with Françoise Gilot, early 1950s.

4 Richard Padovan discusses this phenomenon in his review of six de Stijl publications (*Architectural Review* no 1055 January 1985):

> In the past the plastic arts have always been concerned with 'imaging'; with representing the world, or the bodies of animals and men. This was no less true of architecture than of the painted or carved image; a house or a city was, as Joseph Rykwert says of Adam's House in Paradise, 'an image of the occupants' bodies and a map, a model of the world's meaning'. The bases of architecture's power of representation, its function as image, were the *polarity* of inside and outside, and the *concentricity* of architectonic space and of the solid elements by which it was marked out around its human occupants; it represented man as a being *separate from*, existing in and surrounded by the world. The *nieuwe beelding* reversed this 'Classical' idea of the function of art. Instead of the depiction of the world of phenomena, its aim was the direct representation of the *noumenal* world of pure thought.

5 John Summerson, '*The Case for a Theory of Modern Architecture*' (London, *RIBA Journal*, June 1957).
6 These are terms coined by Colin Rowe, Denise Scott Brown and David Watkin.
7 Demetri Porphyrios *Classicism is not a Style* (London, Academy Editions/St Martins Press,1982) p. 52.
8 Axel Schultes, 'Observations on Berlin and Bonn' (*The Journal of Architecture*, Volume 2, Number 2, 1997) p. 104.
9 Henry-Russell Hitchcock and Philip Johnson *The International Style; Architecture since 1922* (New York, W.W. Norton & Company,1932) p. 20.
10 Adrian Forty, 'Le Corbusier's British reputation' (*Le Corbusier, Architect of the Century*, Arts Council, 1987, London) pp. 40–1:

> By the early 1970s, the notion that what was wrong with modern architcture was that it did not allow housing tenants to express their individuality was becoming a journalistic cliché. . . . In its place was to appear a very different critique of modern architecture: namely that it was making people ill, turning them to crime, and driving them mad. . . . melodramatic newspaper headlines 'Lonely High Rise Flats are Marriage Wreckers' (*Evening News*, 19 July 1976) and countless other stories bore an identical message, that modern architecture was responsible for social ills of all kinds.

11 John Entenza, *Arts & Architecture* (December, 1949) p. 27.
12 Waldemar Januszczak, 'Just a Pervert with a Pointed Moustache' (*The Sunday Times*, 14 September 1997).
13 Daniel Bernstein, Paolo Carrozzino, Joel Loïal, Carine Natali and Fabrice Pilorgé 'Using Twentieth Century Masterworks in School' (*The Journal of Architecture*, Volume 2, Number 2, 1997) pp. 145–9:

> This paper describes methods of learning based on the use of architectural masterpieces of the first half of the twentieth century. A particular case, involving the rehabilitation of Le Corbusier's Unité d'Habitation in Firminy, is presented in detail to demonstrate that the benefits of such methods encompass more than learning technology and detailing, and to show that such student work may have an intrinsic interest beyond the pedagogical.

14 Helmut Lethen, 'Between the Barrier and the Sieve: finding the border in the Modern Movement' (*The Journal of Architecture*, Volume 1, Number 4, 1996) pp. 302–3.
15 Lord Gowrie, *Building Design* 21 September 1994.
16 This issue is elaborated in Robin Evans' essay 'Translations from Drawing to Building' pp. 154–63 in '*Translations from Drawing to Building and Other Essays*' (AA Documents 2, 1997). He states the situation thus:

> My own suspicion of the enormous generative part played by architectural drawing stems from a brief period of teaching in an art college. Bringing with me the conviction that architecture and the visual arts were closely allied, I was soon struck by what seemed at the time the peculiar disadvantage under which architects labour, never working at it directly with the object of their thought, always working at it through some intervening medium, almost always the drawing, while painters and sculptors, who might spend time on preliminary sketches and maquettes, all ended up working on the thing itself which, naturally, absorbed most of their attention and effort. . . . The sketch and maquette are much closer to painting and sculpture than a drawing is to a building, and the process of development – the formulation – is rarely brought to a conclusion with these preliminary studies. Nearly always the most intense activity is the construction and manipulation of the final artifact, the purpose of preliminary studies being to give sufficient definition for final work to begin, not to provide a complete determination in advance, as in architectural drawing. The resulting displacement of effort and indirectness of access still seem to me to be distinguishing features of conventional architecture considered as a visual art . . .

PART I
CONJECTURES AND REFUTATIONS

Any presumption to theory in architecture is suspect first, because normative expectations sit uneasily in any creative context and second, because the record reveals much architectural theory as contrived, *post hoc* justification. Popper challenged the certainty which theory implies, introducing the dynamic procedure of conjecture and refutation as a means towards the progress of scientific knowledge which tempers notions of truth, a process requiring open-mindedness, imagination and a constant willingness to be corrected. The criticism of conjectures is a means of revealing mistakes and clarifying the nature of the problem on hand. The conservation movement, far from proceeding on such a methodological basis, has been dominated by pragmatism, in many cases of a finger-in-the-dyke order, because the tide of decay and its economic consequences has obliged urgent response. Neither the public or, in most cases, building owners, are susceptible to culturally originated pleas. Clarity must be sought, however, in order to inform action. Conjectures around conservation abound, but refutations are not, as yet, ordered or accessible. The three papers included in this section offer first, a *modus operandi* which proposes a means of ordering priorities, second, a plea to re-evaluate the *raison d'être* of conservation in terms of utilitarian human need and finally, an exploration into the paradox of conserving modern architecture. In the film *Twelve Angry Men*, a juror, desperate to reach a verdict, offers a Popperian procedure: 'Let's run it up the flag pole and see who salutes it!' It is with those who do not salute that the conservation cause must engage in debate.

1 The icon and the ordinary

Hubert-Jan Henket

Introduction

Although the approach towards preservation[1] in general does not differ between traditional and Modern Movement buildings, there are some specific aspects which demand tailor-made strategies for its relics. Those strategies relate to the selection of buildings to be retained, the level of intervention and to the paradox of conserving[2] Modern Movement buildings. In broad outline this chapter aims to structure a specific approach towards the Modern Movement.

If an architectural object is not properly maintained, however durably it may be built, it will either be changed functionally beyond recognition over time, or will, in a technical sense, fall to pieces. The two almost always go together, because when a building is functionally or economically obsolete, nobody will spend money on its upkeep. For example, great Roman temples were demolished when religious ideas changed; their columns were often reused as building materials for the foundations of Christian churches. Great Gothic cathedrals, like Notre Dame in Paris, were degraded to storage buildings or contractors' yards at the end of the eighteenth century. They were technical ruins by the time Viollet-le-Duc started his conservation work in the middle of the nineteenth century. And his efforts were only possible because interest in the Gothic heritage revived, so there were those prepared once again to spend money on these buildings. Ever since, the conservation of old and valuable buildings has become an increasingly accepted phenomenon. Twentieth century buildings, in particular Modern Movement buildings, are more vulnerable to the influences of time than their predecessors, and as a consequence, this exposes even more, the paradoxes of conservation.

A static object versus changing demand

Most buildings are erected to serve a purpose, otherwise no one would be prepared to invest in their realisation. In other words a building's *raison d'être* is being a utility. Yet we want a building to be more, we want it to touch our feelings, we want to elevate the utility above its everyday reality. Nietzsche said it clearly in 1872: 'The truth is ugly. We have art so that we aren't drowned by the truth.' In other words one might define architecture as utility art. And we could argue that this utility art becomes worthwhile if it has managed to capture the soul of a particular need and a particular context at a particular time, if it has managed to bring the prosaic and the poetic into equilibrium.

Yet, a given fact of existence is that the only constant in life is change. Sooner or later the requirements will alter, which means that increasingly the original utility doesn't fit the changing demand. We are faced with the paradox that whereas we, as living creatures, are dynamic by nature, the buildings we make, in fact most artefacts, are static by definition. Before the nineteenth century, in general, this was not particularly disturbing, because requirements were mostly limited and only changed slowly. Besides, both the durable building fabric and the neutrally positioned load bearing structures enabled easy re-use. However, since the Industrial Revolution, building requirements have increased dramatically (and keep on doing so) in order to raise the quality of the facilities being provided and to cut their costs. The response to this dramatic increase meant that buildings began to be designed to suit ever more specific requirements. As a consequence, this resulted in an enormous explosion of building typologies. In a short survey carried out some years ago only seven university building types for the seventeenth and eighteenth centuries were identified and, for the second half of the twentieth century over 250 types were counted. These twentieth century buildings are not, of course, constructed any longer with technologies which are meant for eternal durability, but for the dynamic and economic reality of the day. A vast range of new materials and technologies hitherto unknown in the building industry have appeared, with a limited life span. This means that the transition of twentieth century buildings is both a functional and technical phenomenon. A few examples will suffice as illustration: today, offices have a useful life of approximately ten years, factories eight years and shops only five years. The dynamics of building change today are so fast that, for example, a museum extension we designed seven years ago in Rotterdam is now to be altered into a restaurant. Our client for the new Law Court building in Middelburg was a property developer from whom the Dutch State rents the premises for a period of ten years, because ideas and requirements change too fast to make ownership profitable.

One might, therefore, conclude that whereas before the Industrial Revolution the most important buildings were intended to last for eternity, since then we are increasingly making 'throw away' buildings. As a consequence, regarding twentieth century buildings, the emotional appreciation of a building is often longer-lasting than its functional viability.

'Throw-away' buildings for eternity

As touched upon above, as soon as building requirements start to change, the match between demand and utility will fade. Adapting the building fabric might result in an economically and functionally satisfactory solution. If not, the final verdict will be demolition. Yet, if the emotional or historic value of the building is sufficiently apparent, we must be prepared to temper our functional and economic desires. In which case it is the work of art we primarily want to keep, rather than its utility. Here we are faced with another paradox which is that we are aspiring to keep 'throw away' buildings for eternity, buildings that were intentionally designed for a short functional and technical life expectancy.

Before thinking about a conservation approach to suit these new facts, it is important, first, to establish a preservation strategy for Modern Movement buildings. It is necessary, therefore, to consider what to preserve and how to preserve it. Conservation, with its various levels of intervention, is only one option within the total preservation approach.

A preservation approach

At the start of a new century, it is important to decide what of the recent past we should preserve for future generations. First there is a qualitative aspect. In the nineteenth and increasingly in the twentieth century, architects have devoted the main part of their efforts to a domain which, in previous ages, was left to anonymity. Their attention is not so much focused on the extraordinary any longer but on the ordinary, on the everyday artefacts elevating the life of the masses, on mass production, on housing for the lower income groups, on factories, offices, hospitals, sports complexes, schools, etc. There is also a quantitative aspect. In this century, far more has been built than in all previous ages put together and it is not possible, or desirable, to keep it all.

How should we approach this phenomenon? The first question is why do we want to keep objects of the past if they are not funtionally and economically useful? As mentioned, it is primarily our appreciation for the work of art, our love and fascination for its beauty, its mystique and its presence. There are also more scientific reasons for doing so, such as assembling knowledge and understanding the way of life of our predecessors, their technical innovations, the physical performance of their buildings, etc. Everything we do, imagine, make or invent, has its roots in the past. So proper knowledge and understanding of our (recent) past is a key to development in the future.

The next question is, which twentieth century

buildings should be selected to preserve and how should we preserve them? To keep everything for eternity makes functional, economic and cultural nonsense. We have, therefore, to be selective. Not everything has to be preserved in the same way and not all buildings or building types of importance have to be physically conserved. In most instances, proper documentation in terms of drawings, photographs, models, interviews, videos or computer-aided virtual reality can be an effective way of conservation. And this is particularly so when saving the architectural heritage of this century, since people who were involved in the design, realisation or occupancy of these buildings might still be alive and large quantities of relevant information are often still available.

Although it is extremely important that a selection is made of all relevant twentieth century buildings as regards an approach towards preservation, the DOCOMOMO movement only concentrates on buildings, neighbourhoods, cities and landscapes of the Modern Movement. Consequently, this is the primary concern of this chapter. Several well-known critics have made attempts in the past to arrive at a workable definition of the Modern Movement, but without success. What we can establish is that the pioneers of the Modern Movement and their successors have always had a proto-typical approach, experimenting with new social concepts, with new technologies and materials and with

unconventional forms and colours. Modernity, in an architectural context, might therefore be defined as that which is innovative in its social, technical and aesthetic intentions.

For a building which fits this definition of modernity to be selected for preservation, it should also be historically clear that the object concerned was innovative at the time of its conception and thereafter. In other words it should prove to have been more than a whimsical idea of the moment, it should have demonstrated withstanding the test of time. Thus, a certain time distance from the date of its original design conception is required, a period of say twenty years, before a decision can be taken with some degree of objectivity. There is, however, a certain danger in this approach. Some buildings or neighbourhoods, whatever conception of 'ordinariness' might have inspired their conception, have become icons in themselves, objects that have been elevated through cultural appreciation to an extra-ordinary level, due to the heroism they represent, due to their manifest quality, or simply due to sheer beauty. Other buildings, however, which are also manifestations of historically important ways of thinking, are not culturally appreciated partly because they are no longer topical, because they don't fit the cultural concepts of our time (comparable with Gothic cathedrals and their lack of appreciation in the late eighteenth and early nineteenth century), or simply because they are

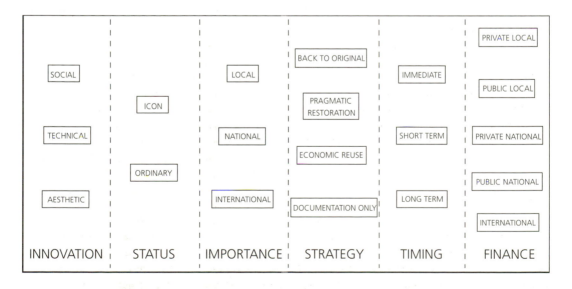

Figure 1.1 Diagnostic chart for assessing preservation and conservation priorities

publicly disliked. This situation obtains particularly in a century which has witnessed such a vast building production.

Where many untested experiments were carried out, and where social and cultural concepts change rapidly, it is to be expected that a certain number of buildings or neighbourhoods are generally unpopular. These buildings might, however, be of extreme importance to preserve for future generations. For example, although post-war public housing blocks in Glasgow, Lyon, Moscow, or Saint Louis might not appeal to us today, they are representative of our recent social past, some of which are surely necessary to preserve one way or another.

Priority

Obviously, we should be extremely selective which buildings and building types we do preserve. The main criterion seems to be that any example should represent an important way of thinking in a country or region in social, technical and aesthetic terms: for example, the postwar public housing drive witnessed the introduction of mass produced panelblocks, the abolition of decoration etc. Documentation is an effective way of preservation in most instances, particularly when a building or a neighbourhood is socially unsuccessful and becomes, consequently, despised.

In a few cases, actual conservation is justifiable economically or is desirable for emotional and scientific reasons. The most important reason for conserving a building is when its innovative influence has gone beyond national or regional boundaries although it goes without saying that it can also transpire that a building is conserved simply because it is loved and financed locally.

Furthermore, it seems to make sense to introduce a hierarchy of interventions, since not all buildings have to be conserved to the same degree of authenticity. Only a few buildings in any country have to be restored as close as possible to the original. This is necessary only when an inter-nationally important building is involved, for example Terragni's Casa del Fascio, Mies van der Rohe's Tugendhavilla, Ginzburg's Narkomfin building or Duiker's Zonnestraal Sanatorium. In most cases where conservation is required one may accept a more pragmatic approach towards intervention, if

the building is nationally or regionally important but does not justify ultimate top priority. Provided the alterations or additions are designed with great respect for the original and are worthwhile in themselves, these are acceptable in order to make the building suitable again for new functional requirements.

A problem frequently to be faced when conserving a building is the question of authenticity. First and foremost there is the authenticity of the original material. Of course one should always try to keep as much of the authentic material as possible, but this is not always realistic. Particularly if the original architect has tried to use as little material as possible, salvage of the authentic material might be impossible; equally deterioration of a short life construction may prejudice its structural stability and not meet current building codes. But does this always matter? In the case of Modern Movement relics isn't the authentic idea of its social, technical and aesthetic presence the most important value? Isn't the representation of that idea the most important aspect of a conservation act? Isn't the authentic visual appearance, its detailing, its dimensions, its colours and textures, its weathering etc. of prime importance? This is why reconstruction can also be a very acceptable means of intervention if that is the only way to come closest to the authentic representation. It is primarily the work of art we want to preserve.

To keep a building just as a work of art without any future use is usually unrealistic and not necessarily only for economic reasons. As previously defined the idea of a building is that it should serve a functional need particularly if we want to appreciate the artistic value of its utility. But that creates problems. The more a building is specifically designed to suit prescriptive requirements, the more difficult it becomes to find a new match between the original materialisation and the new uses and technical functions. These new requirements have increased enormously as compared to those of, say, fifty years ago. We are now being confronted with the results of some important ideas of the Modern Movement. Whereas the original forms in Modern Movement buildings mostly followed designated functions, in re-use the original form dictates its new function. A consequence of the adage 'less is more', is that the original fabric is designed with a relatively short life expectancy in mind.

It also means that there is very little room to manoeuvre both in a spatial and in a material sense to suit the new, inevitably increased requirements. As Aldo van Eyck once said: 'You don't just add 1 mm to the thickness of a line on a Mondrian painting. If you do, it isn't a Mondrian any longer, but just an ordinary painting.'

One is constantly faced with value judgements between the various aspects of authenticity, the actual condition of the materialisation and new demands. The paradox to retain 'throw-away' buildings for eternity forces the architect and the technician to get back to the basics, to locate the true soul of the original, to establish the conceptual, key elements and to find the small limits to which their poetry can be stretched. A new match has to be created between the soul of the original (the *raison d'être* of the preservation act) and the soul of the new utility, (the *raison d'être* of any building act), resulting in a new work of art. This complex balancing act requires sound technical knowledge, combined with good design, craftsmanship, an open mind and sensitivity. When the margins get really small it is professional skill that counts.

To recapitulate, there are three ways of conserving socially, technically or aesthetically innovative buildings of this century. Only very few buildings of international value have to be restored to their original state. A limited number of buildings can be restored pragmatically, because they have a national or regional value. Most buildings with a socio-cultural significance can be economically re-used and, eventually, demolished if they are at the end of their economic life, provided they are thoroughly and properly documented. It goes without saying that the first two categories ought to be documented as well.

Economic interest

Apart from these conceptual aspects of preservation and conservation, there are also some strategic aspects. The fact that a building is not included in a regional conservation register might mean the death penalty for that building. Equally, a building which is included in such a register is not automatically safeguarded from destruction. Therefore it seems to make sense not only to consider the consequences of listing a building but, equally, what the level of urgency for action is. Is the urgency immediate, is short term attention required, or is attention in the longer term sufficient? Since preservation is directly related to economic interest and financial means, important buildings can disappear overnight, not-withstanding democratically approved legislation or bureaucratic safeguards. Gone is gone. The case of GIL building at Campobasso in Italy is a striking example.

That leads to the last important aspect, which is the financing of preservation. Without sufficient funds, public or private, preservation of whatever internationally significant building cannot succeed. If no economically viable function for the building concerned can be found, it is extremely difficult to conserve it for future generations. In such cases only public outcry can help, because love for the spirit or the beauty of a building can sometimes be so strong, that the economic priorities of authorities, or private institutions, are shifted in a cultural direction.

Notes

1   Preservation is the total effort of keeping the memory of an artefact for future generations. This might be in the form of keeping the physical object, or in the form of documenting it.
2   Conservation is the act of keeping the physical object.

2 MOMO's second chance: the revaluation of inner urban housing in Britain

John Allan

This is a speculative chapter that juxtaposes some recent research on British housing need with some of my own reflections on the challenges that seem likely to face the modern conservation movement as it enters its second decade of activity. I will refer to a particular project being undertaken by Avanti Architects, as a tentative example of my 'thesis', but my conclusion is not prescriptive, and given the peculiarities of British housing policy and history, its application is unlikely to be universal. On a more 'generic' or philosophical level, however, it does raise issues that may be of wider interest to others both inside and outside the modern conservation fraternity.

As the said 'thesis' will be approached somewhat obliquely via a preliminary review of DOCOMOMO's first decade, it may be helpful to summarise my main conclusion in advance. This is that in the area of comparatively 'unrare' MoMo buildings there may be a coincidence of economic, social and technical trends that strengthen the conservation cause where a conservation argument on its own is unsustainable. Specifically, it appears that an anticipated demand for central urban apartments for single people or small households for leasehold or market rental may create a new and more favourable context for revaluation of some of that considerable legacy of post-war housing which might otherwise face an uncertain future. If so then the modern conservation movement may be faced with the broader challenge of addressing a part of its inheritance that it has up to now largely ignored.

DOCOMOMO was founded on and is motivated by the conservation ideal. Its tools are art history, its posture is evangelical, its reflexes are defensive. Its intellectual home territory is the world of culture, its approach to its portfolio honorific, and its sensibilities probably nostalgic – or at least elegiac. The efforts to infuse its charter with the idea of fostering an ongoing Modernism have been inconsequential and many of its supporters cannot accept today's leading 'modern' architects as rightful heirs of the MoMo tradition.

Now I want to stress that the above observations are not intended as criticism, nor are they meant to detract from the invaluable theoretical and practical work that has been done to identify and develop conservation principles and an understanding of technical procedures – in short, to establish the scope and content of the discourse, and indeed, to proclaim it to a wider audience. I am simply trying to clarify my own perception of what the modern conservation movement has really achieved.

Its first decade of activity has been preoccupied with the identification and protection of key MoMo works under threat or in need of rescue. And rightly so, for not to concentrate first on the best, the most culturally significant monuments of its period would have been to neglect its primary responsibility and risk losing some of the most powerful justifications for its cause.

In so doing conservationists have usually adopted the role of asserting cultural and artistic values over economic or commercial pressures as if these differing imperatives were intrinsically irreconcilable. When they have needed friends or allies they have generally looked for and found them in the period survivors, the special interest groups and the statutory authorities, notably English Heritage, who provide the legislative weapons to defend conservation territory against aggressors – most of whom come from the large constituency of interests that has been hostile or indifferent to modern architecture since its first arrival in Britain.

There is a curious resonance to this predisposition to selective militancy. What does it remind us of? Could it be the crucial strategic shift that occurred within the Modern Movement between the 1920s and the 1930s? Reyner Banham identified this phenomenon with typical precision, tracing the emergence of the term Functionalism in modern architecture's original struggle for recognition and citing two main reasons for its 'decision to fight on a narrowed front'.[1] The first was the late arrival of the movement's main 1930s apologists – Giedion, Sartoris, Mumford – and their unfamiliarity with the local circumstances and symbolic or cultural loadings of the early movement in its countries of origin – Holland, Germany and France.

The second reason, Banham writes, 'was that there was no longer any choice of whether or not to fight'. The virtual limitation of MoMo initiatives in the 1930s, when the style and its friends were fighting for a toehold in 'aesthetically indifferent England and depression-stunned America', meant that 'it was better to advocate or defend the new architecture on logical and economic grounds than on grounds of aesthetics or symbolism that might stir nothing but hostility.'

There is a paradoxical symmetry between this early consensus of inhibition on MoMo's cultural mission and our current propensity to defend the inheritance on this pretext alone. Conversely our grandfathers' emphasis on modern architecture's functional and economic justifications contrasts poignantly with our own embarrassment over the technical and operational validity of MoMo buildings – confronted as we are by the bleak track record of their actual performance in so many cases.

Banham was careful to distinguish between the European and the American 'take' on technology – the force for artistic abstraction versus the harbinger of operational liberation – citing Buckminster Fuller's devastating critique of the International Style and its Bauhaus adherents. (Is it a coincidence that current 'high tech' leaders such as Foster, towards whom British modern conservation apologists feel such

ambivalence, should have experienced crucial formative associations with Bucky?)

However that may be, this difficult dichotomy in MoMo's tradition of self-defence caused me to glance through DOCOMOMO's first book of abstracts for evidence of early uncertainty within the modern conservation lobby. I found it in the very first item – in my preamble to the paper I was preparing for the first DOCOMOMO Conference in Eindhoven, 1990. I quote:

> It is quite common for the owners of early modern buildings to be unaware of, or unconvinced by, their interest and importance as works of architecture. They are understandably more preoccupied with the value of the building as an operational amenity, and may well find that its usefulness is constrained by the same characteristics that are the basis of its cultural significance. As the Modern Movement proliferated and lost its early idealism, so also developed the process of alienation between its practitioners and the public. Those promoting a new conservation initiative in modern architecture must be careful to prevent history repeating itself.

By this I meant that modern conservationists might do better to orientate their cause to the realities of current need than seek to convert 'sinners' simply by evangelical fervour.

It appears to me that the challenge I was trying to define nearly ten years ago remains relevant and indeed is due for enlargement. If my own experience over the first decade of involvement points to any single conclusion it is that the economic and social arguments for retaining a MoMo building will almost always dominate the cultural ones. Time and again it is the modification, adaptation and intervention, sanctioned by the need to re-engineer sustainable use, that have provided the real conservation task and challenge – not the 'simple' repair and restoration.

I have cited many examples[2] but I still think 2 Willow Road (Figure 2.1) is one of the best, diminutive though it may be, because it shows how even a client like The National Trust – whose whole *raison d'être* is conservation with a capital C – was actually obliged, after all our feasibility study options, to restrict its conservation activities to only part of Goldfinger's house in recognition of the

Figure 2.1 2 Willow Road, London. Private flat conversion by Avanti Architects to generate revenue for conservation of the rest of Erno Goldfinger's House as a public museum. Photograph by Nicholas Kane

commercial necessity to generate a rental income from the other part of the property by converting it into a private apartment. 'Ideally' we would have restored the whole house as a Goldfinger exhibit, so our natural reaction is to regard the outcome as a slight compromise. But might it not better be understood as 'enabling works', indeed the crucial ingredient that actually enabled the main conservation objectives to be accomplished?

Put more broadly, it is surely not inevitable that DOCOMOMO, like other period interest groups, functions as just an antibody in the process of urban renewal. It need not only look backwards or at best seek to interpose itself between the heroic relics it seeks to protect and the relentless pressure for change that is synonymous with modern life itself.

The syllabus for the fifth DOCOMOMO conference in Stockholm – (entitled VISION & REALITY) – invites analysis of 'how social aspirations *have* influenced architecture and urban planning in the half century *up to* the 1960s'. This definitely widens the scope of discussion to embrace the whole sweep of modernism's legacy – not just its best known monuments. But what of the present and the future? How are *current* social aspirations influencing the architecture and urban planning that *remain* from that period? It is the force of these aspirations in institutional form and empowered by finance (private, public or voluntary) acting upon the

built environment in a given political matrix that is determining today's unfolding urban reality.

Take a couple of British examples. Marathon House (formerly Castrol House) (Figure 2.2) is, or rather was, a tolerably representative MoMo office complex on London's Marylebone Road designed by the British 'Miesians', Gollins Melvin Ward, and completed in 1960. It is no longer an office block, it is now a block of flats. Why? Because its previous commercial value as an office building could not compete with its potential residential value as an apartment complex. A conservation agenda would certainly have given precedence to retention of this building in its original use, even if there had to be modifications to conform to current operational requirements. But this would have ignored its *current* economic value as a real estate asset. It is the latter reality which has determined the outcome.

Is this a tragedy for conservation? Is it even a setback? I would not say so, though as a practising architect I would have little difficulty in criticising details of the conversion. But the question is, has the modern conservation movement anything to learn from this episode?

Take a second example. Alexander Fleming House, (Figure 2.3) the huge office complex designed by Erno Goldfinger (1963), has been a conservation *cause célèbre* in Britain for over a decade, and at various moments within this period was threatened with either imminent demolition, or a full post-modern makeover – the latter being regarded by some of its defenders as an even worse fate than outright loss. But Alexander Fleming House has been neither demolished nor disguised.

In the event the denouement has been more subtle. The building has been repaired, upgraded and converted into a major new apartment complex, offering studios, one, two and three bedroom apartments at prices ranging from £63,000 to £205,000. 'The lifestyle that London's really bought into', reads the developer's literature, '999 year leases, on-site car parking, residents health club, fitness centre and swimming pool, 24 hour uniformed concierge video monitoring and swipe-card entry system, minutes from the Underground, 2 stops from the City, 5 stops to Piccadilly Circus'.

Once again, any card-carrying conservationist could criticise certain aspects of the conversion – the spandrel replacements, the overcoating of the concrete, etc. But set against the fact that Goldfinger's *chef d'oeuvre* after a decade of uncertainty has now acquired a viable future, these misgivings are surely trivial. The form of the complex, its massing, its urban presence and overall identity have been preserved, and what is more, it now once

Figure 2.3 Alexander Fleming Housing, London. Given a new economic future as desirable urban apartments. Photographs by John Allan

Figure 2.2 Marathon House, London. A redundant office block becomes a marketable apartment complex. Photograph by John Allan

again supports a social reality – it resumes a useful function as an element of live urban tissue. It is even conceivable that the alterations may conform with the conservation principle of reversibility.

Now it is relevant to note that both these buildings had been proposed for listing and both been rejected. And one cannot but ponder whether it was their very failure to achieve listed status that actually enabled these buildings to be recycled, in the sense that it 'liberated' their commercial potential to offer a route out of pure obsolescence. What does this tell us about how modern developments of this scale and type are actually saved? Surely that there may well be viable futures for such buildings if a wider agenda than that of 'straight' conservation is brought to bear. This is not the same as saying that conservation issues play no part.

At many conservation meetings and in many publications the debate has continued over whether MoMo buildings are to be regarded as 'monuments or instruments'. This was a useful and stimulating argument initially, but in my opinion has become a sterile one now. Obviously there are some buildings which are such precious documents of our recent past that virtually everyone can agree they must be preserved in as complete and permanent a way as is humanly possible. I recall that even arch-iconoclast Martin Pawley, when challenged, admitted in public at the Eindhoven Conference that Corbu's Villa Savoye (Figure 2.4) should be saved under any circumstances. Equally there are other MoMo

caisse nationale des **monuments historiques** et des **sites** ◇

villa Savoye à Poissy

YVELINES • FRANCE

La villa Savoye dite « les heures claires » a été construite par les architectes Charles-Edouard Jeanneret-Gris dit Le Corbusier et Pierre Jeanneret entre 1928 et 1931. Chef-d'œuvre de renommée internationale, elle est la parfaite application de la théorie des « cinq points d'une architecture nouvelle ».

Ouverte tous les jours sauf mardi et jours fériés
1ᵉʳ avril au 31 octobre
9h30 à 12h30
et 13h30 à 18h
2 novembre au 31 mars
9h30 à 12h30
et 13h30 à 16h30.
Dernière admission
30 mn avant.
Accès
RER ligne A gare de Poissy, puis bus 50 direction La Coudray, arrêt Les Œillets ou Lycée Le Corbusier ; autoroute A14, retour vers Poissy.
Accueil
Visite libre, réservation obligatoire pour les groupes (groupe de 20 personnes maximum).

The Villa Savoye, known as «les heures claires» was built by the architects Charles-Edouard Jeanneret-Gris, better known as Le Corbusier, and Pierre Jeanneret between 1928 and 1931. A masterpiece of international renown, it is the perfect application of the theory of the «five points of new architecture».

Open every day except Tuesdays and public holidays
1 April to 31 October
9.30 a.m. to 12.30 p.m. and 1.30 to 6 p.m.
2 November to 31 March
9.30 a.m. to 12.30 p.m. and 1.30 to 4.30 p.m.
Last admission
30 minutes before closing.
Access
RER line A to Poissy, then bus 50 direction La Coudray, stop Les Œillets or Lycée Le Corbusier; motorway A14, return towards Poissy.
Attractions
Unaccompanied visit, booking essential for groups (maximum 20 people per group).

La villa Savoye denominada «Las Horas Claras» fue construida por los arquitectos Charles-Edouard Jeanneret-Gris llamado «Le Corbusier» y Pierre Jeanneret entre 1928 y 1931. Obra maestra de fama internacional, es la perfecta aplicación de la teoría de los «cinco puntos de una arquitectura nueva».

Abierta todos los días salvo el martes y los días festivos
1 de abril al 31 de octubre
9.30 h a 12.30 h y 13.30 h a 18 h
2 de noviembre al 31 de marzo
9.30 h a 12.30 h y 13.30 h a 16.30 h
Hora tope de admisión
30 minutos antes.
Acceso
RER línea A estación de Poissy y luego autobús 50 dirección La Coudray, parada Les Œillets o Lycée Le Corbusier; autopista A14, regreso hacia Poissy.
Acogida
Visita libre, reserva obligatoria para los grupos (grupo de 20 personas máximo).

photos © FLC. E. Revult © CNMHS Impression Aquaform, juin 1997 conception LM Communiquer

culture

Villa Savoye
82 rue de Villiers
78300 Poissy
tél. 01 39 65 01 06
fax 01 39 65 19 33

caisse nationale des **monuments historiques** et des **sites** ◇

Figure 2.4 Villa Savoye, Poissy, France, visitor's admission leaflet. A national monument sustained by tourism and state support. Photos © FLC.E. Revault © CNMHS. Impression Aquaform, Juin 1997. Conception LM Communiquer, Carte IGNno 901 © 1997

buildings of the postwar period – too many alas – which are so irredeemably awful in every conceivable respect as to be wholly indefensible by even the most ardent Modernist supporter. Indeed it might help their cause if modern conservationists were more forthright in disowning such work as unworthy of their ideals.

But between the easy extremes is the more difficult middle ground embracing a vast range of work neither significant enough to list nor worthless enough to abandon. Now the conservation move–ment may lack the resources or enthusiasm to confront this vexing and undifferentiated legacy, but to ignore it altogether would be hardly justifiable for a society like DOCOMOMO whose mission statement commits it, amongst other things, to 'explore and extend the knowledge of the Modern Movement'.

After all, we are referring to the movement's most prolific period, the twenty-five years from 1945 to 1970 when it enjoyed a more supportive political, economic and social climate than ever before or since. Building activity flourished in the public and private sectors in creating much of Britain's essential contemporary infrastructure in the housing, education and healthcare sectors and of course in the field of commercial property development.

And yet, perhaps ironically, the project on which Modernism staked its primary claim and pinned its highest hopes – the provision of social housing – became the area to attract the greatest criticism. From the late 1960s to early 1970s the consensus for comprehensive redevelopment fragmented and finally collapsed, and the products of this prodigious state investment became the object of public vilification and official neglect.

However, this situation is beginning to change. Two of Britain's largest and most controversial housing estates – Alexandra Road, London (Figure 2.5) and Park Hill, Sheffield (Figure 2.6) have been or are due to be listed. Goldfinger's high rise block Trellick Tower, once an object of derision, is becoming a cult address, while his other notorious estate in London's East End, Balfron Tower, is attracting funds for conservation work.

This suggests a discernible shift in architectural values. But the more significant underlying causes are surely demographic, economic and social, and it is these factors which I contend should inform the conservation approach to this larger and more

problematic part of the MoMo legacy. My two earlier examples indicate that a cultural agenda would not have saved the buildings in question on its own. Indeed it may even have been counter-productive.

There are a number of pointers to suggest that re-investment in the inner city will be a more significant predisposing factor in the future. The application of new official planning policy (PPG6) will discourage further development of out-of-town retail com-plexes at the expense of Green Belt land. The impact of SRB (Single Regeneration Budget) projects and work of Housing Action Trusts may also be cited. The Labour government has declared its urban priorities to promote the concept of 'the sustainable city' and is committed to establish a new governing agency to succeed the Greater London Council, abolished by Mrs Thatcher.

This is also the moment to refer to the findings of the Joseph Rowntree Foundation. This leading independent social research agency has identified a significant trend in housing demand toward compact inner-urban apartments for single people, childless couples and small families at affordable rents.[3]

Various strands of the Foundation's investigations in the UK combined to underpin this prediction, including changing patterns of family life, a preponderance of growth of single-person households in the period 1991–2011; the rise in divorce rates and single parenthood; uncertainties in the labour market leading to loss of confidence in the job security necessary to sustain long-term mortgages; the deterrent effect of the house purchase slump with its associated evils of payment arrears, negative equity, and property repossession.

Conversely there are new incentives to increase private renting, including the deregulation since 1989 of all new lettings, and the extension of the Business Expansion Scheme to encourage greater institutional investment in this sector.

The consequential advantages of increased mobility, a more flexibly housed central workforce and the social attractions offered by urban types of leisure facility (pubs, clubs, cinemas, theatres, galleries, restaurants, 'cafe life', speciality shopping, etc, etc) are cited as further factors in reinforcing this trend.

The JRF has collated at least twenty research projects pointing to the benefits of creating substantial numbers of rental homes for smaller

Figure 2.5 Alexandra Road Housing, London. First admired, then despised, now listed. Photograph by Martin Charles

Figure 2.6 Park Hill, Sheffield. An estate being revalued and considered for listing (see 'Park Hill: What Next?' AA Documents 1, Architectural Association, London, 1996). Photograph by John Allan

households in inner-city locations, and to underscore its recommendations launched its own competition for a demonstration project that would combine the appropriate financial, management and design ingredients – CASPAR, City Apartments for Single People at Affordable Rents. And whilst the emphasis here is certainly on rental tenure I do not intend to exclude the parallel impact of leasehold as an essentially urban mode of tenure in considering the extraordinary growth of 'loft apartment' conversions – often involving adaptation from industrial or commercial use.

What I *am* suggesting is that there might be an interesting 'read-across' between these ostensibly 'pro-urban' phenomena and the large postwar inner-city MoMo social housing legacy which I mentioned earlier. It seems most unlikely that the predicted demand could be satisfied by an experimental JRF model project, the further new-build development that this might stimulate and such other contributions as loftspace conversions, etc., could supply on their own. The existing stock of viable urban apartments will surely also be drawn into the equation. Those considerable tracts of central, or near central, housing – usually in local authority ownership, or the product of an earlier era of public sector investment – will become the next relevant potential source of supply. Indeed, right-to-buy legislation or the transfer of parts of this stock to other types of social landlord have already begun to break down the monolithic tenure pattern within this sector.

This recalls my opening proposition, namely that other criteria than those usually adopted by conservation agencies will need to be deployed in the process of evaluating this huge but undifferentiated resource. Such factors as urban connectivity, susceptibility to tenure mix, structural versatility, accommodation configuration, re-serviceability, unit mix, capacity for thermal upgrade, density retention, fabric renewal, infrastructure longevity, embodied energy, transport linkages, access audits, management issues, ratio of patent to latent value, space syntax, etc., will be the determinants of which of these existing properties

offer viable refurbishment and improvement options – just as such considerations were instrumental in the 'salvation' of Marathon House and Alexander Fleming House.

I repeat, modern conservationists should not shrink from confronting these realities. The location of an existing housing estate relative to an urban centre or sub-centre, its spatial provision in terms of room size and proportion, avoidance of the environmental disbenefits and infrastructure renewal costs of demolition are arguments likely to be at least as cogent in settling its future as any art-historical lecturing to a sceptical audience for recognition of its cultural significance. And it is such factors, that is functional (if not Functionalist) factors, – as well as conservation criteria where appropriate, to be sure – that should inform the revaluation of MoMo's legacy of inner urban housing.

In conclusion I should like to illustrate my 'thesis' with the example of Wynford House, an inner urban apartment regeneration project undertaken by Avanti Architects in the London Borough of Islington.

Wynford House (Figure 2.7) is part of a large early postwar housing estate, Priory Green, designed by

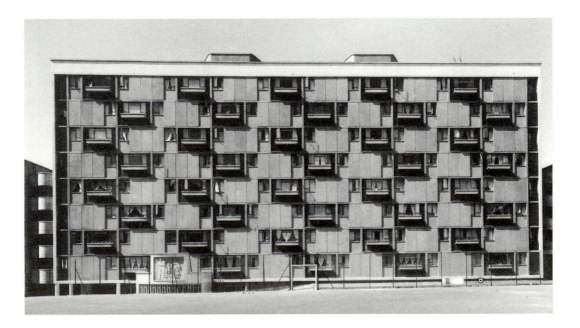

Figure 2.7 Wynford House, London 1957. Robust social housing at an appropriate density for its central location. Photograph by John Maltby

the Russian architect Berthold Lubetkin and his partnership Tecton for the Metropolitan Borough of Finsbury. Although the project originated in the 1930s, building of the eventual scheme did not start until 1947, being completed ten years later in 1957.

It is the largest and least successful of Lubetkin's three housing projects for Finsbury. Significantly it is also the only one of the three not to have been accepted for listing. It is not however without considerable architectural interest and urban design significance as the first substantial attempt to reinterpret the traditional London square in the modern idiom.

Though popular with its original tenants the estate has long suffered from problems of neglect and management and had reached the point where a major strategic response on the part of its owners, Islington Council, was postponable no longer. In 1996 Islington promoted The Wynford House Challenge, an open development and design competition to settle the future of this part of the estate. After a three-stage competition stretching over a year in which thirty-five alternative sets of proposals were considered, including several for total demolition and redevelopment, the challenge was won by Avanti Architects working with Community Housing Association – one of London's leading social landlords in the housing association sector which superseded local authorities in the 1970s as providers of affordable housing through public funding from the Housing Corporation, itself established by Parliament in 1964.

The Avanti design (Figure 2.8) is based on retention and rehabilitation of the Lubetkin buildings, with adaptation of some flats to maisonettes and the addition of four duplex

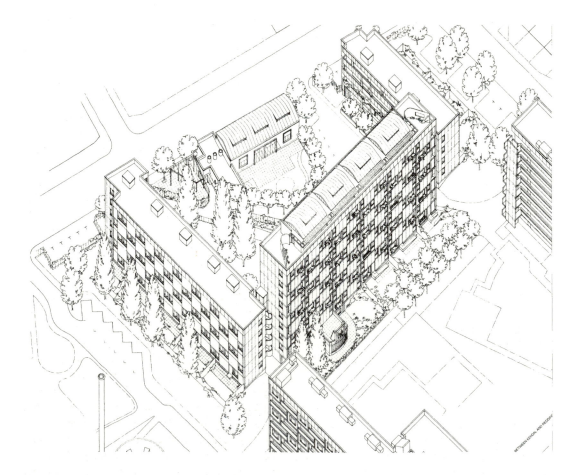

Figure 2.8 Wynford House, London as repaired, modified and revalued by Avanti Architects, 1997

penthouse units in place of redundant rooftop tank rooms. A comprehensive programme of specialist concrete remediation will be undertaken, with fully upgraded fabric and service measures to meet and exceed current energy standards. The estate landscape will be reconfigured on Lubetkin's original strategy to provide amenities and security. A new community centre is also proposed. The new scheme will provide a total of 84 units in a mix of fully managed social and market housing.

Why has this scheme beaten off the thirty-four other contenders? *Not*, I have to admit because its original designer is the most venerated pioneer modern architect in England, with more listed buildings to his credit than any other architect of his generation – modern or otherwise. (As something of a Lubetkin devotee myself I would have been glad to think such a justification would be sufficient.) *But* for reasons – taking all the previously mentioned criteria into account – which include:

- financial arrangements (a major capital receipt for the Council for disposal of the freehold)
- management proposals (a systematic non-paternalistic service by an experienced provider)
- technical solutions (an informed response balancing upgrade requirements with legitimate conservation concerns)
- social fit (meeting precisely the kind of apartment demand foreshadowed by the Rowntree Foundation Research)
- added value (the potential to access a private market through the incorporation of penthouses, the installation of a concierge and the provision of social amenities)
- an 'ideal' location (within yards of the forthcoming European railway terminal at St Pancras)

It offered the best balance of mutual advantages to its vendors and its purchasers. In short, Wynford House will be saved by being changed, by being made relevant and responsive to today's market requirements.

Now I am not claiming that this example represents some sort of panacea. There is ample and costly proof that in housing there is no such thing. What I am arguing is that a more realistic set of factors than purely considerations of conservation will have effectively been the key to saving and revitalising this estate.

To sum up, I suggest the modern conservation movement must enlarge its cognisance of the MoMo inheritance. It should not avoid grappling with its more difficult, less glamorous aspects. It must extend its interest from buildings-as-vessels-of-culture to buildings-as-a-social-resource and thereby acquire more and firmer critical handholds on the neglected, submerged, part of the MoMo iceberg.

John Summerson once defined the distinctive contribution of modern architecture as *social* and suggested that its source of unity was to be found in the architect's programme – 'the one new principle involved in modern architecture'. The programme, he argued, has become a 'description of spatial dimensions, spatial relationships and other physical conditions required for the convenient performance of specific functions . . . and the resultant unity . . . is the unity of a process'.[4] The action also of economic functions in this process is clearly implicit.

It seems to me that it is in this critical area of programmatic priorities that the future of middle-ranking MoMo heritage will be settled, not in the rarified ether of SPAB, ICOMOS or even Burra. The conservationist mindset, drilled in the scrupulous protocols of dealing with Grade I masterpieces, recoils from the commercial 'logic' of market forces but may overlook the fact that buildings at a lower stratum than those in listed categories may actually have a better chance of useful survival if embraced and exploited by that market. And those fearful of such a rapprochement should remember that useful survival need not exclude conservation values, for repair technologies are advancing too. Concrete remediation and window upgrading no longer automatically entail overcladding and uPVC.

Architects' motives are seldom identical to those of their clients, but this does not exclude the possibility of 'win–win' outcomes – to adopt the current flip-chart coinage – in situations where material conservation criteria are widened to include social and operational renewal. In short, modern conservationists might follow their heroes' example and deploy Banham's 'economic and logical arguments' for conserving modernism, instead of the special cultural and symbolic pleading that has tended to characterise their activity to date.

If the ambitions of conservationists go beyond that of merely fighting a damage limitation rearguard action they will have to run faster, get ahead of narrow commercial imperatives and master the full range of economic, social and technical tools available for intelligent conservation with a small 'c'. Specifically in the field of social housing they might function more as an enabling agency in devising ways of fitting the reusable elements of MoMo's heritage to an evident oncoming social demand.

Notes

1   Reyner Banham – *Theory and Design in the First Machine Age* (Architectural Press, London 1960–1982 edition) pp. 320–1.

2   *Modern Matters*, (English Heritage/Donhead 1996) ch. 16.

3   Joseph Rowntree Foundation ('Housing Research Findings 214', June 1997).

4   John Summerson 'The Case for a Theory of Modern Architecture' (*RIBA Journal*, June 1957).

3   Transitoriness of modern architecture

Hilde Heynen

Section 1

Bernard Tschumi once published an 'Advertisement for Architecture' (Figure 3.1), showing a photograph of the Villa Savoye in a state of heavy deterioriation with the caption: 'The most architectural thing about this building is the state of decay in which it is.'[1]

Tschumi clearly intended his statement to be provocative and paradoxical, but he nevertheless has a point. There is something very appealing, even sensual in a building which is gradually becoming a ruin. Such a building does reveal the influence of the passing of time, it reminds us of the fleeing away of the past. It thus awakes very strongly – much stronger than a historical building which has been restored – our awareness of history, of past generations, of people living and dying before us.

Tschumi however was not the first to offer such an observation. When the historical restoration of old buildings emerged as a common practice in the nineteenth century, John Ruskin was a declared opponent of the whole enterprise. According to him restoration means the most total destruction a building can suffer: 'It is impossible, as impossible as to raise the dead, to restore anything that has ever been great or beautiful in architecture.' This is because:

> that spirit which is given only by the hand and the eye of the workman, can never be recalled. . . . If you copy what is left, . . . how is the new work better than the old? There was yet in the old some life, some mysterious suggestion of what it had been, and of what it had lost; some sweetness in the gentle lines which rain and sun

had wrought. There can be none in the brute hardness of the new carving.[2]

There was moreover Antonio Sant'Elia, the most famous among futurist architects, who, for quite

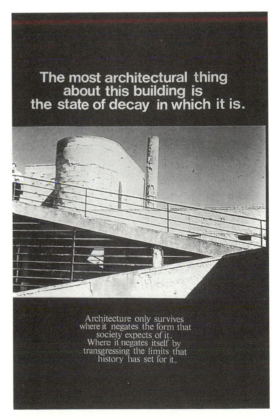

Figure 3.1 Bernard Tschumi, Advertisement for Architecture, 1976

other reasons than Tschumi or Ruskin, rejected any restoration of historical monuments or ancient buildings. In his manifesto of futurist architecture, he disfavours '*classical, solemn, hieratic, theatrical, decorative, monumental, frivolous, charming architecture*' and also '*the preservation, reconstruction and reproduction of monuments*'.[3]

Tschumi, Ruskin and Sant'Elia are authors with very different positions *vis-à-vis* architecture. They nevertheless seem to agree on this precise point: all three of them oppose striving towards the restoration of monuments, be they ancient or modern. All three stress that transitoriness, the ability to be affected by time, constitutes an essential characteristic of architecture. Ruskin's view is based upon a romantic outlook, in which craftmanship is considered the most determining element for the quality and even for the very identity of a building. His plea reveals a certain melancholy: it is clear for him that the idea of memory is most important. Buildings should be able to reveal a certain presence of the past, and they can only do so authentically when nothing is changed or added to them.

Sant'Elia on the other hand enjoys transitoriness, not because it awakens remembrance, but because it points towards the future: remembrance should be broken, tradition rejected, a completely new condition of life is emerging and should be embraced, necessitating a completely new architecture. The past should be forgotten, nothing is worth remembering in the face of this glowing new future.

As for Tschumi, his argument is a more complex one, in that it is very consciously brought into a paradox. Tschumi completes his caption by stating that: 'Architecture only survives where it negates the form that society expects of it. Where it negates itself by transgressing the limits that history has set for it. . . .' Tschumi thus considers architecture as a kind of paradigm for the experience of what is illogical or irrational. The pleasure of architecture, in his opinion, is rooted in the very paradoxes and ambiguities it embodies. His appreciation for the decaying condition of Le Corbusier's masterpiece is based on a sensibility for the erotic qualities which he recognizes in such contradictory situations.

The parallelism between these otherwise divergent authors, forces us to reflect about the ideas and legitimations underpinning the modern conservation movement. Why are modern buildings to be conserved or restored? What is it that makes this undertaking worthwhile? Isn't it much more simple to leave them in peace and let them become ruins? Or wouldn't it be much more convenient to destroy them and build anew? This last solution moreover would be in line with the position of the Modern Movement itself, for there were quite a few of its proponents who were prepared to do away with almost everything that was inherited from the past.

To my mind it is Walter Benjamin who gives the most adequate argumentation to support the latter line of thought. Particularly relevant in this connection is his essay on '*Erfahrung und Armut*'.[4] Written in 1933, this essay contains the most radical and intriguing formulation of Benjamin's liquidationist stance. He argues in this text that humankind is confronted with a 'poverty of experience'. This poverty has to do with the decay of tradition and with the overwhelming presence of technology and information. Rather than mourning this condition, however, one should seize on it as a new opportunity, as a possibility to make a fresh start. Benjamin states that 'a new barbarism' has come into being, which he considered as the most authentic reaction to the poverty of experience. For the new barbarism goes beyond a culture that is false and that cannot be called human any longer. This new outlook is, according to Benjamin, at the core of avant-garde art and architecture. The architecture of the Le Corbusier and the Bauhaus, with its rigid lines and smooth surfaces, is thus a correct answer to the necessities of the age, because it rightly expresses the poverty of the new condition and refuses to rely upon a false inheritance of the past.

Section 2

How then should we react to the buildings of a recent past, to these exponents of a new tradition the declared intention of which was to break with all previous traditions and to start all over again? A reflection on the meaning of modernity could offer some illumination at this point, not only because it might clarify some cardinal ideas affecting the architecture of the Modern Movement, but also because the idea of restoration seems to be a particularly modern one. It is no coincidence indeed that the idea of restoration achieved momentum only in the nineteenth century, with major figures such as Viollet-le-Duc. The care of old buildings is directly related to the threat to their continuing existence. As long as economic development is slow and the pressure to build is low, historic buildings simply continue their existence without being questioned. Modernity disrupts this peaceful condition, the need for new buildings often implies the demolition of older constructions.

Marshall Berman sketches a fascinating picture of the ambivalent nature of modernity in his seminal book *All That Is Solid Melts Into Air.*[5] For him the experience of modernity has to do with living in a world which is constantly changing and trans-forming itself. Berman is quoting Marx with the title of this book, but the same idea is expressed in Baudelaire's famous dictum, 'La modernité c'est le transitoire, le fugitive, le contingent'.[6] Modernity is intrinsically contradictory, according to Berman, because it is characterised by a continuous oscillation between the struggle for development and the nostalgia for what is irretrievably lost. This tension is determining for the individual experience of modernity too:

> To be modern is to find ourselves in an environment that promises us adventure, power, joy, growth, transformation of ourselves and the world – and at the same time, that threatens to destroy everything we have, everything we know, everything we are.[7]

The intriguing character of modernity has to do with the overlapping of these different aspects. Modernity paradoxically links a strong orientation towards the future with a sensibility for the ephemeral and the transitory. These different feelings and attitudes can be recognised in the wide range of modernisms which testify to very different degrees of empathy with modernity.[8] It is useful in this respect to distinguish between at least two different concepts of modernity, the programmatic and the transitory. The programmatic concept considers modernity as a project aiming at the liberation and emancipation of mankind, whereas the transitory concept rather highlights the fugitive aspects of modern reality and disconnects the continuous change from a conscious pursuit of progress. Both reflect the experience of a changing reality, but their emphasis is either on purposefulness and progress or on ephemerality and transitoriness.

The ideas propagated by the Modern Movement in architecture bear traces of a programmatic as well as of a transitory concept of modernity. In the work of Sigfried Giedion, for example, one can discern a certain oscillation between these different concepts, although the first is more forcefully present than the latter. Giedion is nowadays most well-known for *Space, Time and Architecture* (1941), a book revealing a linear view of history, as well as a programmatic and pastoral concept of modernity. However the two books that he wrote on modern architecture prior to that[9] are less univocal and betray ideas and notions that were clearly coloured by transitory experiences of modernity. The key expression that Giedion used to describe the qualities of the new architecture in *Bauen in Frankreich* (Building in France) (1928) is *Durchdringung* (interpenetration). The almost archetypal spatial experience that gave rise to this expression was the result of the sensations aroused by nineteenth century girder constructions such as the Eiffel Tower.[10] Giedion's fascination with these structures arose from the sensation of motion and from the experience of an intermingling of spaces. His description of the Eiffel Tower emphasises the unique effect of a 'rotating' space that is produced by climbing the spiral flights of steps (Figure 3.2). Exterior and interior spaces are as a result constantly related to each other, to such an extent that in the end one cannot make any clear distinction between the two. This new kind of spatial experience is fundamental in the New Building:

> In the air-flooded stairs of the Eiffel Tower, better yet, in the steel limbs of a *pont*

Figure 3.2 Siegfried Giedion, photograph of the Eiffel Tower taken by the author and published in several of his books

transbordeur, we confront the basic aesthetic experience of today's building: through the delicate iron net suspended in midair stream things, ships, sea, houses, masts, landscape and harbor. They lose their delimited form: as one descends, they circle into each other and intermingle simultaneously.[11]

This sensitivity to the transitory aspect of modernity, is still more pronounced in Giedion's next publication. *Befreites Wohnen (Liberated Dwelling)* (1929) is a small book that gives a picture of the aims and achievements of the New Building with the aid of photos accompanied by a commentary (Figure 3.3). Whereas the first book is at some points hesitant to embrace full-heartedly the new spatial sensibility,[12] the second takes it up in a more radical fashion. Here Giedion opposes in an explicit manner traditional ideas such as that the house should be attributed an eternal value. Instead he argues: 'The house is a value of use. It is to be written off and amortized within a measurable time.'[13] This is feasible, according to Giedion, when building production is organised on an industrial basis, so that building costs and rents are reduced. Houses should not look like fortresses then; rather they should allow for a life that requires plenty of light and wants everything to be spacious and flexible. Houses should be open; they should reflect the contemporary mentality that perceives all aspects of life as interpenetrating:

> Today we need a house, that corresponds in its entire structure to our bodily feeling as it is influenced and liberated through sports, gymnastics and a sensuous way of life: light, transparent, movable. Consequentially, this opened house also signifies a reflection of nowadays mental condition: there are no longer separate affairs, all domains interpenetrate.[14]

Giedion explicitly refers in this text to Sant'Elia whose idea it was that a house should only last one generation. In the Futurist Manifesto on Architecture that Sant'Elia authored in 1914 it is indeed stated that:

> We have lost the sense of the monumental, of the heavy, of the static; we have enriched our sensibility by a 'taste of the light, the practical, the ephemeral and the swift'. . . . An architecture

Figure 3.3 Cover of *Befreites Wohnen* (1985 edn) by Siegfried Giedion

so conceived cannot give birth to any three-dimensional or linear habit, because the fundamental characteristics of Futurist architecture will be obsolescence and transience. 'Houses will last less long than we. Each generation will have to build its own city'.[15]

There is however something strange in this passage, something of which Giedion himself was not aware at the time of his writing, but which has since given rise to discussion among scholars. The question is whether it is indeed Sant'Elia himself who is the author of this famous last paragraph of the Futurist Manifesto. There exists another text by Sant'Elia – called the *Messaggio*, which probably was the basis for the Manifesto and which does not contain the last two sentences of the Manifesto. Many scholars therefore assume that the differences between both texts are due to the extensive editing of the Manifesto by Marinetti. In that case the latter would be responsible for the radicalisation of the issue of transitoriness that transpires from the Manifesto.[16]

Sant'Elia argues in the Messaggio that profound changes in our conditions of life make it necessary for architecture to break with tradition: one should begin all over again, getting advantage from new possibilities such as 'the lightness, the superb slenderness of the beam, and the fragility of reinforced concrete'.[17] Architecture should show a taste for the light and the practical, it should be flexible, mobile and dynamic in every part. This text by Sant'Elia indeed hints at several of the most important themes of modern architecture: *tabula rasa*, rationality, no decoration, new materials, dynamism, a house as a machine. The idea of an

Figure 3.4 'Study for a Monument' (1914) by Antonio Sant'Elia. Reproduced with permission from Esther Da Costa Meyer, *The Work of Antonio Sant'Elia*, p. 52

architecture for consumption within one lifetime however is not there – that seems to be solely Marinetti's. This is confirmed when one takes a look at Sant'Elia's designs, which corroborate his description of a new architecture to come. His buildings are unadorned, they express a certain dynamism and a machine-like character, they rely upon the use of concrete, etc. There is however nothing in his drawings which refers to transitoriness in a literal sense: these are not buildings meant to last for only twenty or thirty years, these are buildings witnessing power and strength, they are conceived as artistic expressions of a new age. Transitoriness is present in a metaphorical way: several of these designs have to do with movement, with traffic, with energy – Sant'Elia designed railway stations, airport buildings, power stations and elevator-buildings. Most certainly however these projects do not reveal any trace of easy consumerability (Figure 3.4). Looking at these pictures, one has to assume that Sant'Elia did not really wish to extend the condemnation of monuments to his own creations.

The ambivalent position of modern architects *vis-à-vis* the issue of transitoriness can be traced elsewhere too. Marcel Breuer gives a reasonable summary of the prevailing attitude:

> The solutions embodied in the forms of the New Architecture should endure for ten, twenty or hundred years as circumstances may demand. . . . Though we have no fear of what is new, novelty is not our aim. We seek what is definite and real, whether old or new.[18]

The idea of transitoriness thus was not celebrated in itself: it indeed occurred to modern architects, that changes were inevitable and that architecture should adapt itself to changing circumstances, but in most cases consumerability as such was not the aim. That means that the proponents of the Modern Movement themselves were not univocally in favour of a very short life-cycle for their buildings. It would be wrong therefore to refer to the Modern Movement's presumed preference for one-generation-buildings, in order to legitimize the demolition of young monuments. Apart from the fact that the argument as such would be insufficient – that a building is meant for thirty years after all does not imply that it *should* be demolished after that lifespan, regardless of other considerations – it is also incorrect insofar as the architects and theoreticians involved are at least ambivalent in their opinions and practices regarding the issue of transitoriness.

Section 3

When Sant'Elia's cherishing of the 'houses that last only for one generation' appears to be invalidated, there remains nevertheless another basic idea underpinning the Modern Movement – the idea that architecture is to start all over again, that one should make *tabula rasa* of the existing and construct a completely new world. When we transfer this idea to our actual situation, it would certainly not justify any restoration of young monuments. If we have learnt something however, from the recent history of architecture, it is precisely this: that a *tabula rasa* architecture is not capable of fulfilling all human needs, that there is some deeply felt human desire which has to do with a sense of history, with a feeling of belonging, with a need to establish a relation with the past. One could say – as Félix Torres has it[19] – that modernity has grown up now, that it is entering a stage of adulthood. Modernity now is no longer a matter of combat, the fight has been fought, now the issue is rather how to deal with a modernity that has implemented itself. This new stage of modernity brings along a certain historical consciousness which embraces modernity itself. In the words of Marshall Berman:

> Modernists can never be done with the past: . . . If modernism ever managed to throw off its scraps and tatters and the uneasy joints that bind it to the past, it would lose all its weight and depth, and the maelstrom of modern life would carry it helplessly away. It is only by keeping alive the bonds that tie it to the modernities of the past – bonds that are at once intimate and antagonistic – that it can help the moderns of the present and the future to be free.[20]

Next to the simple observation that modern buildings are part of history and are therefore entitled to a careful treatment, these remarks of Torres and Berman constitute in my opinion the strongest arguments legitimating the conservation

and restoration of the Modern Movement inheritance. The buildings and urban complexes that form our young monuments are important, because they reveal an attitude towards modernity which can enhance our own awareness of the present-day situation and of architecture's stance *vis-à-vis* this condition. Referring to Walter Benjamin, I would say that we have moved ahead from the idea that the depressing state culture is in necessitates a new barbarism. Even if the actual state of culture is scarcely less depressing than it was when Benjamin wrote his essay, it has nevertheless become clear that it is impossible to start all over again, for the attempt to do so bears heavy totalitarian overtones which cannot be ignored. In order to avoid the danger of totalitarianism, one has to take history into account as an important source for the future. We cannot establish an identity from scratch, we need to rely upon the experiences of the past in order to be able to build a future.

That means that we should treat our modern monuments with respect and care, as well in terms of their material presence as in terms of the ideas they embody. It means that restoration can be the best solution – given e.g., a recognized masterpiece such as the Villa Savoye or the Rietveld-Schröderhouse. Nevertheless the specific attitude adopted in both these restorations – a careful reproduction of the building-as-new – seems to me unfaithful to the spirit of the Modern Movement. Both buildings are frozen in a certain state of perfection, killing all the life they once contained, weeding out all traces of use and inhabitation. Such a treatment belies the ideas of dynamism and functionality which were at the core of their original conception. I would argue therefore that an honourable attitude towards the inheritance of the Modern Movement implies a position balancing between a truthful reproduction of the original design and a dynamic renovation which accepts new functions and thus honestly reflects the buildings' primary conceptions.

Conclusion

Although Tschumi, Ruskin and Sant'Elia are authors with quite different positions on architecture, they seem to agree on one point: that buildings are not to be restored but rather left in peace and given over to a sensual affectation by time. Add to this the

Modern Movement's often-voiced opinion that architecture is a matter of building-for-one-generation, and one is confronted with some strong arguments against the urge to restore young monuments. If the experience of transitoriness was a quality modernists valued highly and if ephemerality was a characteristic they explicity strived to achieve in their architecture, what can be the reason to prevent their buildings from falling down?

After having traced some of the arguments that supported the idea of transitoriness, most notably in the writings of Giedion and Benjamin, I conclude that they nevertheless should not be taken at face value. The discourse of modern architecture is rather contradictory with its practice in this respect. We should treat this most recent of our built inheritance with care, for it has become clear that the *tabula rasa* attitude of the Modern Movement cannot be legitimated throughout. Modernity has grown up, and it needs the remnants of its youth to develop its own identity with the necessary depth and substance.

Notes

1 Bernard Tschumi, 'Architecture and Transgression', *Oppositions*, 7, Winter 1976, pp. 56–63.

2 John Ruskin, *The Seven Lamps of Architecture* (1849). I quote from the reprint of the second edition (1880) (New York, Dover Publications, 1989) pp. 194–5.

3 Antonio Sant'Elia, 'Manifesto of Futurist Architecture' (1914), in Luciano Caramel, Alberto Longatti, *Antonio Sant'Elia. The Complete Works* (New York, Rizzoli, 1988) pp. 302–3.

4 Walter Benjamin, 'Erfahrung und Armut', Walter Benjamin, *Illuminationen. Ausgewählte Geschriften* (Frankfurt a.M., Suhrkamp, 1977) pp. 291–6.

5 Marshall Berman, *All That Is Solid Melts Into Air. The Experience of Modernity* (London, Verso, 1985).

6 Charles Baudelaire, *Oeuvres complètes* (Paris, Seuil, s.d.) p. 553.

7 Marshall Berman, op. cit. 15.

8 I follow here the definition of Marshall Berman, who gives the term 'modernism' a rather generic meaning. According to him, modernism refers to ideas and movements which are in sympathy with modernity's orientation towards the future and with its desire for progress, and which strive to enable men and women to assume control over the changes that are taking place in a world by which they too are changed.

9 Sigfried Giedion, *Bauen in Frankreich, Bauen in Eisen, Bauen in Eisenbeton* (Leipzig, Klinkhardt & Biermann, 1928) (hereafter *Bauen in Frankreich*); translated by J. Duncan Berry, with an introduction by Sokratis Georgiadis, Sigfried Giedion, *Building in France, Building in Iron, Building in Ferroconcrete* (Santa Monica (Cal.), The Getty Center for the History of Art and the Humanities, 1995) (hereafter *Building in France*). Sigfried Giedion, *Befreites Wohnen* (1929) (Frankfurt a.M., Syndikat, 1985).

10 Sigfried Giedion, *Bauen in Frankreich*, p. 39 ff.; Sigfried Giedion, *Space, Time and Architecture. The Growth of a New Tradition* (1941) (Cambridge (Mass.), Harvard University Press, 1980) p. 281ff.

11 Sigfried Giedion, *Building in France*, p. 91; Sigfried Giedion, *Bauen in Frankreich*, pp. 7–8: 'In den luftumspülten Stiegen des Eiffelturms, besser noch in den Stahlschenkeln eines Pont Transbordeur, stösst man auf das ästhetische Grunderlebnis des heutigen Bauens: Durch das dünne Eissennetz, das in dem Luftraum gespannt bleibt, strömen die Dinge, Schiffe, Meer, Häuser, Maste, Landschaft, Hafen. Verlieren ihre abgegrenzte Gestalt: kreisen im Abwärtsschreiten ineinander, vermischen sich simultan.'

12 Giedion certainly has reservations with respect to the applicability of the new ideas on housing. He states for instance that 'One would not wish to carry over into housing this absolute experience that no previous age has known. Yet it remains embryonic in each design of the new architecture: there is only a great, indivisible space in which relations and interpenetrations, rather than boundaries, reign.' (*Building in France*, pp. 91–3); German version: 'Man wird diese absolute Erlebnis, das keine Zeit vorher gekannt hat, nicht auf Häuser übertragen wollen. Keimhaft aber liegt in jeder Gestaltung des neuen Bauens: Es gibt nur einen grossen, unteilbaren Raum, in dem Beziehungen und Durchdringungen herrschen, an Stelle von Abgrenzungen' (*Bauen in Frankreich*, p. 8).

13 Sigfried Giedion, *Befreites Wohnen*, p. 8: 'Das Haus ist ein Gebrauchswert. Es soll in absehbare Zeit abgeschrieben und amortisiert werden.'

14 Sigfried Giedion, *Befreites Wohnen*, p. 8: 'Wir brauchen heute ein Haus, das sich in seiner ganzen Struktur im Gleichklang mit einem durch Sport, Gymnastik, sinngemässe Lebensweise befreiten Körpergefühl befindet: leicht, lichtdurchlassend, beweglich. Es ist nur eine selbstverständliche Folge, dass dieses geöffnete Haus auch eine Widerspiegelung des heutigen seelischen Zustandes bedeutet: Es gibt keine isolierten Angelegenheiten mehr. Die Dinge durchdringen sich.'

15 Antonio Sant'Elia, Filippo Tommaso Marinetti, 'Futurist Architecture' (1914), in Ulrich Conrads (ed.), *Programs and Manifestoes of 20th century Architecture* (Cambridge (Mass.), MIT Press, 1990) pp. 34–8.

16 For a detailed discussion of the authorship of the Manifesto and the Messaggio, see Esther da Costa Meyer, *The Work of Antonio Sant'Elia. Retreat into the Future* (New Haven, Yale University Press, 1995) especially pp. 141–68.

17 The text of the *Messaggio* is in translation available as an appendix to the book by Esther da Costa Meyer (pp. 211–12).

18 Marcel Breuer, 'Where do we stand?' (1934), in Tim and Charlotte Benton, Dennis Sharp (eds), *Form and Function. A Source Book for the History of Architecture and Design 1890–1939* (London, Crosby Lockwood Stapler, 1975) pp. 178–83, p. 180.

19 Félix Torres, *Déjà vu. Post et néo-modernism: le retour du passé* (Paris, Ramsay, 1986).

20 Marshall Berman, op.cit. p. 346.

PART II
STRATEGIES AND POLICIES

Just as Modernism in architecture is random in its scope and location, so the legislation and mechanisms which serve the purposes of its conservation are shaped by political, cultural, legal and economic vagaries. Internationally the device which focuses attention and provides a degree of insurance in favour of preservation and a datum against which value judgements may be measured, is a public register of those buildings, or groups of buildings, which are deemed to reflect the spirit of their age. The process of selection is, in itself, a clarifying, critical procedure for those involved. The World Register has been compiled in the ambit of various charters which have been formulated at international, national and local levels (see Appendix B). The Eindhoven Statement (Appendix A) which launched the DOCOMOMO movement in 1990 was devised in order to establish common territory for the disparate agencies and countries devoted to the cultural heritage. The five chapters which constitute this section provide insights not only relating to mechanisms but also to inherent national attitudes towards Modernism. The contrast between South America, Hungary, the United States, Canada and the Netherlands could not be greater. These chapters can at best provide vignettes which hint at the range of political, cultural, economic and professional commitments all of which are in constant flux and also help in initiating a shared basis upon which levels of expectation can be established.

4   The problem of conservation in Latin America

Hugo Segawa

Christopher Columbus crossed the ocean in search of the Orient. He was not just looking for a shorter navigation route. According to his keen imagination, he was also pursuing Paradise. When Columbus landed for the first time, he could have believed he had reached his desired destination. The Italian commander, however, was not in his beloved mythical place – he had touched America.

America was 'invented' by Europe. Thomas More settled his Utopia somewhere in South America. He was not alone in envisaging something quite different from the reality of that unknown part of the world. For the sixteenth century European the new land was the promised land.

Columbus had his visionary ideals, but he actually paved the way for the European conquerors. Henceforth, the mythical paradise was to be fragmented, separated into different regions, each one responding to its coloniser, establishing a Spanish America, a Portuguese America, an Anglo-Saxon America, a Dutch America, a French America, and, incidentally, an Afro-America. Waves of immigration in the nineteenth and twentieth centuries set in motion a re-ordering of the ethnic and cultural cartography of the New World.

Why Latin America?

A French dictionary refers to a 'Latin America' in opposition, presumably, to an 'Anglo-Saxon America'.[1] No dictionary registers the latter entry, but an American one defines 'Latin America' as 'the countries of North America (excepting French-speaking parts of Canada), South America and Central America where French, Spanish and Portuguese are spoken'.[2] The curious inclusion of North America unnecessarily extends the entry: it would have been enough to say 'every country from Mexico below, etc'. Although a Latin culture is present in Quebec, it would not make sense for anyone to include that province or even Canada as part of Latin America. But it is not less Latin than Haiti (or its French colonised residue), similarly as Latin as the US territory of Puerto Rico, and certainly more Latin than Belize. Why are Guyana, the Bahamas, and Trinidad and Tobago, all English speaking states, considered Latin American by the Inter-American Development Bank? Is Latin American everything south of the Rio Grande? But, as mentioned before, why do those English-speaking states, and Netherlands Antilles or Surinam deserve the 'Latin' treatment? How should we categorise people with Indian ancestry that speak their mother-tongues in Guatemala, Mexico, Ecuador, Peru, etc. or the German people in Brazil and Chile, the Japanese community in Peru and Brazil, and the Italian accent everywhere in America?

No geographic or sociocultural criteria support such a wide range of countries under the Latin America identity. Among the 'Americas' (as one could say after the particular conditions all over the continent), the term *Latin America* carries a socioeconomic and geopolitical denotation, those countries that are apart from the developed domain, not in the 'centre' as wealthy nations, but in the 'periphery' of the industrialised world; under-developed or developing countries with historical backgrounds as sources of raw materials and food suppliers in the Occidental economy.

Scopes of modernity

So what is the role of modernity in such a context? Is there any sense in speaking of a modern movement in architecture in underdeveloped or developing countries? Vittorio Magnago Lampugnani from an article published in *Docomomo Newsletter* states:

> Modernity, we believe, stems from the new society that has emerged since the nineteenth century: a mass society confronted with the task of housing and serving previously unthinkable numbers of people in rapidly growing cities. Modernity stems from industrialisation, from the increasingly automated production processes that have been introduced to mass-produce goods and provide products on a wider scale at lower prices and higher profits. Modernity stems from technical progress: enormous advances in mechanical engineering, civil engineering and architecture have permitted completely new types of structures capable of completely new types of task. So far, so good. Sounds familiar, too – after all, these assumptions are entirely in line with the tenets of orthodox twentieth century architectural history. There are, however, some other, less obvious factors. We believe modernity involves social, if not socialist, ideology. It involves an ideology that seeks to share the planet amongst a vastly increasing amount of people. We believe modernity involves the political and technological problems of ecology: the need for prudence and economy in managing the infinite and eroding resources of our planet. Finally, we also believe that modernity involves the cultural phenomenon of all-pervading simplification: a reductionalist tendency forced upon us by new social and technical needs, exalted by progressive culture and elevated to the rank of an artistic principle.[3]

This quotation, taken from a reinterpretation of modernity by Lampugnani in relation to the exhibition *Moderne Architektur in Deutschland 1900 bis 1950*, is a useful statement to compare a current and to a certain extent renewed comprehension of modernity, and to realise another perspective.

If one takes account of the first part of the enunciation (modernity as a matter of industrialisation, technology, low costs, etc.) it clearly defines a European historical term, but scarcely concerns the Latin American context. It is not by chance that Lampugnani remarks that it is dealing with an orthodox architectural position: no ethnocentric history considers the understanding of beliefs and practices other than that established in the light of their own culture. The second part of the statement deserves careful consideration. Perhaps it could be read in a more unrestricted manner, to deduce a conclusion that would match some current Latin American points of view.

Identity

'Avant-garde' versus 'tradition' and 'modernity' versus 'conservation' were habitual dichotomies in the cultural debate during the first decades of the twentieth century. But Latin American modernity was not only affected by the current European avant-garde aesthetics. Writers and artists were gazing at the American pre-Columbian and colonial past.

In an essay of the mid-1960s, Jean Franco asserts: 'In Latin American countries, where the national integration is already a process in definition and the social and political problems are immense and beyond dispute, the artists' feel of responsibility for the society exempts any justification. Any evaluation of Latin American movements must be related to the social and political concerns that originated them. While it is reasonable in Europe to study art as a tradition by itself, which can generate new movements thanks to mere formal problems, this attitude is not possible in Latin America, for even the names of literary manifestations differ from the European ones: '*Modernismo*', '*Nuevomundismo*', '*Indigenismo*',[4] define social viewpoints, and 'Cubism', 'Impressionism', 'Symbolism' refer only to expressive techniques. This distinction is of extreme importance because the artistic movements, in general, are not detached parts of the preceding movement, but they emerge as responses to developments beyond the arts.'[5]

Perhaps those European movements are not as socially irrelevant as Franco supposed, but Modernism in Latin American art had also a quite peculiar content as a *manifesto*. In 1925, Prudente de Moraes, Neto, the young editor (together with

Sérgio Buarque de Holanda) of the Brazilian avant-garde literature review, *Estética*, declared: 'Civilization came up to Brazil by graft. That's why here a false tradition surfaced that is no better than an alien tradition. . . . We need to find our own way by ourselves. Well, Modernism, besides its universal meaning, is now corresponding everywhere to the rise of nationalism, it is magnificently fitted to confront this problem.'[6]

A new tradition in architecture

Most of the books on the twentieth century history of architecture report on the Mexican and Brazilian Modern Movement of the 1930s basically as emanations of European trends. Few of these writings take into account the social and political meaning of the works of Villagrán Garcia, Legorreta, O'Gorman, de la Mora and Yañez (housing, schools, hospitals) to the Mexican Revolution. Rarely do these studies demonstrate any awareness of the experiment led by the Brazilian Luiz Nunes in the state of Pernambuco, at the Department of Architecture and Urbanism, designing and building hospitals, schools, and other public buildings; or that Lucio Costa, the master of Brazilian modern architecture, personally knew Frank Lloyd Wright, read about Gropius, Bauhaus and Soviet Modernism, but was truly enchanted with the social range of Le Corbusier's rhetoric – as were Luiz Nunes and probably the Mexicans. The orthodox histories of architecture are more interested in emphasising the influences of Le Corbusier in Latin America than his change of mind after his South American tours; or disregard that in the 1930s, Le Corbusier was much more influential and intellectually appreciated in Latin America than in his own continent, ahead of the 'discovery' of the Swiss-French master all over Europe (and Japan) by the young architects and students of the immediate post-World War Two generation. It was not by chance that the first vernacular-inspired design by Le Corbusier was the 1930 Errazuriz House in Chile; that it was he who recommended Lucio Costa to use regional granite and not Italian marble at the Ministry of Education and Health building in Rio de Janeiro. These are some curious details, but what was behind this dialogue?

The development of the Modern Movement in Europe from the 1920s was due to the aims of reconstruction following World War One. While the effort of the European architects resulted in a policy of reorganising destroyed landscapes and dealing with postwar needs, Latin American architects were embroiled in another kind of struggle: the challenge to build a new world, to overcome the material and social necessities in underdeveloped countries that were in search of ways to increase their self-confidence. European architects had the task of modernising a destroyed urban structure; Latin American architects had the task of modernising a barely urbanised subcontinent. The roots and the scope of the challenge were different, the results were quite distinct, but the desire for change was the same: the ideals among them were close.

Blooming modernities

The New World, out of the battlefields, welcomed scientists and artists who fled Europe, and was also an experimental ground for modernity. This is particularly true in Latin America, where the healthy economic circumstances triggered some outstanding architecture. While Europe was again a wasted land, engaged in the hard task of reconstruction after World War Two, Latin America was constructing on almost virgin territory in the forefront of the Modern Movement. An examination of the modern architectural manifestations in the subcontinent shows the significant presence of European *émigrés* behind some pioneer buildings or ideas (even before World War Two). The concepts evolved between the wars in Europe flourished in Latin America in the 1950s and 1960s. But in a different climate and geography and its own distinct culture, Latin American modern architecture bloomed differently.

The chapters on the architecture of the period from 1945 to 1970 in the textbooks (particularly those written in Europe) usually register the late production of the masters of the Modern Movement in terms of the United States panorama, postwar European reconstruction and housing development, and the debate on the Italian scene. Within this traditional scope, Latin American achievements remain almost unmentioned. The abstract theoretical and circumscribed discussions presented in such books are quite limited compared to the actual realisation in Latin America. Large ensembles, for example some university campuses created in the 1950s are true monuments of modernity in their own right. Where else in the world can one appreciate on one site open-air and indoor pieces of art by Wilfredo Lam, Mateo Manaure, Alejandro Otero, Jesus Soto, Jean Arp, Alexander Calder, Henri Laurens, Fernand Léger, Antoine Pevsner, Victor Vasarely, among others? The Venezuelan architect, Carlos Raul Villanueva, upheld the ideal of the synthesis of the arts ideal on a monumental scale when he set up the architectonic and artistic principles for the campus of the Central University of Venezuela. A different kind of monumentality is presented at the UNAM campus in Mexico City, where spaciousness and art integration (e.g., the famous Mexican mural painting) can be comprehended only by reference to pre-Columbian culture and mid-twentieth century Mexican art. The Rio de Janeiro Federal University campus is a one-of-a-kind Le Corbusier/Brazilian architecture blend. All these campuses were not only the confines of sciences and arts, they were places of a new modernity in Latin America.

Urban modernities

No cities other than Chandigarh and Brasilia equally express the spirit of the Modern Movement and yet both of them are out of the developed world. The latter is the greatest milestone of Modern Movement urbanism. It is not well known that Le Corbusier offered himself as master planner of Brasilia, before the competition was held and which was won by Lucio Costa.

More unknown is that the Swiss-French master was due to plan the reconstruction of Concepción, a city destroyed by an earthquake in 1939 in Chile. The commission was grasped in the end, by a group of young Chilean architects who improved, over a period of twenty years, a mixed proposal for its reconstruction; over the pre-existent urban grid pattern, all the new public or important buildings displayed flat roofs, screen walls, large glass and ribbon windows with either discreet or no applied decoration, and form and regularity of concrete structures. I say 'mixed proposal' for it was not a Corbusier-style *tabula rasa* urbanistic solution that arose from the new plan, but an adaptation by the Chilean architects of the traditional urban structure; they were much more engaged with International Style aesthetics concerning the buildings. Does this constitute a 'fault' in their search for modernity? Is

Tel Aviv acclaimed 'an open-air' museum of the International Style' for its buildings or for its urban structure or rather for the architects involved in it, disciples or followers of recognised European masters? Should Concepción be considered 'less' modern because its architects did not have pedigrees as those employed in Palestine? In neither case (Chile or Israel), are the contexts attuned to some convenient interpretation of the Modern Movement or modernity.

These cases – and many others, including the vast amount of experience emanating from the developed world – are unknown by-products of investigation, from a local or regional point of view (so-called *regionalism*), and now or in the near future we need to insert them in a more complex understanding of the phenomenon of modernity. They are 'by-products' although we are not certain of their nature and significance, and we must distinguish 'regional', in a new interpretation, in other words *regionalism* as something pertinent to a wider range of interconnected phenomena. Everywhere in the world (including Europe, North America and Japan) the sense of modernity has its peculiarities, each one with a particular time scale, a distinct cadence, unlike vectors behind the modernisation scene. So modernity is a diffuse phenomenon – it is change – it is breakthrough – it is progress – it is rejection of the past – and it is failure, as well.

The paradox of conservative Modernism

'Conservation', 'preservation', were not keywords in the Modern Movement repertoire. Registration and protection actions were archaeological and museological attitudes concerning the past. In Latin America, there is, likewise, a distinguished background. Marina Waisman's comment represents a local point of view that is effective all over the subcontinent (regional characteristics apart):

It has been frequent in Argentina to consider the colonial epoch as the only period worthy of esteem in the past, probably for the social myth of a more honorable culture, or Argentina as a result of a unique and great bygone Hispanic moment. Adjoining to this, a concealed embarrassment for the real immigration root of the majority of the population, which motivated a nationalist reaction among some intellectuals, evoked perhaps for the first time the conscience of the necessity for an appropriate nationality. Due to such confusing origins, a popular belief that all aged architecture that deserves deference and conservation is 'colonial' emerged, and even when safeguarding actions toward nineteenth and early twentieth centuries architectures had begun, the general public followed along the same standard of the 'colonial' as distinctive value that sanctions patrimonial status.[7]

The paramount monuments worthy of notice by national registers are predominantly pre-Columbian and colonial remains in Latin America. Few Modern Movement structures are the focus of attention, as the Benedictine Chapel in Santiago de Chile, designed in 1963 by Martín Correa and Gabriel Guarda, and the campus of the Universidad Central de Venezuela in Caracas, the enormous and long-term effort by Carlos Raul Villanueva – both considered national monuments in recent years.

Brazil is a distinct case: as early as 1947 the Saint Francis Chapel of Pampulha in Belo Horizonte, by Oscar Niemeyer, completed in 1943, was registered as a National Monument; a year later, the Ministry of Education and Health building, designed by the team led by Lucio Costa (having Le Corbusier as consultant) and inaugurated in 1944, was also registered. Later, another Modern Movement landmark, the Flamengo Park in Rio de Janeiro, designed by Roberto Burle Marx and Affonso Eduardo Reidy, was registered in 1965, almost immediately after its completion. Governmental cultural heritage preservation proceedings were elaborated in the mid-1930s by a group of modernist intellectuals, with the advantage of the brilliant participation of Lucio Costa. Distinct from any other experience in the world, the intelligentsia that introduced modern art, architecture and literature in Brazil was responsible also for matters of preservation. Recent analysis on the subject revealed controversial positions about the registers promoted during the 60 years of PHAN, the national cultural heritage institution.[8] The sole contemporary urban complex registered by UNESCO as World Heritage Monument is Brasília, the Brazilian capital planned by Lucio Costa.

Modernity depth

Modernity and Modern Movement architecture in Latin America are already chapters in an untold story. As in other parts of the world, we will find in Latin America different kinds of modernities in architecture: programmed modernity, pragmatic modernity and even a random modernity. No hierarchic rank is possible among them. It is not reasonable to think of modernity attached to a few hypothetical unerring conditions. Completely different contexts bear no comparison; on the contrary, the differences among them could enlighten and magnify the meaning and the range of modernity.

Notes and references

1   Le Petit Robert 2: *Dictionnaire Universel des Noms Propres*, 1990, s.v. 'Amérique'.

2   *The New Lexicon Webster's Dictionary of the English Language*, 1990, s.v. 'Latin America'.

3   V.M. Lampugnani, 'Another Modernity', *Docomomo Newsletter*, 8 (Jan. 1993), pp. 39–41.

4   In English, these terms could be: Modernism, New-Worldism, Indianism.

5   J. Franco, *La cultura moderna en América Latina* (México, Grijalbo, 1983), p. 15 (author's translation).

6   P. de Moraes, Neto, 'Idéias de hoje: 'modernismo não é escola: é um estado de espirito'. In F. de A. Barbosa (ed.), *Raízes de Sérgio Buarque de Holanda* (Rio de Janeiro, Rocco, 1988), p. 71 (author's translation).

7   M. Waisman, *El interior de la Historia* (Bogotá, Escala, 1990), pp. 133–4.

8   M.V.M. Santos, 'Nasce a academia SPHAN', *Revista do Patrimônio Histórico e Artístico Nacional*, 24 (1996), pp. 77–95: S. Rubino, 'O mapa do Brasil passado, *Revista do Patrimônio Histórico e Artístico Nacional*, 24 (1996), pp. 97–105; L. Cavalcanti, 'O cidadão moderno', *Revista do Patrimônio Histórico e Artístico Nacional*, 24 (1996), pp. 105–16.

5 Recording and preserving the modern heritage in Hungary

András Ferkai

The idea of preserving our recent heritage was pioneered very early in Hungary compared with other European countries. The first nation-wide list of Hungarian historic monuments, published in 1960, contained some items from the turn-of-the-century and even from the inter-war years, although the most recent ones did not belong to the Modern Movement. The Committee of Architectural History and Theory within the Hungarian Academy of Sciences applied to the National Board for the Protection of Historic Monuments with the request to enter twentieth century buildings on the list, as early as 1963. The committee drew up a list of twenty-two additional buildings from which ten were modern, and all of them were included in the 1967 national list. Though the committee expressed its intention to continue the work of registering and upgrading the list with new items, almost ten years passed until the next step was taken.

At the beginning of the 1970s, a working group was formed by the same committee and was given the task of presenting a new collection of work from the recent past which could be protected as national landmarks. This group declared that the process of registering buildings as 'monuments' was never-ending, the sole limit being that works by a living architect cannot be listed since they are protected by authors' royalties. Nevertheless, members of this working group set the age-limit of 1950, almost certainly because they did not want to get entangled in the evaluation of the Stalinist period which would have been awkward at that time, in every respect. The final list, presented in 1974, comprised twenty-three buildings from the countryside and around 120

from Budapest, of which only a fraction were from the Modern Movement. As a consequence of this activity, the total number of MoMo buildings in the enlarged 1977 edition of the National List of Hungarian Historic Buildings reached 38 solo buildings and one ensemble (the Napraforgó Street model housing estate from 1931), in the case of Budapest, and only two buildings from the countryside. In December 1976, the Municipal Office for the Protection of Monuments organised an exhibition with the title '20th Century Monuments in Budapest' which presented the public with new entries to the list. This material was later published in the form of a brochure.[1]

It is to be regretted that this pioneering work was not resumed until the 1990s. It is true that a conference on the monuments of the last 100 years was organised in 1982 in Budapest and Kecskemét by the Hungarian section of ICOMOS. One of the lecturers there, Gábor Winkler, was commissioned by the Ministry of Construction and Urbanism to prepare a methodological guide for the protection of monuments from the same period. The huge work carried on between 1982 and 1984 resulted in five volumes covering every aspect of the theme and including a preliminary list of countryside buildings. Unfortunately, no one institution took on the task outlined in this guide.

As far as the publications are concerned, the first monograph on the inter-war period, written by one of the members of the Hungarian DOCOMOMO working group, came out in 1983.[2] The National Board for the Protection of Historic Monuments which had traditionally published topographic works according to counties and city districts, concentrated exclusively on listed monuments; hence modern heritage is very poorly represented in these volumes. The Art History Research Institute of the Hungarian Academy of Sciences also considered launching a Dehio-type series of topography that would have comprised the modern heritage too, but only one volume has been prepared for publication. The same institute undertook the task of managing, financing and publishing the topographic researches of an 'outsider', the author of the present article on the inter-war architecture of Budapest, a comprehensive work, half of which came out in 1995 with most of the highlights of the Modern Movement in Hungary.[3] The publication of the other half on Pest-side architecture of the same period is scheduled for 1999.

The new Municipal Act of 1991 and the transformation of the National Board for the Protection of Historic Monuments in 1992 paradoxically gave an impetus to the affair of listing by removing jurisdiction from the Budapest Municipal Office and passing it to the National Board. The Budapest Office was then reorganised as the Department for the Protection of Settlement Heritage which was concerned with a wider range of buildings, ensembles and parts of the cityscape worthy of protection, excluding those figuring on the National List. A municipal decree in 1993 introduced the notion of 'local or municipal protection' and about 50 solo buildings and three greater contiguous urban areas of the Modern Movement in Budapest entered the list. Although local protection is weaker in legal respects, it is still rather effective because a fund was established for the renovation of listed buildings, thus their owners and dwellers can apply for subsidies or loans. From its establishment in 1994 up to now, many Victorian and Art Nouveau monuments have been restored with the help of this fund but not one from the Modern Movement.

The Hungarian working party of DOCOMOMO started work immediately following the first conference in Eindhoven. Its members were mainly recruited from among architects and art historians working for the National Board, the Department for the Protection of Settlement Heritage and the Hungarian Museum of Architecture. The most important outcome of the group's activity has been the Hungarian National Register and the brochure

with about 60 top items which was published for the DOCOMOMO Fourth International Conference in Bratislava and Sliac.[4] Members of the working party promoted several civic and professional initiatives such as the architects' meeting in the Pasarét district of Budapest organised on the Bauhaus-inspired tendency of 1996 and on the other tradition of Modernism in 1997, or the celebration of Farkas Molnár's (1897–1945) and Fred Forbat's (1897–1972) centenary in their native town of Pécs in 1997. Quite recently, we managed to stop the brutal alteration of the villa by József Fischer, a member of the Hungarian CIAM-section, in the Napraforgó Street model housing estate. The Hungarian working group, however, did not succeed in becoming a factor in the events related to modern monuments. In spite of every attempt, DOCOMOMO members have not been invited as consultants to discussions organised by the authorities. Quite a lot remains to be done in the field of propaganda in favour of modern architecture which is far from being popular among the people.

In preserving our modern heritage, a serious problem is the hostile attitude of the public towards everything belonging to the Modern Movement. Of course, Western countries also faced this problem but they appeared to get over it, whereas in Eastern Europe the banality of modern forms in architecture during the 1960s and 1970s, coupled with the bureaucratic mass production of prefab housing and public buildings, discredited modernity for a long time. The common people prefer Postmodernism, organic or regional style, or anything which is decorated, to the purist modern, and they hold in high esteem nineteenth century Historicism and Art Nouveau from the turn-of-the-century. However, they deem modern buildings ugly, be they old or new. It is very difficult to explain why a flat-roofed cubic house, generally ruined by alterations, merits the status of a historic monument. Especially so, when they hear the world famous architect of the Hungarian Organic Movement speaking about 'crimes of the Bauhaus' and blaming the pioneers of Hungarian modern architecture for importing patterns from abroad.

Many people cannot understand why the 'ugly modern building' of the coach terminal in Budapest Erzsébet Square, next to the site where the new National Theatre is to be constructed, ought to be kept and refurbished as an exhibition hall. This modernistic terminal built in 1949 was the first postwar building listed in Hungary (1977) and as such it must be preserved on its original site although many competition entries for the National Theatre proposed its demolition or removal.

Strange though it may appear, not only the man in the street but some professionals, even in the field of preservation, are not able to evaluate potential 'young monuments' in an objective way. Architects and experts of the older generation who personally experienced nasty periods from our recent past, cannot separate products from the political background taking into account exclusively the architectural and historical value of the given building or complex. 'The historical approach is badly missing from the field of the protection of monuments' – writes a young art historian working for the National Board in a polemical article about the preservation of recent heritage[5] – as opposed to a subjective approach, let us call it neo-purism, which picks out certain elements of a work to keep as determined, and the fate of the building depends exclusively on arbitrary attitudes and the aesthetic considerations of our day. It often happens that an architect is not able to appreciate an early work of his own *oeuvre* and assist in its alteration. A potential monument of the 1960s was damaged when the former Chemolimpex offices in the city centre of Budapest (7–9 Deák Ferenc Street, 1960–63. Architect: Zoltán Gulyás) had to be renewed in 1992 for a new client, the National Savings Bank. Since the original architect was living and he also participated in the team of the designers, the authorities did nothing to stop alterations that seriously affected the original concept (the grey granite cladding was replaced by a reddish one, the proportions of the windows were changed, the skylights fitting in a reinforced concrete grid on the ceiling of the banking hall were turned into a copy of the glassed pyramid of the Louvre, etc.). This 'accident' could have been prevented if the authorities had made efforts in time to put this building on a 'waiting list' so that they could establish conditions.

A common feature of the present situation in the whole Central Eastern European region is the menace to modern buildings issuing from rapid and mass changes in the ownership after the collapse of Communism. The privatisation of former state properties often means that foreign developers are purchasing real estate just to obtain an inner-city

territory of high value and in order to realise their dream (generally a complex of commercial, administrative blocks and luxury apartments or hotels) they will pull down all the existing buildings with absolutely no concern for their historic value. This happens in the case of previously prospering industrial plants occupying important sites in Budapest, such as MOM (Hungarian Optical Works) with concrete factory buildings from the period 1920–50 or Ganz Electrical Works also with steel-and-concrete halls and one of the best high-rise factory blocks from around 1949. Huge textile and engine works were sub-divided and sold in parts and now accommodate a great variety of trades that have transformed buildings or segments of buildings on their own. The same thing happened to a central department store (former Pioneers' Department Store in Kossuth Street, 1951) which has a magnificent modern interior and has been purchased by an Australian developer consortium, together with four adjacent plots, to serve as the site for a new shopping centre. The protest of the civil heritage movement and demonstrations by university students against the demolition resulted in a climb-down by the developer and the building still stands. Nevertheless, its future in 1998 is uncertain since it has not yet been listed and for lack of a prospective client; the ground floor has been let to several dozen small retailers endowing the interior with the ambience of an Eastern bazaar.

The case of the power plant of the Municipal Electricity Works in Budapest-Kelenföld shows that the preparation of scientific documentation does not necessarily result in the listing of the monument. The complex, built in several phases between 1910 and 1934 in a rationalist manner reminiscent of early Peter Behrens industrial buildings, was prepared for privatisation and the Municipality commissioned a detailed documentation on the history and architectural values of the plant so that they could initiate the process of listing. Two years passed and the documentation has not yet arrived in the offices of the National Board, five miles away. It is plain to everybody that neither companies nor developers like monuments, or rather, they do not like authorities which might restrict them in the realisation of their grandiose projects, and they therefore do everything they can to prevent the listing of a building or complex to which they have taken a liking. In recent years, some political circles could be seen to be putting pressure on local and national institutions for the protection of historic monuments and launching press campaigns against so-called 'inflexible' officials.

In Hungary, modern buildings more exposed to damage than works of former periods are generally in very bad repair, especially because, after being nationalised, their maintenance has been neglected over many decades. One-family houses and large apartments have been divided into several flats and crude alterations made. After the political changes of 1989, most of the nationalised flats and houses were reprivatised, or rather, sold to those living in them. This political decision froze the existing situation and the new ownership made very difficult the reconstruction of the original conditions on the one hand, and did not improve the state of preservation of the buildings on the other, for the low level of average income and unfavourable credit conditions do not permit occupants to spend on careful renovation. As a consequence, most Modern Movement housing is in such a bad state of preservation that we feel ashamed when showing it to visitors and have had to use archival photographs in the architectural guide of Budapest.

Particularly delicate is the situation of postwar housing. New housing types of the reconstruction period (1947–50), the first standard designs developed for housing estates and new towns during 1950 and 1951 in a modern spirit, as well as slabs and towers from the period 1956 to 1965, are far from being recognised as of historic value. Their prestige has decreased considerably in the course of time and since small flats in them barely meet the living standards of the day, everybody who can afford to, moves out. The lower income groups who then take their place, further increase the deterioration. Even conservation experts often disregard that part of our young heritage for it does not correspond to the 'modern imagery' and spectacular character associated with modern monuments. Hungarian conservationists have hitherto concentrated on, and selected from among 'impressive' examples, an attitude that was convenient in the beginning but should now be revised.

Interior design is too rarely considered by Modern Movement conservationists. Both the trade and the catering industries (plus entertainment) have kept architects and interior designers busy with smaller

scale design works such as shops, shopfronts, cafés, restaurants, cinemas, etc. They all represent a transient genre. Whenever fashions and demands change, interiors and the front are also changed or rebuilt. Masterpieces disappear from one day to the next. The loss in Hungary is immense. Nevertheless there are some surviving interiors and shopfronts from the inter-war period. The former Münchengrätz shoe shop in Budapest (15 Kossuth Lajos Street) has retained its main features from 1937. While the shopfront was reconstructed not in the most accurate way, the listed interior looks almost the same as it did at the time of its completion. The cherry wood wall panelling and built-in furniture with a gallery was all made in a modern, streamlined style. Another remarkable shopfront built in 1935 has also remained in a condition that justified a thorough reconstruction.[6]

Figure 5.1 ERMA shopfront, Budapest 1935, architect Pál Rákos

Figure 5.2 ERMA shopfront, Budapest early 1980s

Figure 5.3 Semi-detached house, (Gyula Rimanóczy 1933) Pasarét, Budapest

Figure 5.4 Semi-detached house, (Gyula Rimanóczy 1933) Pasarét, Budapest, before restoration

The lavish textile store named ERMA (4–6 Teréz Boulevard) had a 7-m-square shop window at the corner, with an engine-driven revolving stage (Figure 5.1). The logo originally appeared at the two most striking positions, above the entrance the metal letters were 1.5 metres high, while on the corner somewhat smaller. The omission of these signs after the shop was nationalised, as well as the blue paint on the upper glass sheets of the shop windows together with the new neon signs, altered the nature of the design (Figure 5.2). In the mid-1980s the company had the shopfront restored according to its original condition. They even had the signs of their legal predecessor re-made. Parallel to the reconstruction the process of listing occurred and this is now the sole shopfront of the inter-war period that is complete with original signs.

Of the very few good examples concerning the reconstruction of a 1930s modern building, one excels in quality and thoughtfulness.[7] The semi-detached house, built in the Pasarét garden suburb of Budapest in 1933 and designed by a gifted architect of the then younger generation, Gyula Rimanóczy (Figure 5.3), was bought by the Inter-Europa Bank some years ago. The president of the bank, an admirer of the Modern Movement (which is a rarity among this rank in Hungary) and the architects (Tamás Dévényi and Katalin Németh) who

Figure 5.5 Semi-detached house, (Gyula Rimanóczy 1933) Pasarét, Budapest, after restoration

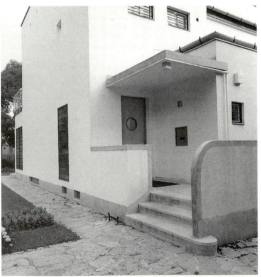

Figure 5.6 Semi-detached house, (Gyula Rimanóczy 1933) Pasarét, Budapest, after restoration

are also sympathetic to this tendency, decided to restore the exteriors (Figures 5.4–5.6) as accurately as possible while the interiors had to be adapted to function as branches of the bank. Later additions were removed, windows manufactured anew on the model of the original but with Thermopan panes, and even the original colour scheme was restored, based upon carefully exposed original areas. Not only the building but the surrounding garden, also designed in the period, was reconstructed (landscape designer: Ágnes Herczegh).

Notes

1   *20th Century Monuments in Budapest* (ed. Piroska A. Czétényi) Budapest 1979 (with an English preface).

2   Nóra Pamer, *Magyar építészete a Két világhábotú között* Hungarian Architecture between the two World Wars (Budapest 1983) with an English summary.

3   András Ferkai, *Buda építészete a Két világhábotú között* 'The Architecture of Buda between the two World Wars' (Budapest 1995).

4   Modern Architecture in Hungary 1930–49, ed. Edina Horváth – with English Preface (Budapest 1996).

5   Pál Lövey '*A Közelmúlt emlékeinek Müemléki védelméröl*' (About preservation of the recent past) (Müemlékvédelmi Szemle No 1 1996).

6   See: Üzletportál rekonstrukciója (Reconstruction of shopfront) (Magyar Építömüvészet No 6, 1987).

7   See: Pasaréti ikervilla rekonstrukciója – müemlék a huszadik századból (Reconstruction of a semi-detached house at Pesarét) a twentieth century monument (Épités Felújítás No 6, 1994).

6   Vancouver's recent landmarks

Robert G. Lemon and Marco D'Agostini

Introduction

Vancouver is a young city, incorporated in 1886. The population of the metropolitan area – the lower mainland of the province of British Columbia – is about 1.5 million people. It is Canada's third largest city and a major port on the west coast of North America. In its centennial year, 1986, a heritage inventory was established of buildings built prior to 1940. In the decade since its establishment, there has been a growing recognition of the value of the city's buildings from the modern, post-World War Two era. The West Coast of Canada, and Vancouver in particular, had an important period of development in the late 1940s through to the early 1960s which produced a rich legacy of buildings of modern regionalism and technical innovation.

In order to raise the awareness of the buildings of the post-World War Two era, the city's Heritage Commission undertook a survey of buildings built after 1940. The study was known as the Recent Landmarks Study and was completed in 1990. It considered over 250 buildings in the City of Vancouver to determine if they met heritage criteria established for older buildings on the Vancouver Heritage Register. Of those surveyed, 100 were evaluated in detail and according to stylistic categories established for the era. This became the master list of Recent Landmarks. To date, 20 of these buildings have been formally listed on the City's Heritage Register and three are legally designated. This chapter describes the modern era in Vancouver, the Recent Landmarks Program, outlines the stylistic categories established, the evaluation methodology

and the public awareness component. The chapter concludes with brief case studies of the rehabilitation of the former BC Hydro Building and the former Vancouver Public Library.

Vancouver's heritage

In 1986, Vancouver's centennial year, the Vancouver Heritage Register or VHR (originally known as the Vancouver Heritage Inventory) was completed. The VHR listed over 2,200 buildings and sites that were considered to have heritage value to the City of Vancouver. Consistent with most communities in Canada, the VHR included only buildings built before 1940. However, this time frame limited potential heritage resources to those built in Vancouver's first fifty-four years. The following three-decade period produced a notable legacy of progressive, modern buildings many of which were architectural and cultural landmarks and, due to contemporary publications and awards, were highly influential in modern Canadian architecture.

Because these buildings had not been included as part of the record of Vancouver's 'heritage', a true sense of the historical development of the city was incomplete. Furthermore, as these buildings began to approach fifty years of age they increasingly became threatened with demolition and inappropriate alteration.

The modern era in Vancouver

The post-World War Two era in Canada was marked by rapid population growth, a rising economy, and an extraordinary period of building and development. Design in this period was influenced by the Modern Movement which had begun in Central Europe in the 1920s and 1930s and celebrated modern technology and innovation. Vancouver proved to be a fertile ground for Modernism as a generation of young architects and artists embraced Modernist thoughts and ideals. Local architects began to experiment with the use of new materials and with the relationship between building and site. This new breed of designers adopted the goals and objectives of Modernism in the design of both commercial and residential buildings.

Commercial and institutional buildings in the post-1940 era employed these emerging Modernist technologies allowing for glass curtain walls and flexible interior space. Modern buildings, preferring unadorned surfaces over non-essential decoration relied on materials, form and detailing for design expression (Figure 6.1).

A distinct new residential building style, which became known as West Coast Regional, emerged during this period. This style was characterised by a wooden post and beam construction system, the use of local materials, and the extensive use of landscaping to integrate interior and exterior spaces (Figure 6.2).

Many of Vancouver's postwar buildings were recognised by contemporary critics for their excellence in design and their importance in the evolution of twentieth century Canadian architecture. While some buildings from this period had been recognised previously, no detailed study of the period existed. The purpose of the Recent Landmarks Program was to document and acknowledge the most significant buildings from this time.

The Recent Landmarks Program

The Recent Landmarks Program was initiated by the Vancouver Heritage Commission (the city council's appointed volunteer advisory body on heritage matters) in 1990 to expand the scope of the Vancouver Heritage Register to include modern buildings, i.e., those built after 1940. One of the objectives in undertaking this study was to raise public awareness of the architecture of the period. In a city like Vancouver it is often difficult to generate

Figure 6.1 The Vancouver Public Library (Semmens and Simpson Architects, 1956–57, is a very good example of an institutional building from the Modern Period. Some of the building's more notable design features include a reinforced concrete structural system with curtain wall glazing creating an open interior design, a distinctive perimeter cantilever and roof projection with a knife edge profile and a unique two-storey glazed corner at street level that provides openness and encourages public accessibility. The Vancouver Public Library was also one of the first in the city to incorporate public art in the design of the building. The building was rehabilitated for retail, restaurant and TV studio uses in 1995–97. See Figure 6.10. Listed on the Vancouver Heritage Register and a municipally designated building. Archival photo c. 1958 courtesy Vancouver Public Library

Figure 6.2 The Copp House (Ron Thom of Sharp Thompson Berwick and Pratt, 1951) has many of the characteristics of the West Coast Regional Style and is noted for its experimentation and economy, using a timber framing system on an eight-foot module, extensive glazing, and an open plan with horizontal wings built into a sloping site. Listed on the Vancouver Heritage Register and a candidate for the DOCOMOMO International Register

appreciation for turn-of-the-century buildings let alone those that were built only a few decades ago.

Prior to this initiative, several events helped to lay a foundation for a better understanding of the

Modern period and to increase public awareness. In 1986 a symposium on Award Winning Vancouver Architecture was organised by the Architectural Institute of BC and Simon Fraser University. In 1989 the Heritage Commission became increasingly concerned with the future of Modern buildings and promoted the theme of 'Our Recent Heritage' as part of Heritage Week activities in early 1990. At about the same time, an important Modernist building, C.B.K. van Norman's Custom House office/warehouse building of 1950–55 was slated for demolition.

In June 1990, the city council directed the planning department to review buildings that were more than twenty years old for the possibility of adding them to the VHR. Twenty years was thought to be a critical period of time to allow for assessing the heritage merit of a building. Shortly after this, the Heritage Commission received a grant from the BC Heritage Trust to assist in the completion of the study.

The study's inventory was co-ordinated by the planning department of the City of Vancouver and the school of architecture at the University of British Columbia who provided staff to oversee the completion of the study and to provide administrative support. The grant from the BC Heritage Trust allowed for the hiring of four student researchers.

A steering committee made up of scholars and architects,[1] including some who designed Recent Landmark buildings and were familiar with modern architecture, provided input and guidance. The study commenced with a review of architectural, design and popular journals from the period to identify notable buildings and to obtain a better understanding of the aesthetic values, technological innovations, and social and cultural currents of the day. Additional research included a review of architectural guide books and publications and archival documents from the period to assist in determining lesser known or forgotten examples. Other buildings were identified through field reviews and from steering committee suggestions. Over a three-year period more than 250 buildings were reviewed and evaluated according to criteria established for the Heritage Register.

In 1992 Vancouver city council brought its definition of 'heritage' up-to-date by resolving that buildings at least twenty years old could qualify for

heritage status and could be eligible for listing on the Heritage Register. The register is a policy document which does not assure the protection of the building, but does make the building eligible for the city's heritage incentives. (By negotiating the long-term protection of listed buildings through the use of these incentives, primarily by-law relaxations and density bonusing, planning staff have facilitated the preservation, with protection afforded by the council's heritage designation by-law, of over 160 listed properties in the past two decades.)

With the Recent Landmarks study complete and the political support to consider modern buildings as 'heritage', the next step was to begin the process of formally listing the buildings on the Heritage Register. In 1994, after planning staff had discussed the potential listing of some of the Recent Landmarks with the property owners, Council approved the addition of eleven of them to the Heritage Register. Since then an additional nine were added in 1996, bringing the total number of listed buildings to twenty (or 20 per cent of the priority modern properties). Of these, three have been designated – protected – as part of negotiated rehabilitation approvals. These include the Gardner House, the former BC Hydro Building and the former Vancouver Public Library. The rehabilitation of the last two is the subject of the case studies below. In addition, an information brochure detailing the significance of these buildings and the period in which they were built has also been printed.

Development of stylistic categories

The steering committee decided early on in the study that the heritage value of modern buildings should be determined using the same criteria as older buildings already on the Heritage Register. This meant that an assessment would be done, according to the parameters of the Register, with respect to the building's architectural value. As architectural style and type were important components of this evaluation, it was necessary to establish stylistic categories within the MoMo period so that relative architectural merit could be determined.

This task charted new ground in Vancouver and there was very little conclusive documentation in this area of MoMo architecture. It proved to be a challenge for the team and considerable thought was given to how the various stylistic periods and variations had evolved locally, in the larger context of the modern period.

The stylistic categories were determined after researching architectural style guides and writings on the period and a review of buildings with similar design features constructed internationally during the era. The draft categories of styles were refined by grouping the buildings by functional type. Photos of each of the building candidates were pinned up to facilitate the working sessions with the steering committee. After considerable rearrangment of the photos of each of style and type, the following stylistic terms were selected: Moderne, International, Late Modern, Expressionist, and West Coast Regional. These styles would be used later in the evaluation process to determine relative heritage merit.

The styles found in Vancouver's building stock can be identified by the following characteristics:

Moderne

Following Art Deco, and sharing some of its characteristics, this vernacular style was popular from the 1930s through to the late 1940s in Vancouver. Design is expressed through the building's geometry and massing with common design elements including flat roof forms with horizontal massing; horizontal shadow banding; asymmetry in smaller examples; and monumental symmetry in large scale and institutional buildings.

International

This represents the early Modern Movement (1950s). These buildings are characterised by unbroken surface volumes, non-bearing screen walls and a structure that is not expressed on the surface. Roofs are flat or slanted and windows are flush often set in ribbon banding with light simple metal frames and placed flush with the surface of the building (Figure 6.3).

Late Modern

Can be described as a later development of the Modern Movement (from the late 1950s) with three sub-categories: Late Modern – Cage; Late Modern – Curtain Wall; and Late Modern – Brutalist.

Figure 6.3 Hycroft Towers (Semmens and Simpson Architects, 1950) is a good example of the International style with a non-load-bearing screen wall made of alternating bands of metal spandrel panels and flush metal frame windows

a) Late Modern: Cage   The surface of these buildings is highly articulated with exaggerated load bearing structural elements. Emphasis is on both horizontal and vertical elements (Figure 6.4).

b) Late Modern: Curtain Wall   Surface effects and purity of shape are accented by non load-bearing glass curtain walls (Figure 6.5).

c) Late Modern: Brutalist   These buildings have a distinctive sculptural form with large-scale elements and coarse materials and finishes. The shape and design of Brutalist style buildings has a strong reference to cubist form (Figure 6.6).

Expressionist

Characteristics include an overall dynamic sculptural form, expressed roof structure and the use of contrasting materials to emphasise form (Figure 6.7).

West Coast Regional

Found primarily in residential design, its main attributes include the dominance of an exposed timber structural system, open plan, shed-like roofs, the extensive use of indigenous timber, lots of glass, integration of interior and exterior spaces and the use of native trees and landscaping (Figures 6.8 and 6.9).

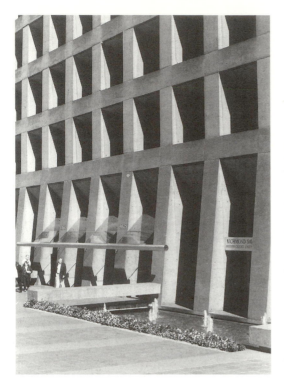

Figure 6.4 The MacMillan–Bloedel Building (Erickson-Massey and Francis Donaldson, 1968–69) was designed as two off-set towers made of unfinished concrete that tapers from eight feet in thickness at the base to 8 inches at the top of the building. Listed on the Vancouver Heritage Register and a candidate for the DOCOMOMO International Register

Figure 6.6 The Moore Business Forms Building (McCarter Nairne and Partners, 1968) is the best example of the Brutalist style in Vancouver and features unfinished concrete and an unusual triangular plan

Figure 6.5 The Dal Grauer Substation is one of Vancouver's most striking and visible works of modern architecture. It was designed by Sharp and Thompson, Berwick and Pratt architects in 1953. The glazed skin exposes the workings of the hydro substation, however plexiglass panels have replaced the original glass (for safety reasons). Listed on the Vancouver Heritage Register and a candidate for the DOCOMOMO International Register (with the adjacent former BC Hydro Building – see Figure 6.9)

Figure 6.7 This triodetic dome is notable for its sculptural form and roof structure. The roof on the Bloedel Conservatory (Underwood McKinley Cameron Wilson Smith and Associates, 1969) consists of triangular frame elements of aluminum pipe infilled by plexiglass panels. Listed on the Vancouver Heritage Register

Figure 6.8 This interior view of the Unitarian Church shows the use of natural materials, flat roof forms, large glazed areas and the integration of exterior and interior spaces typical of the West Coast Regional style in a religious building of great simplicity and beauty. It was designed by Wolfgang Gerson, with Richard Hale architect in 1964. Listed on the Vancouver Heritage Register and a candidate for the DOCOMOMO International Register

Figure 6.9 The BC Hydro Building (1955–57, Thompson Berwick and Pratt) has a unique lozenge shape with a reinforced concrete core located at the centre of the building that supports the cantilevered floors. A glass and metal spandrel curtain wall is also supported by thin metal piers on the exterior curtain wall. Mosaic tile murals are used at the base and in the interior lobby areas as public art. Listed on the Vancouver Heritage Register, this building was Vancouver's first designated Recent Landmark. It is a candidate for the DOCOMOMO International Register with the adjacent Dal Grauer Substation (see Figure 6.5)

Evaluation methodology

Evaluations of buildings were made using the criteria that had been established as part of the original Heritage Register completed in 1986. The steering committee concluded that it was important to use the same evaluation criteria in order to maintain consistency between the existing Heritage Register and the buildings identified in the Recent Landmarks study. The evaluations considered the (1) architectural characteristics; (2) historical and cultural value; (3) importance of the building's context or setting and; (4) degree of original building fabric that remained. A group of about 250 buildings were identified as having heritage value and preliminary evaluations for each of them was prepared.

Using the Register's numerical evaluation system, the buildings were evaluated and assessed in the 'A',

'B', 'C' or 'X' categories. The results were vetted by the steering committee and planning staff. Buildings were then compared by style and type and scores were adjusted as necessary. A priority group of 100 buildings, comprising all the 'A' and ''B' rated buildings was compiled. The preliminary evaluations were reviewed by the Heritage Commission and the findings were reported to the city council in September 1992. The council instructed the director of planning to initiate a notification programme of the 100 priority buildings.

The first group of eleven Recent Landmark buildings was added to the Heritage Register by the city council on 20 January 1994, with another nine added in September 1996, for a total of twenty listings to date. Listing is a significant step towards a building's protection in that it is then eligible for preservation incentives.

Public awareness

An important part of the Recent Landmarks Program was the public awareness component. To help describe the period and the value of its buildings, an information brochure on the Modern Movement and its significance to Vancouver was prepared. It included descriptions of the more notable buildings and the various architectural styles that evolved during the period. The brochure has been useful in the notification programme as well. Meetings with affected building owners and with the architectural community and the general public were also part of the notification process.

Case study 1: Former BC Electric Building

Designed in 1955–57 by architects Thompson Berwick and Pratt as the head office for the BC Electric Company (later BC Hydro), the building was rehabilitated as a condominium residential tower known as as The Electra in 1994 (Figure 6.9). A landmark tower of twenty-three storeys, the building's unusual lozenge shape had a concrete core and very shallow cantilevered floor plate – no desk was further than six metres from a window.

Figure 6.10 The rehabilitation of the former Vancouver Public Library shows the addition of a penthouse level, satellite dish and some of the neon signage. The sunscreen louvres on the Robson Street (right hand) facade have been removed. The curtain wall glazing has been sympathetically replaced with new double glazed panels in aluminum mullions which match the originals

Slender external column-mullions clad in aluminum provided structural support to the floor slab at the perimeter. A curtain wall system of single glazed fixed windows in aluminum frames with enamel-coated steel spandrels was installed between the structural mullions. Extensive use of glass mosaic tiles in decorative patterns of green, blue, grey, mauve and black were featured on the elevator core, external planters, foundation walls and the elevator penthouse.

In the course of the rehabilitation designed by Paul Merrick Architect, the structural mullions were retained in situ. The curtain wall system was replaced with a double glazed system in frames to match the material and colour of the original. The proportions of the window and spandrel area were altered – after extensive research and mock ups – to introduce new opening window units for ventilation to the apartments. While this change altered the proportions of the original curtain wall system, it was done in a way which does not change the building's original design aesthetic. The project also included the restoration of the tile mosaics. A density bonus (with the ability to transfer density to other downtown sites) and parking relaxations were incentives used to assist with the economics of the building's rehabilitation. In return, the owner agreed to protect the building through heritage designation, becoming the city's first designated Recent Landmark.

Overall, the project has achieved a successful balance of preservation and adaptation, seeing a modern landmark rehabilitated for a viable new use.

Case study 2: Former Vancouver Public Library

Vancouver's former Public Library was sold to help finance the construction of a new central library. The former library building was built in 1956-57 to designs of the architects Semmens and Simpson (see Figure 6.1). Aspects of West Coast Regionalism can be found in their adaptation of the International Style to this civic institution in downtown Vancouver. A glazed corner opened the building to view from the street, while a solid granite base, vertical sunscreen louvres and a knife-edged roof canopy combined to create an assymmetrical but balanced composition. An important mosaic tile mural was commissioned for the building's lobby as well as an illuminated bronze sculpture on the exterior.

The purchase of the building for conversion to retail and restaurant use saved the building from demolition. A package of incentives, including density bonusing (transferable to other downtown sites) as well as parking relaxations were agreed to by the owner in exchange for the building's heritage designation. However, the designation excluded the granite base, the vertical sunscreen louvres and the mosaic mural.

The building has been rehabilitated by James Cheng Architect. Many changes were requested to the exterior and interior of the building as part of its conversion for a Virgin Records Megastore and a Planet Hollywood restaurant (see Figure 6.10). In rehabilitating the building, much of the exterior has been retained or replaced (curtain wall glazing) in-keeping with the original aesthetic. Despite efforts to preserve the granite base, sunscreen louvres and the mosaic mural, these were altered. While the new glazed openings in the granite base have been well designed, the new signage elements overwhelm the appearance of the building and detract from its architectural significance. At the insistence of Virgin Records, the glazed double-height corner space was enclosed to create a 'black box' retail environment. Worse, the blank wall to the street is less than one metre inside the windows and the wall is used to display huge posters, framed in red neon tubing. The exterior is further marred by a new metal canopy, complete with an illuminated blue and red globe, over the Planet Hollywood restaurant entry. The discreet and handsomely detailed penthouse addition is overwhelmed by a satellite dish installed atop the building.

While the valiant and progressive efforts to preserve a landmark building of the Modern era are diminished by the manner in which inappropriate signage and external additions have been handled, the distruptive changes are fortunately largely reversible.

Conclusion

The Recent Landmarks Program has proved to be an effective tool in increasing public awareness of buildings from the Modern period in Vancouver. The Recent Landmarks Program has served not only to identify, but also assist in creating a greater appreciation of buildings from the post-1940 period.

Of the twenty buildings that have been added to the Heritage Register, three have been legally designated as protected heritage sites ensuring their preservation for the future. Without the study it would have been much more difficult to obtain support from the buildings' owners as well as political support for the retention of the buildings. Despite the mixed results of the two rehabilitation projects undertaken so far, the Recent Landmarks Program has been effective in raising the awareness of the issues and potential of the preservation of Modern Movement heritage in the city.

For a city like Vancouver, which is little more than a century old, the Recent Landmarks Program has provided an opportunity to document its development in the postwar period. Together with the existing Heritage Register, the Recent Landmarks Program has completed the historical record of Vancouver's first century and identified the landmark buildings that represent an important part of its evolution. It also ensured that the continuity of the city's heritage is maintained into the twenty-first century.

Note

1   The steering group included Abraham Rogatnick, Hal Kalman, Wolfgang Gerson, Barry Downs and Sherry McKay.

Bibliography of British Columbia modern architecture

D. Beers, 'The Way We Lived', *Western Living* (summer 1993).

L. Berelowitz, 'Fade to Modern', *Boulevard* (Nov/Dec 1990).

M. D'Agostini and R. Lemon, 'Vancouver's Recent Landmark Program', *DOCOMOMO Journal* (June 1994).

M. D'Agostini and R. Lemon, 'Recent Landmarks in Vancouver – The Post-1940s Inventory', *CRM – Cultural Resources Management* Vol. 16, No. 6 (1993).

C. M. Ede, *Canadian Architecture 1960/70* (Toronto, Burns and MacEachern Ltd, 1971).

A. Erickson, *The Architecture of Arthur Erickson* (Vancouver, Douglas and McIntyre, 1988).

E. Gibson, *Award Winning Vancouver Architecture* (Burnaby: Simon Fraser University, 1986).

A. Gruft, 'Vancouver Architecture: the Last Fifteen Years', *Vancouver: Art and Artists 1931–83* (Vancouver: Vancouver Art Gallery, 1983).

E. Iglauer, *Seven Stones: A Portrait of Arthur Erickson, Architect* (Seattle, Harbour Publishing/University of Washington Press, 1981).

R. Lemon and M. D'Agostini, 'Recent Landmarks: Identifying Vancouver's Modern Heritage Buildings', *ICOMOS Canada Bulletin*. Vol. 5, No. 1 (1996).

H. Kalman, *A History of Canadian Architecture* (Toronto, Oxford University Press, 1994).

H. Kalman, R. Phillips and R. Ward, *Exploring Vancouver: The Essential Architectural Guide* (Vancouver, UBC Press, 1993).

R. W. Liscombe, 'Modes of Modernizing: The Acquisition of Modernist Design in Canada', *Bulletin of the Society for the Study of Architecture in Canada,* Vol. 19, Number 3 (Sept. 1994).

R. W. Liscombe, *The New Spirit: Modern Architecture in Vancouver, 1938–1963* (Vancouver: Douglas and McIntyre in association with the Canadian Centre for Architecture, 1997).

S. McKay, 'Western Homes, Western Living', *Bulletin of the Society for the Study of Architecture in Canada,* Vol. 14, Number 3 (September 1989).

S. Rossiter, 'The Building Boomers', *Western Living* (August 1988).

D. Shadbolt, *Ron Thom: The Shaping of an Architect* (Vancouver, Douglas and McIntyre, 1995).

D. Shadbolt, 'Postwar Architecture in Vancouver', *Vancouver: Art & Artists 1931–83* (Vancouver, Vancouver Art Gallery, 1983).

D. Simpson, 'Toward Regionalism in Canadian Architecture', *Canadian Art,* Vol. X, No. 3 (1953).

City of Vancouver, *Recent Landmarks brochure* (Vancouver, Planning Department, 1992).

G. Warrington, *Contemporary West Coast Architects.*

7 Preserving modern architecture in the US

Nina Rappaport

Introduction

Many communities in the United States are addressing the challenge of the preservation of prewar and postwar modern architecture. With the realisation that our recent past has become historic, and that many buildings of this period deserve preservation, also comes the realisation of the need to re-analyse preservation regulations, registries and methodologies as they apply to modern architecture. The totally different aesthetic, use of new materials and new building types in the modern era also require a new approach to preservation. In the US the contrast between the public regulations and private owners' desire to have freedom for commercial success also comes into play, as does a public which does not understand the significance of buildings that they remember being constructed. Groups and individuals around the country are taking initiatives to identify significant modern buildings for registries and find ways to best document and restore these landmark buildings.

Regulatory systems in the US

In the United States regulations to preserve modern buildings follow the same federal and local government guidelines and organisational structures as those for all historically important architecture. There are local city designations as well as national designations which began with the founding of the National Historic Preservation Act in 1966 to institutionalise the National Register of Historic Places. The National Register is organised under the National Park Service, part of the Department of the Interior with State Offices of Historic Preservation, to help implement nominations in each state. To qualify for national listing a building must be significant to the history of the country; or be associated with an important historic person; or be the work of a great creative master. Historic designations can be proposed by individuals, associations and the government. A structure can be listed on a historic register at the national or state level depending on the degree of its significance. The US government doesn't provide financial support for preservation projects and grants are hard to find.

To qualify for the National Register, a building should be fifty years old, but over 1,000 exceptions have been made where other aspects are significant enough to make them eligible, such as the Art Moderne Ford Building in San Diego designed by Walter Darwin Teague in 1935 which was given historic designation in 1973.

The National Register is primarily an honour and only a protection in regards to any federal development work which might occur in that historic area. When an owner undertakes the restoration of a commercial property, tax benefits can be available when the restoration meets the Secretary of the Interior's standards for historic preservation. This is the way the government offers its financial support. The standards are guidelines which describe the manner in which a restoration is to be implemented, such as how the original elements must be repaired, then restored and, when that is not feasible, that the elements may be replaced. Some of these regulations need a re-evaluation with regard to modern buildings since often a material can be replaced without changing the appearance of the building.

Many local city preservation codes are actually stricter than federal codes and have more protective clout. New York's preservation laws are often held up as a model. The New York City Landmarks Preservation Commission (LPC) was founded in 1965 after the demolition of Penn Central Terminal designed in 1906 by McKim, Mead & White. The LPC designates structures as historic, regulates alterations to historic buildings and provides technical assistance to building owners. A NYC Landmark may not be altered without prior approval, through a lengthy review and permit process.

In New York City a building can be designated a City Landmark when it is only thirty years old. But as of 1998, only a handful of buildings from this period have been designated because the interest is so new, as are the buildings, in comparison to the previous eras and often people feel that older buildings should take precedence. Within modern architecture preservation there is a new dialogue about the value of prewar and postwar buildings.

It is much easier to come to an agreement concerning the significance of the prewar, 'white' modern buildings, often designed by European immigrants, which are not, however, the totality that makes up American modern architectural heritage. Postwar architecture is really where the challenge and philosophical questions lie, as to what should be preserved and documented. Many of these buildings built for corporate America, were not meant to last forever, and are now in need of major upgrades for computerised and electronic office technologies. In the US, so much preservation activity is controlled by real estate values and private ownership issues rather than the idea of a 'public good', that it makes it difficult to create district designations in areas where the real estate values are high and the owners are important to a city's stability. So there must be educational outreach to develop a consensus about which buildings are most important to be saved and what is 'Modern' in American architecture of the period.

As they come of age, these postwar buildings and their architects are receiving attention through writings by contemporary architects such as Rem Koolhaas, who has focused on the work of Wallace Harrison, or exhibitions are held and auto-biographies appear by architects such as Morris Lapidus. When architects such as Paul Rudolph pass away more attention is given to their work in retrospect. These architects of the postwar era, are now considered significant to the history of architecture as the representatives of a previous generation. In addition they are gaining importance as Postmodernism loses respect and architects look to the pre-Postmodern years to find form and theory, continuing from where Modernism truly left us, with technological experimentation and innovations.

Historical background

American modern architecture has distinct technological developments which were then transformed into a new aesthetic in the postwar period. The steel frame buildings of the turn-of-the-century led to the development of 1920s skyscrapers which have eclectic Art Deco, Classical and Art Moderne decorations. Pre-fabricated construction such as Frank Lloyd Wright's 1920s glass block and concrete houses and Buckminster Fuller's Dymaxian House of 1927 developed technological experiments in modular and cost-efficient forms. The development of new materials and improvement with concrete construction in factory buildings by Albert Kahn and Ernest Ransome lead the way for architects to adapt it to all building types both in Europe and the US.

The social concern to provide housing for all people came later to the United States, after many architects like Clarence Stein and Henry Wright toured Europe and returned to build communities such as Sunnyside Gardens in 1926. This was more innovative in its planning, whereas a modernist aesthetic developed with the 1938 Williamsburg Houses by William Lescaze in New York and housing developments by William Wurster in California. However, this new aesthetic could not be fully explored within the confines of US housing regulations.

When in the 1920s and 1930s, European architects, Marcel Breuer, Mies van der Rohe, Walter Gropius, William Lescaze, Richard Neutra, Rudolf Schindler, Eliel and Eero Saarinen and Albert Frey all emigrated to the USA, their new Modern style was easily transplanted. In 1932, architect Philip Johnson and historian Henry-Russell Hitchcock organised an exhibition on what they called the new 'International Style' at the Museum of Modern Art which served as a catalyst for architects in other countries to adopt the avant-guard style and promoted the new designs in America.

As Kenneth Frampton observes:

> . . . the International Style never became truly international. Nonetheless, it implied a universality of approach which generally favored lightweight technique, synthetic modern materials and standard modular parts so as to facilitate fabrication and erection. It tended as a general rule towards the hypothetical flexibility of the free plan, and to this end it preferred skeleton frame construction to masonry. This predisposition became formalistic where specified conditions, be they climatic, cultural or economic, could not support the application of advanced light-weight technology.[1]

This 'International Style' monumentalised techno-logy through the use of steel and glass and became more prevalent in the postwar period with corporate buildings such as the Lake Shore Drive Apartments in Chicago by Mies van der Rohe of 1950; his Seagrams Building with Philip Johnson in 1955; and Lever House by Skidmore, Owings and Merrill in 1952, both in New York. At the same time Louis Kahn began designing with a more personal interpretation of Modern, the Yale Art Gallery of 1951 in New Haven, softer glass, steel and masonry façades with concrete and masonry interiors.

Preservation advocacy

In the US, preservation activity is conducted not only by government agencies, but by interested individuals and preservation professionals often through not-for-profit organisations. In cities such as New York, Denver and Los Angeles groups have been formed to address issues such as a specific period of architecture, work of an architect, a neighbourhood, a building, or specific materials. Modern architecture is well documented in archival collections at universities, museums and historical societies. Conferences, seminars and publications focus on modern architecture to identify resources,

share experiences and find new preservation techniques.

But preservation of modern architecture is practically a contradiction to the way the historic preservation movement began in the United States. Individual efforts at grass-roots level initiated the preservation movement because of the lack of respect for the historic fabric of previous eras with the destruction in the 1950s and 1960s of so many inner city historic districts by grand master plans and highways. Some of these same developments which were contemporaneously criticised are those which are getting a second look by the preservation community now. The earliest historic designations in the US were those of significance to the founding of the country, very patriotic and conservative, but now designation encompasses everything from roadside buildings to vernacular homes.

Chester Liebs, Director of the University of Vermont Preservation Program, in a 1976 article in the journal, *Possibilities,* writes that, 'today we are in a period of reaction to this era (the modern), and historic preservation is challenging modernism and urban renewal as a national aesthetic order. It is at this juncture that preservationists can learn a philosophical lesson from the modern era.'

Modern examples

Preservation of modern architecture has been more prevalent around the saving of private houses, perhaps because of the facility to preserve at a smaller scale and due to the pride of the owners. The National Trust for Historic Preservation, a not-for-profit umbrella organisation, provides technical assistance to local associations and owns historic houses open to the public. They have two modern houses in their collection, Philip Johnson's 1949 Glass House which will be donated to the trust and Frank Lloyd Wright's Pope-Lehighey Usonian house. The Pope-Lehighey House built near Washington DC, was endangered in the 1960s with the construction of the interstate highway. Mrs. Lehighey donated the house to the National Trust in 1964 with the agreement that she could continue to live there and that the house would be relocated to the National Park Service's Woodlawn Plantation. After the house was moved and restored it had to be de-constructed and re-constructed again to solve the problem of differential settlement on the new site.

Other organisations are also the stewards of individual houses and run model preservation programmes: The Frank Lloyd Wright Foundation maintains Talesin West; the Western Pennsylvania Conservancy recently conducted a restoration programme for Falling Water designed in 1936 by Wright which epitomised the development of modern architecture in technology and form; and the Los Angeles Conservancy has a special association to maintain the house Rudolph Schindler built in 1925–26 for Dr Lovell, with its white reinforced concrete skeleton frames and open plan which fills with sunlight and air.

Walter Gropius' 1938 house designed with Marcel Breuer in Lincoln, Massachusetts was donated to the Society for the Preservation of New England Antiquities (SPNEA) in 1983. The house with its flat roof and white planar façade exemplifies the ideals of the Modern Movement in design and furnishings. For the exterior Gropius used the local vernacular of wood siding, applied vertically, and a fieldstone foundation in a new way. In the interior, the factory materials such as laminates, cork tile floors and plastics had disintegrated and were discontinued. The SPNEA re-manufactured the modern materials and has completed a detailed paint analysis, that involved as much custom restoration work as their Colonial era houses.

Modern houses have also been preserved through the love and interest of individual building owners. One well-known British house collector, Peter Palumbo, has saved a Frank Lloyd Wright house and the Mies van der Rohe Farnesworth House in Chicago. Two early Wright American System Built houses, discovered outside Chicago, are being appreciated by their owners who are in favour of the historic landmark designation. A private owner is slowly restoring Edward Durrell Stone's 1933 Mandel House in Katonah, New York. And, when the Norman House by Lescaze designed in 1941 on East 70th Street in New York, was placed on the market in 1997, the real estate company provided tours for local preservation and architecture groups as a way to promote its preservation.

Commercial buildings of the prewar era have also been successfully saved. In 1992 two Art Moderne buildings, one on the east and the other on the west coast, both owned by the May Company, were saved from demolition. The Los Angeles Landmarks Conservancy negotiated with the owners to restore the 1939 department store designed by Albert Martin and S. A. Marx with a distinctive gold-tile and black granite corner cylindrical tower to save it as part of the adjacent Los Angeles County Museum of Art. The 1937 Washington D. C. Hecht Company warehouse designed by Gilbert Steele with extensive use of glass block and a sixth-floor illuminated glass crown was in dire need of restoration. With the DC Preservation League's urging, the building was landmarked and restored.

Postwar New York

Postwar architecture is the area most difficult to preserve. In 1995 when the North East Regional Working Party of DOCOMOMO was organised in New York City other groups took interest and an informed group of the Municipal Art Society, a 100 year old civic preservation and arts organisation began the 'Post-War Working Group' to evaluate priorities for preservation and landmark designations.

The first issue to address concerns which postwar buildings should be designated as Landmarks. Organisations have begun to submit lists to the LPC. While the Lincoln Center designed by Harrison and Abramovitz, with buildings by Philip Johnson (1962–66), could be considered for Landmark status, most people would find the idea of a Sixth Avenue or Park Avenue historic district inconceivable. As David Dunlop noted in the New York Times on 7 April 1996,

> Not everyone felt kindly toward this crop of architecture, to be sure. The building boom of the 50s and 60s had replaced so much of the city's historic fabric that it spurred a popular preservation movement culminating in the landmarks law of 1965. But even those who said 'glass box' with a sneer would have thought the Park Avenue towers would always be part of the skyline.

Promise is on the horizon with three postwar buildings in New York designated in October 1997: the Ford Foundation Building at 321 East 42nd Street designed by Kevin Roche and John Dinkeloo in 1967 with its use of Cor-ten Steel and garden atrium space, and the CBS Building designed by Eero Saarinen and Associates (1961–5) with its strong verticality and elegance. Both of these designations received prior approval from their owners and caused little controversy. The harder cases will be those border-line buildings such as Two Columbus Circle and the more vernacular buildings by lesser known or under-appreciated architects.

In 1997 a preservation debate ensued around the potential demolition or alteration of Two Columbus Circle designed by Edward Durrell Stone in 1965. Most recently used as city offices for the Department of Cultural Affairs it was built to house an art gallery. The curved concrete frame building with marble cladding hugs the circle and could be described as a bit quirky. Without windows except for porthole openings at the corners and base, and a loggia on the top floors which originally had a restaurant, it has not been uniformly appreciated by the preservation community. The potential for increased real estate development on the site makes the land more valuable than the building, so the city is proposing a development.

Issues

Major restoration issues have arisen in regard to the preservation of modern sites, such as the increased typological obsolescence of buildings; how to conserve materials; the importance of maintaining a building as a whole; the issue of modern interiors in regard to its exterior expression; and landscaped plazas and open spaces.

Functional and typological obsolescence is easily understood when looking at the many specialised building types. The branch bank is being transformed by automative banking that will eliminate the need for large bank halls. Travel has changed so that although Dulles Airport in Washington DC designed in 1941 had expansion built into its original Eero Saarinen design, its SOM's 1996 addition is a continuation of the existing building, but the redesign had to incorporate the need for heightened security, improved circulation and the arrival of jumbo jets while maintaining the metaphor of flight in the overall expansion. Some of these same issues will be addressed when the already landmarked TWA Terminal at JFK Airport designed by Saarinen in 1962 is renovated (Figure 7.1).

The question of restoration techniques with regard to saving original materials is being reconsidered in modern buildings where those have

Figure 7.1. The TWA Terminal Building, (Eero Saarinen 1956–62) JFK Airport. Photograph by Christopher Hall

failed. If replacement is necessary, the preservation of the original design intent becomes a critical conservation issue. When Unilever, owners of the Lever House designed by Gordon Bunshaft of SOM in 1952, did not want their building to be restricted through a landmark designation in 1982, citizens and professionals rallied for its listing. In 1996 Unilever, with SOM as the architects, proposed a restoration plan which included new thermal windows, but it was not approved by either the community or the Landmarks Commission. So, instead, SOM found a way to replace all the spandrel glass and the rusted carbon steel supports of the curtain wall to maintain the original design intent.

Buildings such as cultural institutions or universities constructed as monuments, face the challenge of being individual works of art which are difficult to alter such as Marcel Breuer's Whitney Museum of American Art of 1966 and Frank Lloyd Wright's Solomon R. Guggenheim Museum of 1959 (Figure 7.2). Both buildings were the centre of debates around their expansion programmes in the early 1990s. Architect Richard Gluckman's plans for renovation and additions to the Whitney have been drastically reduced from the museum's original proposal for a Michael Graves expansion. The Gwathmey Siegel & Associates addition to the Guggenheim respected closely Wright's own proposed expansion for the museum. The buildings have been carefully restored as a unified whole, but at the same time were brought up-to-date with appropriate climate controls and gallery spaces.

This pressure for institutions to expand has influenced the sponsorship competitions between

Figure 7.2 The Guggenheim Museum, (Frank Lloyd Wright 1959). Photograph by Christopher Hall (1983)

well-known architects to ease the transitions. This is a concern with The Museum of Modern Art, designed in 1939 by Philip Goodwin and Edward Durrell Stone, which has received numerous additions throughout the years. The Museum is embarking on an expansion and renovation project in 1998 which addresses the concern to save the Sculpture Garden. Illinois Institute of Technology designed by Mies van der Rohe in Chicago is beginning a renovation and expansion project and held an invited competition of fifty-six international architects (won by Rem Koolhaas) for a new campus centre which could potentially alter the original intent.

Modern architecture requires the rethinking of boundaries of what is inside and what is outside where the architects desire transparency. The appearance of the interior is visually an integral part of the envelope which must be considered by the regulatory agencies. In New York, interiors can qualify for historic landmark status – this has saved Radio City Music Hall and the Rainbow Room in Rockefeller Center. And when in 1989, the Seagram Building at 375 Park Avenue with the Four Seasons Restaurant, designed by Mies van der Rohe with Philip Johnson in 1958 was designated, it included some interiors. The deed required the views from the outside, into the building, to be the same at each floor with the same lighting fixtures, ceiling designs, venetian blinds and details for each of the separate tenants. This has required a large budget for maintenance that building owners often do not want to allocate.

But a compromise was made for the October 1997

designation of the Manufacturers Hanover Bank branch at 510 Fifth Avenue at 43rd Street, now a Chase Manhattan Bank, designed by Gordon Bunshaft of SOM in 1954. The Landmark's Commission gave it only an exterior designation because of the client's need for commercial viability. The modern architect's original desire for transparency of the outside wall makes a literal separation of outside and inside an impossibility. At Chase Manhattan, they are working to maintain the ceiling lighting and basic design elements, but much of it is cluttered with unsympathetic furniture and advertising and the Harry Bertoia sculpture is hidden from view. Lack of regulation could surely jeopardise this masterpiece.

Although the PSFS building designed by Howe and Lescaze in Philadelphia in 1932, was given local historic designation in 1968, and was made a National Historic Landmark in 1977, it was not possible to consider the building's interior. When the bank closed, the owners tried to liquidate its assets by selling, at auction, the original interior furnishings, except for the panelling and the board room table which were too difficult to remove from the building. A local museum tried to obtain the furnishings and the building is to be turned into an hotel.

In 1995 the interior of the Chicago Arts Club, designed by Mies van der Rohe in 1948, was demolished because of development pressures on a building whose exterior was not so important.

Lobby interiors are also notable places of significant creativity in postwar buildings. Lobbies such as in 666 Fifth Avenue in New York with its Isamu Noguchi sculpture is endangered with a change in building ownership and renovation plans; most of the lobby has been destroyed.

Urban open spaces are receiving attention in New York for individual designation or as part of a building site, as in the Seagrams Building with its designed plaza and set backs. Architect Richard Dattner's 1966 Adventure Playground with its unique climbing equipment and forms to explore, was threatened in 1996, so a group of concerned residents rallied to save the structures. Richard Dattner was invited to advise on the project which resulted in alterations for safety and maintenance. Other open spaces which need recognition include the plazas of Lincoln Center designed by Dan Kiley and Paley Park designed by Zion and Breen with

Albert Preston Moore in 1966 at 53rd Street near Fifth Avenue, a vest-pocket park it is an outdoor enclosed room and a quiet interval in the city.

In 1997 the US government's own buildings for the Park Service Visitors' Centers, which they developed across the country in a programme called Mission 66, became endangered. These buildings were designed both in-house and by more well-known architects such as Mitchell/Giurgola and Richard Neutra to provide an interpretation programme and landscape siting which was sensitive to their natural surroundings and were a new building type designed to enlighten the visitor. In Neutra's 1962 Gettysburg National Military Park Visitors' Center (Figure 7.3) he created a connection to his Cyclorama Building with a winding ramp which continues through the building to a roof deck observation point that exits to the battlefield. The building is threatened by a new proposal to raise money for the Park Service without concern for the architectural heritage that it was meant to profess. A huge visitors' centre, à la Disney, might be created that would commercialise the park and destroy the heritage of the way in which scenic and historic areas were interpreted.

Although there are many battles to be fought and philosophical issues to be solved, preservationists, architectural historians, architects, private associations and governmental organisations in the United States have embarked on a wealth of activity to restore modern architecture. With an even greater

Figure 7.3. The Gettysburg Visitors' Center, (Richard Neutra 1966). Photograph by Tim Sullivan

awareness of the importance of these buildings, and the recognition that what is contemporary will soon be historic, preservation will be dynamic not static. Preservation is now seen as a continuous process, not just preventing progress, but developing a dialogue and a consensus of what is great about our architectural heritage almost up to the present day.

Note

1   Kenneth Frampton (1980) *Modern Architecture: a critical history* (Thames & Hudson Ltd, London) p. 248.

8 Recording the recent heritage in the Netherlands

Marieke Kuipers

Introduction

This chapter is primarily concerned with the national Monuments Inventory Project (MIP), recording the 'younger' architecture and town extensions of the 'Steam period' (1850–1940) in The Netherlands. Before the MIP started, in 1987, several pilot projects on various themes were carried out and one was particularly devoted to the Modern Movement. The MIP led to new recording and preservation activities and also influenced physical planning. A follow-up project will concentrate on the even more recent heritage of the Reconstruction period (1940–65).

Architect's appeal on modern monuments

By the end of the 1960s the first stage of listing monuments for legal protection was completed, forced by by-laws at the introduction of the Dutch Historic Buildings and Monuments Act. Over 40,000 historic buildings had been inscribed on the national register, for which the base was provided by the prewar Preliminary List (drawn up in 1918–33 by the State Commission). However the heritage after 1850 was hardly represented, due to a covert disapproval of Historicism and the persistent use of the 'fifty-years-rule' which was introduced in 1903 for the composition of scientific inventories, and had become one of the legal criteria for protection in order to ensure an objective evaluation.[1]

This rule did not fit in with the increasing dynamics in the built environment. So, the Dutch Union of Architects (BNA) advocated a shorter period because most buildings are economically debited after thirty years and start a new lifecycle with radical repair or demolition. Also, the BNA published in 1970 in its magazine *Plan*, a selection of 140 eligible 'Young Monuments' built between 1900 and 1940, which was in its opinion 'the most interesting period for Dutch architecture'. The majority of this 'shadowlist' (seventy-eight) consisted of typical buildings of the Modern Movement, e.g., the Open Air school and Cineac (Amsterdam), the Zonnestraal Sanatorium (Hilversum), the Van Nelle factories and Parklaanflat (Rotterdam) (Figure 8.1). But also many expressionist buildings of the Amsterdam School and some traditionalist projects of the Delft School were included.[2] Although the fifty-years-rule still prohibited legal protection of most monuments of the Dutch Nieuwe Bouwen (built in the 1920s and 1930s) for another decade, the *Plan* publication achieved success as a starting point for increasing awareness of recent heritage and was followed by more research on Dutch modern architecture.[3]

First attempts on preserving 'younger' monuments

In spite of the gradually rising interest in recent heritage, many typical buildings of the first Machine Age were pulled down – often without any record of their history – because they could not function any more in their original setting. In the new towns the process of urban renewal and renovation had its effects on countless complexes of social housing (Figure 8.2). These 'younger monuments' had not only to contend with a lack of knowledge and recognition but also with special problems of maintenance caused by their monofunctional design and the (experimental) use of new building techniques and materials. Their number also, was far greater than that of the 'older' monuments and staff available to survey this field was very limited.

Alarmed by the increasing loss of witness to the recent past and pressed by several private organisations of historians and architects, specific actions on preservation were undertaken in the 1970s. With caution, the first attempts on selection and listing of recent heritage were made by means of pilot projects based on thematic surveys (such as neo-gothic churches, railway stations and cast iron lighthouses), until in 1978 a special commission for the 'Younger Architecture' of the Monumentenraad (State Commission on Monuments, the legal advisory body of the Minister of Culture) was installed.

Together with the Nederlands Documentatiecentrum voor de Bouwkunst (NDB, Dutch Documentation Centre for Architecture) and the fresh inventory team of the Rijksdienst voor de Monumentenzorg (RDMZ, Netherlands Department for Conservation) this commission worked out a strategy for survey and selection of the so-called 'younger architecture' of the period 1850–1940. The strategy followed a two-track policy: one concentrating on the selection and preservation of the most important landmarks of the Dutch modern architecture, already known through professional literature, the other aiming at an over-all investigation into the field, taking also cultural and socio-economic historic values into account.

The first operation was set up with special regard to the heritage of the Dutch Modern Movement and therefore a late response on appeal by the Union of Dutch Architects. For the first time the heritage of modernism – however contradictory it may sound – became the preservationist's priority because of its overwhelming significance for the development of today's architecture. The elaborate advice of the special commission led to the legal protection of about sixty 'Modern monuments', which were all privately owned and not all of them in good condition, including such famous buildings as the Van Nelle factories and the former Zonnestraal Sanatorium. Although the RDMZ finally had the means to convince owners to accept the assignment of their buildings as protected monuments, the problems of proper conservation remained (and later

Figure 8.1 Rotterdam, Parklaanflat, designed by Willem van Tijen in 1932, who lived in the upper-apartment for some years; published in *Plan* as an eligible 'Young Monument' and listed 50 years after completion as a protected monument in 1983 *Source*: RDMZ Zeist, Gerard Dukker, 1991

Figure 8.2 Amsterdam, the social housing estate of 'Eigen Haard' (Block III) at Zaanstraat/Oostzaanstraat/Hembrugstraat (1917–21), designed by Michel de Klerk in the typical expressionism of the Amsterdam School and consisting of 102 dwellings, a post office, a meeting office and a small school; listed as a protected monument in 1972. Photograph by Marieke Kuipers, 1990

on provided the impetus for the launch of the DOCOMOMO movement).

However, more education was needed to interest the general public in the specific meaning of our recent heritage. New actions of inventory and preservation were consistently supported through several channels of publicity. This was especially important for the second operation, the national Monuments Inventory Project (MIP),[4] which followed various pilot projects surveying younger architecture and townscapes in specific areas.

MIP purposes and organisation

The MIP-campaign aimed to explore the entire country in a systematic way and within a few years, for existing buildings, neighbourhoods and sites of 1850–1940 which were of at least local value. The first purpose of this project was to overcome lack of knowledge by building up a national database on the recent heritage of the prewar period. Second, the intention was to promote a broader appraisal of 'younger architecture', which was done by involving the local and regional press and authorities, as well as organising excursions, popular exhibitions and other educational activities. It was no coincidence that the introductory excursion of the MIP in Rotterdam started in a well-known functionalist building, the Feyenoord stadium by J.A. Brinkman and L.C. van der Vlugt (1936). Another aim was to advance an integrated policy for the control of our built environment as a whole. This meant that we should not be too restrictive in formulating our inventory standards, only pointing to qualities of 'modernity' or certain architectural merits, and also paying attention to buildings and areas with social or cultural historic value.

In order to guarantee a quick but geographically complete scan, we decided to focus our inventory programme on specific regions instead of specific building types or architectural styles. So the country was divided into almost sixty 'inventory areas' or regions, which were defined by coherent cultural and historic developments as well as by the current provincial or municipal boundaries for administrative reasons. For instance, the sparsely populated province of Drenthe counted just three of such 'inventory areas', while the densely built province of South-Holland had seven regions, as well as two 'major cities' (Figure 8.3).

The organisation of the MIP-campaign had a unique character, because of the intensive co-operation between the national, provincial and municipal departments for conservation of historic buildings and areas. Sixteen partners were involved, our twelve provinces and the four major municipalities (Amsterdam, Rotterdam, The Hague and Utrecht). For the main inventory work, dozens of special assistants of different disciplines had been attracted, thanks to a special grant provided by the minister of culture and benefiting from such different sources as employment plans for unemployed starters, ethnic minorities, re-entering women or alternative military service for conscientious objectors.

The RDMZ retained the initiative for the project, its methodology, budget and progress, within the aegis of a small supervision team, while the daily practice was in the hands of the provincial or municipal MIP teams, supported by a voluntary committee of guidance (which was often related to the provincial or municipal commission on historic buildings and monuments).

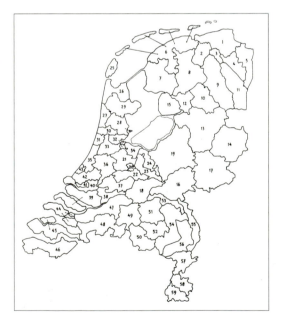

Figure 8.3 Division of MIP-regions in The Netherlands; the four major cities are Amsterdam (32), Rotterdam (40), The Hague (35), Utrecht (20); drawing by Teun Brouwer, 1988
Source: Reproduction by RDMZ, Zeist

General MIP methods

The MIP's central idea was to investigate the whole country on a declining scale - from the level of a region to the level of the municipalities and then to the individual buildings - in a uniform way. For this purpose a detailed MIP manual was available, accompanied by other guidelines and instructions, guiding the inventory work step by step. The initial idea was that before the fieldwork would start two types of description would be produced, based on desktop research through the use of general, easily available sources (books, journals, reports, maps) and indicating interesting places and building types. But in practice there was more interaction and, later on, the descriptions became more elaborated as a result of the growing interest in local history. For a lot of municipalities the MIP introduced for the first time the theme of heritage and preservation. The research began with the regional descriptions, paying special attention to developments during the period 1850–1940. The first part dealt with the geographical aspects (nature and use of soil, drainage), followed by chapters on infrastructure (roads, water, railways, military works), the structure of the settlements with their cores, extensions and scattered buildings. For the second step more detailed descriptions of all municipalities were made according to the same division of contents, with an additional chapter on the main building types, and also illustrated with adapted maps. The municipal descriptions of the four major and about thirty mid-sized towns were more elaborated, both on the level of local districts and the urban structure. In case of large extensions or interesting developments, a so-called 'urban typology' was demanded in addition to the previous descriptions, with a specific map showing the character of these developments by means of a uniform standard. There were prescribed hatching types for marking areas with villas, garden-villages, industrial zones or green areas but other types could be added.

The third step was to evaluate the relevant town and village extensions by applying a uniform scoring list in order to assign so-called 'areas of special values'. This distinction was important for two reasons; one for the future (or even actual) town planning and control of housing complexes, another for the proper fieldworking phase: the 'special areas' should be inventoried intensively (as for the historic centres), while the other parts of the settlements could be inspected in a more rough way. During the project the interpretation of the 'special areas' broadened from mere extensions towards all kinds of new spatial arrangements. The inventorisation of all buildings in the field was perhaps the most labour-intensive part of the project, but from the methodic point of view it was not the most problematic part. After several joint instructions in practice, a general consensus was achieved about what buildings should be recorded and those which should not, demanding certain local valuations.

The fieldwork also had an impact on public relations through contacts with the local authorities (which often provided temporary working rooms for the MIP-contractors) and the local press. Thanks to publications in the local papers the inventorisation work became generally known to the public. This was of great practical importance because most people are strongly attached to their privacy and now doors were more readily opened to the surveyors. On the other hand, many inhabitants (or even local authorities) were often not aware of the particular value of the buildings in which they live or work. However, for reasons of time saving, not all buildings have been inspected inside, but at least most churches, factories, (semi-)public buildings and other buildings where an interesting interior or roof construction was anticipated have been examined. The fieldworkers scanned street by street, even outside the built-up areas, equipped with special forms, maps, manuals and cameras. They took pictures of all valuable buildings (black and white obligatory, colour slides optional) and completed standard forms concerning address, architect, dates of construction, shapes, materials, building type, style and so on to provide all required records for both the reports and the intended national database.

MIP-results

The inventory project was carried out between 1987 and 1994, taking two years more than was originally intended but the results exceeded all expectations, on the amount of traced buildings and areas as well as on the remaining interest in the recent heritage. The results taught us too that we had to adjust some details of our recording framework, which for the first time had to deal with the computarisation of data – a very complicated affair. Roughly speaking, the formal output of the MIP can be divided in digital data and documentation on paper: soberly produced reports (fifty-five regional descriptions, ± 650 municipal descriptions of which those of the four major cities and ± 30 mid-sized towns are more elaborated), maps, pictures, slides, completed inventory forms. These reports can only be consulted by the public in the offices of the municipalities, provinces and the RDMZ. However, a special 'MIP-series' of lavishly illustrated, popular books came out concerning the twelve provinces and four major cities; this series had such a success that several municipalities also decided to join the formula with a separate volume. The province Flevoland, consisting for the major part of postwar 'New land' by reclamation, also participated in the MIP and the publication series for the eldest parts (Urk and Noordoostpolder). Moreover, the municipality of The Hague published a special volume on their MIP-results, full of coloured maps, illustrations and historic information.

In the computerised database only the written parts of the inventory forms (over ± 165,000 buildings and complexes) are stored, for technical and economic reasons. Unfortunately, no maps, pictures and other illustrations of the MIP-reports were integrated in this system because the use of a digital Geographical Information System was at that time regarded as too complicated and too expensive. For the object-related database, we adapted initially the British CAIRS program for separate input on PCs at the offices of our sixteen MIP-partners. Finally, we integrated all collected MIP-data and converted them by use of the BASIS-Plus module Fundamental Query and Manipulation (FQM) for an easy and varied output of the national database in the RDMZ office. Therefore, each object or complex of buildings received a unique code number (alphanumeric). In order to store the records as uniformly as possible we developed a special 'MIP thesaurus' for characterising the building types and styles, but since this came out half-way through the project the consistency in terminology did not reach the optimum. For instance, one should use several terms to obtain all inventoried buildings belonging to the Modern Movement. Recently, we have made some revisions and adapted the Art and Architectural Thesaurus developed by the American Getty Institute for Dutch use and added terms for postwar styles.

Documentation about the assigned 'areas of special value' (c. 650) can only be found in the photocopied reports. The areas can vary both in scale and character – from rather planless reclamation villages like Griendtsveen in the southern high moorlands to carefully planned companytowns (such as 't Lansink at Hengelo or Heveadorp at Renkum) or large town extensions like H.P. Berlage's layout for South Amsterdam (full of expressionist housing estates) and W.G. Witteveen's project for the northern quarters Blijdorp and Bergpolder in Rotterdam (with many functionalist housing estates). Some small housing complexes were also determined as 'special areas', including Modern examples like the Papaverhof at The Hague by Jan Wils (1920–22) (Figure 8.4), the Kiefhoek at Rotterdam by J.J.P. Oud (1925–9) or Landlust in Amsterdam-West by B. Merkelbach and Ch.J.F. Karsten (1933–7), but cultural landscapes as well (for example, the penal colony at Veenhuizen in the north-eastern province Drenthe and the whole area of the Loosdrecht wood site of the former aftercare colony of Zonnestraal at Hilversum). In the last stage of the MIP even more interest arose for non-built areas, such as country estates, public parks, cemeteries, defence lines, canals. These examples illustrate both the broad approach of the inventory campaign, based on a cultural-historical point of view in the first place, and the growing tendency for policy-making with

Figure 8.4 The Hague, Papaverhof, middle-class housing estate for the housing corporation 'Duin en Daal', designed in 1920–22 by the *De Stijl* architect Jan Wils with partial use of concrete walls; restored in 1989–90 with reconstruction of the original colour scheme
Source: RDMZ Zeist, Gerard Dukker, 1991

regard to the environment instead of just single buildings (Figure 8.5).

After MIP-activities

The inventory project was just one step on the long road to obtain more attention (and money) for the documentation and conservation of our recent heritage, but it had a great spin-off. In fact, the main goals are achieved thanks to the great enthusiasm and efforts of all involved MIP teams and their coherent organisation.

Continuing the aim of raising public awareness of our recent heritage two annual events now profit from the MIP-results: the Day of Architecture (1st of July) and the Open Monuments Day (second Saturday of September). By choosing unusual themes (Industrial Heritage, 1996; Schools, 1997), through educational booklets and by mixing historic and recent buildings which can be visited, people slowly learn to appreciate the qualities of young monuments. Such public involvement is very important because most protected monuments in The Netherlands are privately owned, making their future fate highly dependent on the interests and financial position of their owners.

As another result of the MIP the local and provincial departments for physical planning and conservation have begun to share information, especially on the distinct 'areas of special value'. Moreover, new methods have been developed for supporting the idea of 'integrated planning', such as Cultural Historic Value Maps for regional planning (introduced by the provincial departments) and *Cultuurhistorische Verkenningen* (Cultural Historic Reconnaissances), produced by the RDMZ for various complexes, municipalities or regions and indicating the opportunities and risks of the built cultural heritage in future developments. These methods of recording are more superficial than the MIP-methods – not to compare with the profound studies of the *Geïllustreerde Beschrijving* (illustrated description) – but perhaps more effective in preventing demolitions, because the process of (urban) renewal is more rapid than the process of research and legal protection.

For this purpose a second national operation started, directly following the MIP: the current Monuments Selection Project (MSP). The MSP is organised in a similar way to the MIP, but with a

Figure 8.5 Rotterdam, the former Drinking-water production complex with watertower (1874), filtering houses along basins (right) and a younger concrete building for filtering (1925) left (rebuilt with apartments for younger people) and recent flatblocks as an example of integrated re-use
Source: RDMZ, Zeist, Gerard Dukker, 1991

Figure 8.6 Heerlen, former fashion house Schunck with its transparent curtain walls in the heart of the historic centre, designed by Frits Peutz in 1934–36. Photograph by Marieke Kuipers, 1996

greater role for the municipalities and with stricter criteria for inclusion.[5] The project should be finished before the new Millennium. We expect that about 14,000 'young monuments' will be added to our national register and approximately 150 recent conservation areas will be assigned. Among these future protected monuments will be several functionalist buildings, especially those of the late 1930s, which could not be protected earlier because of the legal fifty-years-rule, such as the former fashion house Schunck at Heerlen (Figure 8.6). Often the MSP gives reason to review the MIP-results for both additions and alterations, because of later interventions. The MIP was not always a success-story for proper preservation. Nevertheless, the MIP-model inspired a private committee and the municipality of Rotterdam to initiate a local follow-up, concerning the architecture and town planning of the Reconstruction Period (1940–65), which is today more and more endangered by radical renewal or demolition. Not only has the reconstructed inner city been inventoried, and recorded on CD-ROM (with text and images together), but also studies for future use and renovation have been made of typical buildings and postwar housing estates. Recently, an advisory report came out on the future control of the inner city of Rotterdam with a first summary of the specific features of 'Reconstruction architecture' and with remarkable references to preservation models (the French ZPPAUP developed in Le Havre and the Dutch national MSP).[6]

In the jubilee year, 1995, fifty years after the liberation from German occupation, a *hausse* of publications, exhibitions and manifestations on the recent heritage of Reconstruction appeared. Together with Rotterdam, the RDMZ held a national symposium on this new and huge task for preservationists and researchers, in which the Netherlands Architecture Institute is also involved. For the recording and preservation of the immense number of postwar buildings, neighbourhoods and sites we have not yet found the necessary means and finance, while the process of destruction is continuing. Only the first small step has been taken towards future exploration, but more steps should follow in the coming years.

Defending Dutch Modern monuments

In contrast to some preceding actions on recent heritage, the MIP had no preference for specific architectural styles. For historic and cultural reasons it is essential to preserve not only the highlights of the 'Modern Movement', but also the other typical buildings and areas of the modern period, against which pioneering architects like Duiker, Van Loghem, Rietveld and others agitated, in order to understand the whole context of the struggle for a real new way of building and town planning. For instance, the compulsorily concealed site for the First Open Air School for the Healthy Child in Amsterdam can, because of its radical character, only be experienced if the original surrounding housing block with its restrained interbellum architecture survives (Figure 8.7).

However, a new action on preservation is again drawing special attention to the Dutch heritage of the Modern Movement for its high architectural qualities, even at the international level of the World Heritage List of UNESCO. The first tentatative list, submitted by the Dutch government in 1995, contains three main themes in which several modern monuments are included. The first theme is *Nederland-Waterland*, dealing with the character-istic man-made landscape of the Low Countries. This is symbolised by the windmills at Kinderdijk (nomin–ated for 1997) and the waterline defence system of

Figure 8.7 Amsterdam, Open Air School by Jan Duiker (1931), where the author experienced outdoor teaching on the rooftop during sunny days and was in charge of the listing in 1982
Source: RDMZ, Zeist

Figure 8.8 Rotterdam, Van Nelle factories by J.A. Brinkman and L.C. van der Vlugt (1925–31), placed on the Dutch tentative list for the World Heritage List of UNESCO, but intended to be abandoned by the current user in 1998, challenging future users to maintain this well-known Modern monument. Photograph by Marieke Kuipers, 1996

the Position around Amsterdam (inscribed in 1996) and the recent reclamation area of the *Noordoost–polder* (1942–62), in which one of the eleven towns, Nagele, is entirely modern. The second main theme concerns the civic culture of the seventeenth century Golden Age, but represented by the inner city of Amsterdam with its world famous canals and former City Hall. Here, too, we can find important works of modernity (e.g. Berlage's Stock Exchange and Duiker's Cineac). Remarkably, the third main theme is entirely devoted to the Dutch Modern Movement with three of its highlights: the Rietveld-Schröder-house at Utrecht (to be nominated in 1999), the Zonnestraal Sanatorium at Hilversum and the Van Nelle factories in Rotterdam. The Rietveld-Schröder-house and the Van Nelle factories are even part of the Dutch 'top 100' most important historic buildings in The Netherlands with regard to the UNESCO Treaty of 's-Gravenhage 1954 concerning protection of monuments in case of armed conflicts. Higher recognition is hardly possible, but the last two cases are still troublesome. For the management team of the Van Nelle factories – which now belongs to an American company – the burden of history seems to be too heavy. This complex, which has been well-kept over the last decades and therefore received state subsidies, will be abandoned in 1998 and now common efforts are being made by public and private parties to find an appropriate solution for new uses, which will respect the true functionalist architecture it represents (Figure 8.8).

The Zonnestraal Sanatorium is already largely abandoned and has been waiting for a new use for years, but now there is real hope for restoration and re-use, thanks to the efforts of DOCOMOMO. Through the initiative of some students from the Technical University of Delft the circular servants'

house was restored in 1995, subsidised by the state, and it serves today as an exhibition centre on the history of Zonnestraal.

In the past decade the scope and methods of recording recent heritage have drastically changed, gathering more public support for preservation, the conservation of Modern monuments in The Netherlands remains a great challenge to manage.

Notes

1   The first Dutch Historic Buildings and Monuments Act came into force as late as 1961. For the history see: M.C. Kuipers, 'The Long Path to Preservation in The Netherlands', in *Transactions of the Ancient Monuments Society* 1998 (vol 42) pp. 13–34.

2   *Plan, maandblas voor ontwerp en omgeving* 1970 nr. 4, pp. 220–90.

3   The first survey of Dutch modern architecture (1900–40) was published by an Italian in 1968: G. Fanelli, *Architettura Moderna in Olanda 1900–1940* (F. Papafava, Florence, 1968). After just ten years the Dutch translation came out, published by the *Nederlands Documentatiecentrum voor de Bouwkunst* (precursor of the current Netherlands Architecture Institute), which had organised in 1975 a series of four exhibitions on the roots of Dutch modern architecture accompanied by elaborate catalogues (*Architectura, Americana, Amsterdamse School, Berlage*).

4   For example the historic centre of Amsterdam, the industrialised region of Twenthy in the east and the mining region in South-Limburg and the buildings designed by W.M. Dudok in Hiversum; see M.C. Kuipers, 'Een weerbarstig onderzoeksveld ontgonnen', in *Monumenten van een nieuwe tijd, architectuur en stedebouw 1850–1940, Jaarboek Monumentenzorg 1994* (Waanders Uitgevers/RDMZ, Zwolle/Zeist, 1994), pp. 8–20.

5   See the MSP manual, *Handeiding Selectie en registratie Jongere Stedebouw en Bouwkunst (1950–1940)* (RDMZ, Zeist, 1991).

6   W. de Jonge *et al.*, *Het gebruik v an de stad, Hoe Rotterdam zichzelf kan blijven* (Rotterdam, 1997) (Report of the Commission Evaluation Reconstruction Rotterdam).

PART III
CASE STUDIES

Case Studies provide the most complete representation of the professional process, demonstrating procedures requiring not only open-mindedness and imagination, but also profound understanding of, and sympathy with, the generating principles of Modernism. One may invoke the Taoist dictum 'First perfect technique – then abandon yourself to inspiration' because all-encompassing technological skills do need to accompany design ingenuity when confronting the complexities of conserving buildings, whether icons or the ordinary. Modern architecture privileged certain materials or components for their expressive and functional potential and these inevitably predominate in the descriptions included here, in particular reinforced concrete and metal windows. The first chapter is, consequently, not focused upon a building at all, but on a system – the curtain wall – which, far from being a benign element free of bearing stresses, is subject to severe air pressures, temperature fluctuations, water penetration, atmospheric pollution and the rays of the sun. The second chapter further enriches this theme by examining two New York landmark buildings – the Woolworth Building and Lever House. The chapters on Zonnestraal and Bellerive-Plage are preoccupied with rescue of the elegant but over-optimistic concrete profiles of heroic Modernism. Of the three chapters on individual dwellings, the one on the Aluminaire House traces the survival, following traumatic deconstructions and transformations, of this 'Corbusian' gem, the Prouvé study reveals an eccentric approach towards panel construction, and the third, on Eileen Grey's E-1027 villa, is a unique contribution to the concept and methods of 'virtual' conservation. These chapters are in the fast company of Terragni, Mallet-Stevens, Mendelsohn and Alvar Aalto, an assembly of unique productions demonstrating the rich heterogeneity of Modernism.

9 The metal and glass curtain wall: The history and diagnostics

Stephen J. Kelley and Dennis K. Johnson

The curtain wall can be defined as, 'an exterior building wall made of non-load bearing panels that are supported on a structural frame. The curtain wall spans between floors and transfers lateral loads, such as those produced by winds, to the structural frame, while the structural frame alone carries these horizontal as well as all gravity loads.'

The antecedents of the curtain wall made of metal can be traced to numerous nineteenth and early-twentieth century sources, including glass exhibition pavilions such as the Crystal Palace in London (1851) and masonry infilled metal frame structures such as the early Chicago skyscrapers of the 1880s[1] (Figure 9.1). Its development was governed by technology and economics as well as aesthetics. Technology was dependent upon the evolution of the structural frame, the development of lightweight building materials, and the invention of adequate fireproofing and insulation systems. Economy dictated that the amount and weight of materials used be minimised, that more prefabrication occur, that erection be faster, and that construction become standardised. Aesthetics called for greater expanses of glass. These factors led to the sleek, metal and glass skins that have cloaked the skyscrapers of the era following World War Two.

Precedents

In Europe by the end of the century, architects were exploring the aesthetic possibilities of glass and metal on building facades. An example (Figure 9.2) was Victor Horta's *Maison du Peuple* (Brussels, 1896, demolished) where the metal skeleton was enclosed only by glass or thin panels held in iron frames.[2] Similar themes were explored in the United States. The Boley Building (Kansas City, 1909) by Louis Curtis, incorporated a transparent glass wall enclosing an entire structure. These experiments in the aesthetic possibilities of the metal and glass curtain wall were largely ignored by American architects of the period.[3]

German architects Walter Gropius and Adolph Meyer were commissioned to build the Faguswerke Factory (Alfeld-an-der-Leine, 1911), widely regarded as a founding monument of the Modern Movement. At this factory, each level is indicated by solid spandrel panels that are installed like the glass above and below them, a treatment echoed by post-World War Two high-rise curtain walls.[4] After World War One, the theme of the curtain wall of the Faguswerke Factory, was furthered by the construction of the Bauhaus School (Gropius, 1925) (Figure 9.3) with a studio featuring an impressive metal and glass curtain wall.[5] Contemporary to this, Ludwig Mies van der Rohe, who followed Hannes Meyer as head of the Bauhaus School, prepared a series of unrealised projects in which the most famous came to be known as the 'Glass Skyscraper,' a high-rise enveloped totally in glass.

The Modern Movement, known in the United States as the 'International Style', was formally introduced to American architects in 1932 and created an immediate sensation.[6] Due to the economic constraints of the Great Depression, speed was necessary in design and erection. The International Style was characterised by the elimination of costly decorative features on the façade, and

Figure 9.1 An archetype of the Chicago School and example of the structural innovations of the late nineteenth century can be found in the Reliance Building. The Reliance Building curtain wall of terracotta, a masonry material, is a clear aesthetic expression of the underlying structure and provides a maximum of natural lighting. This facade treatment has been compared to the 1921 'Glass Skyscraper,' study project of Ludwig Mies van der Rohe

Figure 9.2 In Victor Horta's design for the auditorium at the top of the Maison du Peuple, the iron frame was enclosed only by glass or by very thin panels held in iron frames. Its Art Nouveau style strove for lightness, attenuation, and transparency; qualities that were easily expressed by metal and glass on the exterior

was realised on such buildings as the New York Daily News (Hood and Howells, 1930), the McGraw-Hill (Hood and Fouilhoux, 1932), and the Philadelphia Savings Fund Society (Howe and Lescase, 1931) buildings. Curtain wall construction, however, continued to utilise traditional masonry techniques that had been developed by the turn-of-the-century.[7]

One of the architects of the Empire State building (New York City, 1931) wrote of the masonry curtain wall technique:

> We inherited masonry walls and seem unable to outgrow our inheritance. The idea that masonry is the only form of permanent construction was so deeply rooted that practically all building codes made masonry walls mandatory ... The covering of the observation tower ... accomplished by a combination of aluminum, chrome-steel and glass, [was] designed and fabricated into forms entirely free from masonry influences. The extension of similar treatment to embrace all of the inclosing walls of a tall building is quite conceivable and ... will result in a light wall, readily made weather tight, easy to fabricate and erect and requiring practically no maintenance.[8]

The new era of the curtain wall

New technologies resulting from World War Two had a great influence on the acceptance of the glass and metal curtain wall and the realisation of a machine-made building envelope. Lightweight workable and resistant to corrosion, aluminium would become the metal of choice for curtain walls and would rise above the use of other durable metals. Advances during World War Two brought about new processes and techniques for fabricating and working aluminium, and placed unprecedented quantities of the material at an economical price at the disposal of designers.[9] Extruded metal components were suitable for standardisation and could be prefabricated for delivery to the site, and installation was less limited by cold temperatures which prohibited erection of 'wet' walls of brick and mortar. This was important because labour costs had now become a significant part of construction costs.

In 1959 Pilkington Glass introduced their revolutionary float method for the manufacture of plate glass and other existing processes soon became obsolete.[10] In the 1950s, heat absorbent or tinted glass had made major inroads into the commercial building market.[11] Though green was initially the only colour possible in transparent optical glass, by the 1960s other colours were also becoming available.[12] Insulation materials were developed by manufacturers such as Pittsburgh-Corning, Owens-Illinois, US Gypsum, and Johns-Manville. These materials were toted for their significant contribution in reducing heat loss.

Traditional oil and resin-based caulking compounds were the only joint sealants available before World War Two, and they did not provide the flexibility required to accommodate the significant movement in curtain wall joints. War technology[13] spawned a new family of elastomeric sealants such as polysulphides, solvent acrylics, urethanes, and silicones that would fulfil this role. Polysulphides were the first elastomerics to be used for curtain wall construction in the early 1950s. Their use to seal the curtain wall of the Lever House in 1954 signalled their widespread acceptance. Silicone sealants were introduced in the 1960s and urethane sealants were introduced in the 1970s.[14]

Technical guidance in the use of glass and metal curtain walls for 1950s designers was limited.[15] The approach to design that evolved was to make the joints as weather tight as possible, then provide positive means for conducting any water leakage out of the wall through an internal drainage system. At first, caulking compounds, which have become indispensable in curtain wall design and maintenance, were frowned upon for the sealing of joints. It was envisioned that rubber gasket systems would fulfil this role.[16]

Large-scale commercial adaptation of building air conditioning also profoundly influenced the development of metal and glass curtain wall, which now made up the entire envelope, not just a portion. This adaptation initially led to curtain walls which were not provided with operable windows for natural ventilation. Architects of the 1950s had little concern for energy conservation. It was left to mechanical engineers to insure occupant comfort.[17]

One of the first postwar buildings to be constructed with a metal and glass curtain wall (Figure 9.4) was the Equitable building (Pietro Belluschi, 1948) in Portland, Oregon. Belluschi was able to take advantage of leftover aluminium

Figure 9.3 The Bauhaus School designed by Gropius in 1925 utilised a glass and steel curtain wall that was emulated by the Modernists. One reason that the Bauhaus was located in Dessau was the nearby Junkers airplane factory where advances in the use of aluminum in aircraft were being pioneered

stockpiled for World War Two by smelters and to utilise assembly techniques derived from west coast aeroplane plants.[18]

The 860–880 Lake Shore Drive buildings in Chicago (Mies van der Rohe, 1949–51) were among the first residential buildings in the United States to be sheathed entirely in glass, and were the realisation of Mies' earlier proposal for a Glass Skyscraper (Figure 9.5). The steel grid was assembled on the buildings' roofs in two-storey high units and then lowered into place on the facade.[19]

The United Nations Secretariat building (Harrison and Abramovitz, 1950) was conceived as a pure sculptural form – a narrow tower slab set so that its long walls of glass faced east and west, and its shorter walls of white marble faced north and south. The Secretariat building was a thermal nightmare with its all glass facades subjected to the harsh rising and setting sun. Designers learned to consider the orientation of buildings relative to the path of the

Figure 9.5 The 860–880 Lake Shore Drive buildings in Chicago were the realisation of Mies' 1920 proposal for a glass skyscraper, and set the trend for American skyscrapers through the 1950s. The curtain wall uses a mix of exposed steel and metal components, metals that galvanically react with each other. In contrast, the Esplanade Apartments next door and shown above, also designed by Mies and constructed 8 years later, uses an all-aluminum curtain wall. In the period between the construction of these projects, curtain wall manufacturers had begun the process codifying good practice in curtain wall fabrication and installation

Figure 9.4 One of the first post-war buildings to be constructed with a glass envelope is the Equitable building (Pietro Belluschi, 1948) in Portland, Oregon. The Northwest US offered inexpensive power sources and airplane production facilities left over from World War Two. The Equitable Building was constructed with cladding panels made from rolled sheets of aluminum, and glazing frames which were simple extruded shapes. It was an early use of insulated glass

sun, and the size of windows to control heat gain.[20] The curtain wall was glazed with green-tinted glass, which was coming into widespread use in commercial architecture.[21] In detail the curtain wall was an assembly of aluminum windows held in place with a grid of reinforced mullions.[22] The lower portion of the curtain wall at each level was backed up by a concrete block wall to provide fire protection.[23]

At the Lever House (Skidmore, Owings and Merrill, 1952), the curtain wall has an interior frame of mild steel clad with stainless steel. Its simple appearance 'belies its complex internal construction which was cobbled together from off the shelf parts'.[24] Later design of curtain walls was made easier by catalogue

components. The Lever House curtain wall, like that of the Secretariat building, was backed at each floor by a knee wall of concrete block to provide the fire protection that code officials felt was not provided by the curtain wall itself.[25]

Other durable metals were also utilised in the 1950s. New York's House of Seagram, (Mies Van der Rohe, 1957–8) was constructed with a curtain wall of bronze tinted glass and metal grid of bronze. Frank Lloyd Wright's Price Tower (Bartlesville, Oklahoma, 1955) is a mixed-use high-rise with a curtain wall of copper and precast concrete units.[26]

An alternative response to the all-glass curtain wall, the Alcoa Building (Harrison, 1952) in Pittsburgh, used storey-high panels of aluminium penetrated by relatively small windows. The windows were set in aluminium frames and sealed with rubber gaskets. Aluminium panels were formed with a pressed pattern to add rigidity, create relief, and produce scale.[27] This type of sheathing became quite popular during the mid-1960s. Perlite insulation was sprayed on aluminium lath to provide fireproofing instead of using concrete block behind the curtain wall marking the final break of the curtain wall with traditional masonry techniques.

New technologies in the past thirty years have created the economy of using less material and the use of new materials to achieve thermal and cost-effective construction. Thermal efficiency became important in building construction after the energy crisis of the 1970s. By the 1960s reflective coatings of thin metal applied to glass became available to the construction industry. Originally fabricated in silver, the colour palette would eventually include gold, bronze, copper, pewter, grey, and blue.[28] A circa 1980s application is the coating of glass with clear low emissivity (low-e) films that are used to improve the energy efficiency and performance of buildings.[29] 'Pressure equalisation' to prevent water penetration through building envelopes was first published by the Norwegians in 1962 and a year later in Canada. It was not until the 1970s that this principle was first applied to curtain walls.[30] Pressure equalisation applied to curtain walls may one day help realise the abolition of sealants on the exterior of building skins. The use of plastic breaks to improve the thermal performance of metal components of curtain walls was introduced in the 1960s. Structural silicone glazing, which has been responsible for the large expanses of mullionless glass, began to appear on building curtain walls toward the end of the 1960s.[31]

Common problems with metal and glass curtain walls

The curtain wall fulfils one of the most demanding roles in building construction. Not only does it provide the primary image for the building, but also performs the multiple functions required of an exterior skin – form a protective enclosure, keep out the outside environment, and maintain the inside environment in an efficient, economical manner.

Metal curtain walls can be categorised by their fabrication and installation as follows. **Stick systems** (Figure 9.6) are assembled in the field and consist of vertical members (mullions) and horizontal members (rails) which are anchored to the structural frame. Glass, stone or other panels are then glazed into the openings created by the metal grid. **Unit systems** (Figure 9.7) are composed of panels that are assembled and glazed in the factory prior to installation in the field. The units are then stacked together to form the mullions and rails. **Unit and mullion systems** (Figure 9.8) utilise features of both the stick and unit systems by inserting prefabricated units between installed mullions.

The following discussion covers some of the more common problems experienced with curtain walls.

Water penetration

The prevention of water leakage – the failure of which presents the most common problems associated with curtain walls – relies upon either the elimination of leakage into the wall or the control of water flow through the wall. Several different approaches have been developed to achieve a watertight wall, which include interior drainage systems,[32] pressure-equalized systems,[33] and barrier walls.[34] All successful implementations rely upon the understanding of and design for the various forces acting on and attempting to drive water through the wall. Wind, capillary action, and gravity are but a few

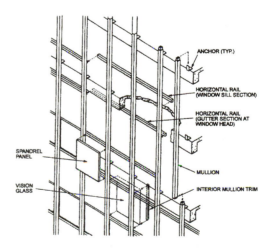

Figure 9.6 Schematic diagram of a typical curtain wall *stick system*
Source: adapted from *Curtain Wall Design Guide*, AAMA: Palatine, Illinois, 1996

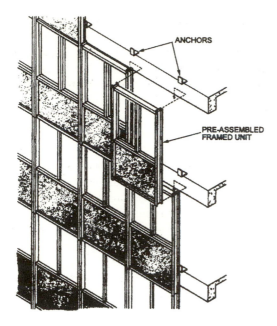

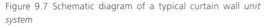

Figure 9.7 Schematic diagram of a typical curtain wall *unit system*
Source: adapted from *Curtain Wall Design Guide*, AAMA: Palatine, Illinois, 1996

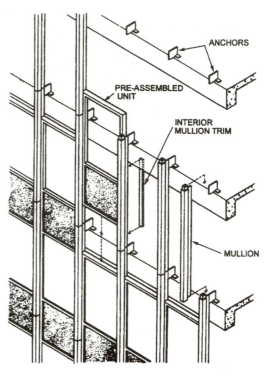

Figure 9.8 Schematic diagram of a typical curtain wall *unit and mullion system*
Source: adapted from *Curtain Wall Design Guide*, AAMA: Palatine, Illinois, 1996

of the forces that must be accommodated. The different approaches must ultimately handle these forces successfully. The following are descriptions of some of the more common causes of water penetration.

Improper design – interior gutters and glazing pockets may not be designed with enough features to accommodate water that penetrates the exterior wall and direct it back to the exterior. Inadequate design sometimes does not accommodate interior water flow or is inadequate to resist the wind induced pressures accompanying the water.

Improper installation – drainage systems rely upon internal gutters or flashings to achieve water-tightness. An interior drainage system cannot perform adequately unless it is properly sealed. End dams that are created where horizontal and vertical members intersect, discontinuities at splices, and penetrations for connections are common sources of water penetration.

Glazing leaks – glazing joints between the metal

frame and glass or other inserted panel is a common source of water leakage into a curtain wall system. In dry glazing systems, glazing gaskets, if installed improperly, will creep away from the corners of the glass or panel over time and allow water to reach the glazing pocket. Unless the glazing pocket is designed to control the resulting volume of water, leakage can occur.

Sealant failures – when contemporary elastomeric sealants, such as silicone or urethane, are properly installed and the joints are designed to be compatible with the sealants, an effective seal can be obtained. Sealant failures, whether they be cohesive or adhesive, can create many problems, especially considering that sealant joints are the final seal to weather penetration. Sealants should also be designed so they can be maintained or replaced, and for the prevention of contamination of adjoining surfaces.

Weatherstripping – weatherstripping is used in operable windows within curtain wall systems as a means of sealing the window vent to the frame when in a closed position. Weatherstripping is commonly the first part of a vent to become worn out and should be designed to be replaceable. Weatherstripping can become worn, permanently set, shrink away from the corners or become unattached. Weatherstripping may have been installed without continuity around the vent or improperly sized so that it is not effective when the vent is closed. All of these conditions can contribute to water leakage problems.

Thermal break shrinkage – this is a condition that occasionally occurs in aluminium frame systems that incorporate a thermoset plastic break to separate the interior metal from the exterior metal. Shrinkage of this plastic 'thermal break' material can compromise the internal gutter system and contribute to water leakage problems.

Improper repairs – previous repairs which seal drainage holes and other joints which were originally provided to allow leaked water to drain from the interior of the curtain wall system can exacerbate leakage problems. When this occurs, leaked water will find another pathway, perhaps into the building rather than through the plugged internal drainage system.

Air leakage and thermal discomfort

One of the main causes of thermal discomfort with curtain wall systems is air infiltration. Air infiltration will result in drafts and discomfort to occupants sitting near the wall. Air leakage can occur around operable window vents, through stack joints at mullions, at defective sealant joints, and in any place where water leakage can also occur. Though the exchange of air is needed in any building, air infiltration must be controlled.

Condensation occurs on curtain wall systems when climatic conditions are such that water vapour turns to liquid or ice on the interior surface.[35] Older curtain wall systems that do not incorporate thermal breaks or insulated glass are more prone to winter frost condensation. They were normally designed with an exposed gutter at the inside base of the curtain wall at each level to collect the condensate

run-off that was then expected to evaporate. Excessive condensation may indicate a poor thermal design, a bridge across a thermally broken system, or areas of excessive air infiltration. Condensation is also a concern because water run-off can cause damage to interior finishes.

Material failures

Failure of such materials as sealant and thermal breaks were discussed previously in conjunction with water penetration. Aluminium has become almost ubiquitous with curtain walls because aluminium forms a tough, protective coating of aluminium oxide as it weathers. This coating arrests further oxidation of the aluminium surface.[36] Older aluminium curtain walls dating from the 1950s or earlier may not have any protective coating or treatment on the aluminium surface. In these cases, pitting of the frame may occur as the aluminium oxidizes in an uneven fashion. There is no method to appropriately treat this unsightly oxidation, however pitting of the frame normally does not cause more than an aesthetic concern.

Though durable, aluminium is a highly cathodic metal. It can deteriorate through electrolytic action when in contact with anodic metals such as lead, copper, or mild steel in the presence of water. Staining, excessive oxidation, or frame failure can result if this phenomenon is not accommodated in frame or connection design.

Other metals such as copper, stainless steel, and bronze have also been used for curtain walls. Like aluminium, these metals are extremely durable as they weather and may only cause problems with staining as they patina.

A difficulty with curtain walls composed of mild steel is the tendency of ferrous metals to corrode. Corrosion of the steel frame over time can cause glass breakage, loss of use of operable vents, and ultimate failure of the structural frame. Steel curtain wall systems can last a long time but only if they are frequently maintained.

Peeling or chalking paint coatings on aluminium or steel can cause chronic maintenance problems. Causes for paint failure include improperly selected paint coatings or poorly prepared surfaces that are to be painted. Metal surfaces are best painted in the factory where all the variables for a successful paint coating can be controlled. Repair of painted metal surfaces in the field must be carefully monitored to approximate these factory controls.

Impurities in the manufacture of glass have resulted in glass failures. Glass that is heat-tempered can spontaneously break due to nickel sulphide inclusions that expand within the glass some time after fabrication. Glass can also break when struck by projectiles such as roof gravel or larger building materials during high winds and hurricanes.

Glass surfaces can become damaged when they come into contact with chemicals that are used to treat other parts of the building facade. Glass coatings such as low emissivity and reflective treatments can become splotchy, discoloured or begin to peel. Glass coatings should be studied to verify compatibility with all components of the glazing system and measures taken to control potentially damaging glass-cleaning operations.

Insulating glass units can fail if excessive moisture collects between the two sheets of glass. They are designed with a hermetic edge seal to prevent moisture access into the unit. However, the edge seal can break down, especially if the unit is subjected to standing water.

Structural failure

Permanent distortion of the curtain wall system due to wind is rare, though curtain wall distortion has occurred as a result of earthquakes. A more common type of structural failure occurs from loss of structural integrity of connections between curtain wall components or the curtain wall to the building frame (Figure 9.9). Areas of the building that receive higher wind loads such as at corners or at the tops of skyscrapers are more prone to curtain wall connection failure.

Curtain wall conservation, restoration and replacement

Although the early advocates believed that curtain wall maintenance would require no painting, caulking or refinishing, this has not proved to be true. Curtain walls like all claddings require work to maintain them in a serviceable condition. With proper maintenance curtain walls can continue to last as long as their masonry counterparts. Sealant replacement is the most prevalent maintenance requirement for the middle-aged metal and glass

curtain wall. Following is a discussion of repair scenarios when measures beyond maintenance are required.

'Band-aid' repairs

A 'band-aid' can be defined as a short-term solution to water leakage on a curtain wall. Band-aids entail the introduction of sealant to the exterior of the curtain wall to retard water leakage or air infiltration. Sealant can be introduced to all metal-to-metal joints, the perimeter of window walls where they meet stone or masonry, or at glazing joints. Properly designed, band-aids verified by testing should only be considered temporary.

Selective reconstruction

In a selective reconstruction only those members of the curtain wall that are defective would be removed and replaced with members that are identical or similar. Examples would be the selective replacement of corroded portions of steel frames, reglazing of existing frames, or the selective replacement of spandrel glass.

Overcladding

With overcladding, the original curtain wall system is left in place and is clad over with a new curtain wall system. The old curtain wall system can become part of the waterproofing for the new curtain wall or it can be abandoned behind the new wall all together.

Figure 9.9 The curtain wall failure illustrated is located on the facade of a building where wind pressures are the greatest. This failure occurred at the connections that attached the curtain wall to the building frame

Overcladding will normally have an impact on the appearance of the building. The increased load of the new curtain wall on the existing structure must be taken into account. It is also important that the connections for the new curtain wall adequately transfer all loads to the building frame.

Recladding

The recladding option has become quite popular with 1950s-era skyscrapers and entails complete replacement of the original curtain wall. It is a popular option because it allows the building owner to completely update the image of the building, as well as install a state-of-the-art curtain wall that will perform in a superior manner to the original curtain walls. This option, however, is bound to become more controversial as our early post-World War Two skyscrapers become landmarked.

Conclusion

A distinction of our era is the relaxation of the guidelines established by the Modern Movement. Though no longer the strict dogma of designers, the appearance and details of the curtain wall remain influenced by the machine-made aesthetic with which the early Modernists were captivated. Curtain wall technology continues to evolve with the result that curtain walls are lighter, more economical, and not only constructed of new materials, but also of these new materials in conjunction with each other. This ever-increasing sophistication will present new challenges in the repair and preservation of curtain walls as the contemporary buildings which they enclose become old and cherished reminders of our building heritage.

Notes

1 These antecedents have been described in previous DOCOMOMO publications. See Stephen J. Kelley, 'An Image of Modernity, An American History of the Curtain Wall,' *DOCOMOMO Journal* 15, July 1996, pp. 33–8.

2 Henry-Russell Hitchcock, *Architecture: Nineteenth and Twentieth Centuries* (New York: Penguin Books, 1982), p. 394.

3 John Burchard and Albert Bush-Brown, *The Architecture of America: A Social and Cultural History* (Boston: Little, Brown and Company, 1966) p. 346.

4 Henry-Russell Hitchcock, *Architecture: Nineteenth and Twentieth Centuries* (New York: Penguin Books, 1977), p. 491.

5 Henry-Russell Hitchcock, *Architecture: Nineteenth and Twentieth Centuries* (New York: Penguin Books, 1977), p. 449.

6 The exhibition on the International Style opened at the Museum of Modern Art on 10 February 1932, in the middle of the Great Depression to a profession that was 85 per cent unemployed. James Marston Fitch, *American Building and the Historical Forces that Shaped It* (Boston: Houghton Mifflin Company, 1966), pp. 247–8.

7 J.M. Richards, *An Introduction to Modern Architecture* (Baltimore, Maryland: Penguin Books, Inc., 1962), pp. 71–2.

8 H.R. Dowswell, 'Walls, Floors, and Partitions in the Tall Building,' *Engineering News-Record*, February 19, pp. 319, 321.

9 Talbot Hamlin ed., *Forms and Functions of Twentieth-Century Architecture, Volume IV* (New York: Columbia University Press, 1952), p. 165. During World War Two, more than 200 extrusion presses produced aluminium shapes and tube. After the war, with the introduction of press heat treatable intermediate-strength alloys having good extrudability, the aluminium extrusion industry entered a period of rapid growth. Kent R. Van Horn ed., *Aluminum, Vol. III. Fabrication and Finishing* (Metals Park, Ohio: American Society for Metals, 1967) p. 81.

10 Float glass is formed by laying molten glass upon a bed of molten metal upon which it floats. Glass formed in this way can be fabricated in continuous sheets that are then cut as part of the fabrication process. Rune Persson, *Flat Glass Technology* (New York: Plenum Press, 1969). p. 4.

11 In the 1925 Sweet's catalogue, Hines Turner Glass Company had introduced 'actinic glass,' an amber tinted glass which was sold as an anti-glare device that would also control ultra violet and radiant energy rays. By the 1930s tinted glass was also available in a variety of colours including blue, green, peach and violet. These speciality glasses were primarily used for interior and mirrored finishes rather than exterior glazing.

12 The colour and heat absorbing qualities were achieved by increasing the iron content in the glass batch. Grey coloured glass was introduced in the 1960s, bronze in the 1970s, and blue in the 1980s. Howard Griffiths, 'Colors of the City', *The Construction Specifier*, August 1987, p. 100.

13 Butyl sealants were developed in the 1930s as part of the process of the production of synthetic rubber. Urethanes were also developed in tandem with synthetic rubber during World War Two. Julian R. Panel and John Philip Cook, *Construction Sealants and Adhesives* (2nd Edition, New York: John Wiley and Sons, 1984), pp. 130, 144.

14 Julian R. Panek and John Philip Cook, *Construction Sealants and Adhesives* (2nd Edition, New York: John Wiley and Sons, 1984), pp. 106–7, 120–1, 130–1, 138.

15 The ideal curtain wall was described as being between two and five inches thick, self-insulating, able to withstand high winds, weatherproof on the outer surface, vapour-proof on the inner surface, ventilated and drained for control of internal moisture, designed for expansion and contraction of the building, easily removable for repair, sound deadening, adaptable to all types of building frames, installed from the inside without scaffolding, easy to

fabricate, ship, and handle, attractive, maintenance free, and moderate in cost. Furthermore, this system was intended to last 40 to 100 years. 'Metal Curtain Walls', *Proceedings of the Building Research Institute* (Washington DC: National Academy of Sciences – National Research Council, 1955).

16 John Hancock Callender, 'The Design of Metal Curtain Walls', *Metal Curtain Walls: Proceedings*, pages 79–97.

17 H. Wright, 'What Next for the Window Wall?' *Architectural Forum*, July, 1955.

18 In 1943, during the planning stages for the Equitable Building, Belluschi stated, 'Our assumptions were affected by the peculiar circumstances found in our Northwest region – cheap power and a tremendous expanded production of light metal for war use, which beg utilization after the emergency'. *Architectural Forum*, May, 1943.

19 Peter Carter, *Mies van der Rohe at Work* (New York: Praeger Publishers, 1974), p. 46.

20 H. Wright, 'What Next for the Window Wall?' *Architectural Forum*, July, 1955.

21 John Burchard and Albert Bush-Brown, *The Architecture of America: A Social and Cultural History* (Boston: Little, Brown and Company, 1966) p. 473.

22 The curtain wall industry of the early 1950s was dominated by manufacturers and contractors whose main expertise was derived from the window industry. *Aluminum Curtain Walls, Volume 5* (Chicago: American Architectural Manufacturers Association, 1979), p. 8.

23 'The Trend to Building with Metal Curtain Walls,' *Engineering News Record*, 20 October 1955.

24 'Icons of Modernism or Machine-age Dinosaurs?' *Architectural Record*, June 1989, p. 142.

25 Trevor I. Williams, *A History of Technology* (Oxford: Clarendon Press, 1878) Volume II, pp. 943–4.

26 The Price Tower was the realisation of the St Mark's Tower project that Wright had designed for Manhattan in 1929.

27 John Burchard and Albert Bush-Brown. *The Architecture of America: A Social and Cultural History* (Boston: Little, Brown and Company, 1966), p. 473.

28 Early reflective glass relied upon a chemical spray deposition process, much like that used for mirrors. In the 1960s, the electron beam evaporation system was introduced which rendered a more durable coating and allowed the process to be performed at the glass factory rather than by the fabricator. In the late 1970s, sputter coating was developed that made the previous processes obsolete. Howard Griffiths, 'Colors of the City', *The Construction Specifier* (August, 1987) pp. 105–7.

29 H.K. Pulker, *Coatings on Glass* (New York: Elsevier Science Publishing Company Inc., 1984), p. 5.

30 *The Rain Screen Principle and Pressure Equalized Design* (Chicago: American Architectural Manufacturers Association, 1979) p. 1.

31 *Architectural Technology*, May/June 1986, p. 46.

32 A drainage or weeped system employs two lines of defence against water penetration. The first line provides a wall that can endure the various movements to which a curtain wall is exposed and still remain relatively watertight. The second line is a series of internal gutters and drainage holes designed to catch and collect water which does bypass the exterior plane of the wall and direct that water back to the exterior.

33 Pressure equalised curtain walls rely upon the inclusion of an interior air space formed between an inner and outer wall of the curtain wall. The outer wall or rain screen is designed to shed most of the water but is not airtight. The inner wall is designed to prevent air and watertight and withstand pressure induced by wind. The pressure within the interior air space between these walls equalises to the outside pressure and prevents the build-up of pressure across the outer wall.

34 A curtain wall which relies upon the elimination of all voids and discontinuities on the exterior plane of the wall to control water penetration is referred to as a barrier system. A barrier system is entirely dependent upon the barrier formed by the sealing of the exterior face. This system contains no drainage wall features or other techniques to improve its watertightness.

35 The type of condensation that occurs in hot weather on the exterior side of a vapour barrier of an environmentally controlled building is not normally of concern with a glass and metal curtain wall. Water and frost can form, however, on the interior side of a curtain wall in extremely cold weather when the interior faces of curtain wall members become cold enough to bring water vapour out of warm and moisture bearing inside air. This type of condensation can be damaging to interior surfaces.

36 Aluminium anodising, a popular aluminium surface treatment, is a factory-controlled homogeneous formation of aluminium oxide that is created integrally with or without a colourant to achieve colours from clear (silver), gold, and the range of light bronze to black.

Bibliography

Aluminum Curtain Walls, Volume 5, Chicago: American Architectural Manufacturers Association, 1979.

Architectural Forum, May 1943.

Architectural Technology, May/June 1986.

Burchard, John, and Albert Bush-Brown, *The Architecture of America: A Social and Cultural History*. Boston, Massachusetts: Little, Brown and Company, 1966.

Callender, John Hancock, 'The Design of Metal Curtain Walls', *Metal Curtain Walls: Proceedings*.

Carter, Peter, *Mies van der Rohe at Work*, New York: Praeger Publishers, 1974.

'Colors of the City', *The Construction Specifier* (August 1987), pp. 105–7.

Dowswell, H.R., 'Walls, Floors, and Partitions in the Tall Building', *Engineering News-Record*, 19 February, 1931.

Fitch, James Marston, *American Building and the Historical Forces that Shaped It*, Boston, Massachusetts: Houghton Mifflin Company, 1966.

Griffiths, Howard, 'Colors of the City', *The Construction Specifier*, (August 1987).

Hamlin, Talbot, ed. *Forms and Functions of Twentieth-Century Architecture*, Volume IV. New York: Columbia University Press, 1952.

Hitchcock, Henry-Russell, 'Architecture: Nineteenth and Twentieth Centuries', New York: Penguin Books, 1977.

'Icons of Modernism or Machine-age Dinosaurs?', *Architectural Record*, June 1989.

Kelley, Stephen J., 'An Image of Modernity An American History of the Curtain Wall', *DOCOMOMO Journal* 15 (July 1996) pp. 33–8.

'Metal Curtain Walls,' *Proceedings of the Building Research Institute*, Washington, DC: National Academy of Sciences – National Research Council, 1955.

Panel, Julian R. and John Philip Cook, *Construction Sealants and Adhesives*, 2nd Edition, New York: John Wiley and Sons, 1984.

Persson, Rune, *Flat Glass Technology*, New York: Plenum Press, 1969.

Pulker, H.K., *Coatings on Glass*, New York: Elsevier Science Publishing Company Inc., 1984.

The Rain Screen Principle and Pressure Equalized Design, Chicago: American Architectural Manufacturers Association, 1979.

Richards, J.M., *An Introduction to Modern Architecture*, Baltimore, Maryland: Penguin Books, Inc., 1962.

'The Trend to Building with Metal Curtain Walls', *Engineering News Record*, 20 October 1955.

Van Horn, Kent R., ed. *Aluminum, Volume III: Fabrication and Finishing*, Metals Park, Ohio: American Society for Metals, 1967.

Williams, Trevor I., *A History of Technology*, Oxford: Clarendon Press, 1878.

Wright, H., 'What Next for the Window Wall?', *Architectural Forum*, July 1955.

10 'Great expectations' Woolworth Building (Cass Gilbert) and Lever House (SOM)

Theodore H.M. Prudon

The preservation of twentieth-century architecture presents some inherent historic ironies. Where preservation is about saving significant historic buildings for the future, modern architecture is about breaking with the past and with great expectations for the future. This new architecture was not to be based on historic precedent whether aesthetically, technologically or socially but was rather, in its new aesthetics and technologies to be reflective of a new social order. Technology was to be the means to provide everyone with a part of the new prosperity. In other words modern architecture was one of 'great expectations' and had good 'prospects'. How good these 'prospects' were is evidenced by the development of the International Style after World War Two when many of the early proponents of the Modern Movement had found their way to the United States. Building and its technology were therefore often seen in the light of so-called first costs. However, much of the emphasis moved away from social aspects and focused on using the design vocabulary and search for appropriate technology in expressing modern corporate ideals such as efficiency and profitability and the personal fulfilment of the American Dream. Ironically these two factors, i.e., financial performance and technology are the very two factors that are the core of the preservation challenge of the next century.

Long-term durability was frequently of lesser concern, or hidden behind a social optimism. The combination of social and therefore economic considerations and the use of often experimental or less durable technologies presents unique challenges today as well as the unique irony of how to make something that was not supposed to endure last still longer without costing too much money. Without a doubt the reconciliation of these two aspects was not only the challenge that faced the original architects and designers but is very much the same problem to be faced in our effort to save the icons and the lesser known icons of modern architecture. The very ideology and forces that made the original design and construction possible are to be harnessed for its preservation. The answer for effective preservation must be found in the very origins of this modern architecture, not unlike earlier preservation philosophies which found their basis in the appreciation of pre-industrial design and craftsmanship.

In considering the economic implications of the preservation of modern architecture two very different aspects need to be addressed, which are the continued usefulness of the original structure and the actual costs to effect the necessary modifications and repairs.

Functional or economic obsolescence

One of the significant parameters for the preservation of more contemporary landmarks needs to be economically viable uses. The sheer number of buildings to be considered combined with the ever growing lack of public funds make it necessary to place greater emphasis on the need to develop preservation plans within the context of the private market place and to find revenue-generating uses. While the 'icons' of modern architecture may be saved without too much effort, the preservation of the more 'vernacular' examples of the period need to be viewed within the context of an economically viable strategy. That strategy may often involve a so-called public–private partnership. This is particularly the case in the United States but will, probably, become an important issue elsewhere in the modern world.

Many of the twentieth-century structures were designed for a specific purpose and function using the design standards that were appropriate at the time. This emphasis on the functionality of the building was very much part of the initial design philosophy. Once these 'custom designed' functions become less desirable or disappear altogether the buildings are likely to become functionally obsolete and no longer economically viable. The enormous growth in technological requirements have further aggravated this process and, for instance, office facilities designed before the 1970s are considered less desirable in New York City (Class B as opposed to Class A). This need for economic viability causes considerable pressure to change the entire configuration and appearance of the structure. While the upgrade may be physically possible it is likely to be costly and to generate considerable sentiment to alter the building architecturally to reflect its new technology externally. Unfortunately the more customised the building type is, the less flexible it is likely to be and the greater the possibility that the structure will become functionally and therefore prematurely economically obsolete.

Where the function has endured, the original design standards and criteria for use are likely to have become outdated and obsolete. Contemporary expectations for social housing, for instance, are entirely different than those considered appropriate before World War Two. A good example of changing expectations is the famous TWA Terminal at the J.F. Kennedy International Airport in New York City (Figures 10.1 and 10.2). This gem of early airline transportation architecture was conceived at a time when the present volume of traffic and the complexities of security were not anticipated. While the type of use remains viable the standards for that use have changed enormously.

Similarly branch banks, those majestic (small) palaces of commerce that began to proliferate at the turn of the century, are rapidly disappearing with the rise of electronic banking. The Manufacturers

Figure 10.1 TWA Terminal Building, JFK Airport, New York City, exterior. Architect: Eero Saarinen, 1956–62. Photograph by Theodore H.M. Prudon 1970. When completed in 1962 TWA Terminal was a dominant feature in the architecture of the airport. Subsequent redesigns of the airport, its layout and infrastructure as well as the number of buildings added or remodeled have altered the context. The addition of a canopy in the front and an additional building for TWA at the back do not lessen the significance of the terminal but make it harder to appreciate

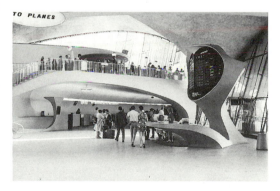

Figure 10.2 TWA Terminal Building, JFK Airport, New York City, interior concourse. Photograph by Theodore H.M. Prudon 1970. The changes in the airline industry have affected the interiors the most. The need to introduce security checkpoints has put limitations on the dynamics of the free flowing space so characteristic of the original design. From an use and economics perspective the sheer volume of traffic to be handled has made buildings like this terminal functionally and economically difficult to maintain in spite of their significance

Hanover facility designed by Skidmore, Owings and Merrill around 1950 and recently declared a New York City landmark is one such modern facility (Figure 10.3). The 'transparency' of the building which at that time 'exposed' banking including its safe, to the outside world, is more difficult to adapt because of the changes in banking as well as its

Figure 10.3 Manufacturers Hanover Trust (now Chase Manhattan Bank), Fifth Avenue and 43rd Street, New York City. Exterior. Architect: Gordon Bunshaft, Skidmore Owings and Merrill, 1954. Photograph by Theodore H.M. Prudon, 1970. Once this building was an innovation in the design of branch banks making the acitivities of the bank fully visible while the presence of the safe right in the wondow suggested that the money was 'safe'. Curtains and blinds were used to 'veil' parts of the building but maintaining the interior of the building very much as part of the external architecture

open and transparent appearance.

Many other buildings where functionality has changed or has disappeared can be identified and may range from early shopping centres or autocourts to military architecture of the Cold War period. Finding appropriate uses or strategies for continued preservation will require all the ingenuity the architects and designers of our era can muster. The lack of a suitable or viable alternative use will often lead to benign neglect at best or outright demolition at worst.

Where, however, changes in the use of a building are to be considered, cost and benefit will also be reconsidered. Pressure to update the structure both visually and technically will re-emerge and create pressure for changes that often eliminate the very reasons the buildings are considered significant in the first place. The analysis of cost and the value of the building once restored will continue to receive close scrutiny and will again require considerable creativity both in design and in financing.

The impact of reduced functionality or the increase in real estate values may not originate directly with the landmark itself. The interior of the Chicago Arts Club was designed by Ludwig Mies van der Rohe in the 1940s and was one of the first of his many projects in the United States. While no doubt

existed about the significance of this interior, the much larger building in which this interior was located was no longer considered economically viable or functionally satisfactory.

The demolition of this early work of Mies van der Rohe also brought out the issue of what actually can be saved physically and what these parts may mean outside their original context or container. While the reconstruction of the Barcelona Pavilion could possibly be justified because it concerns an 'icon' of modern architecture, for many structures that may not be enough justification. The reconstruction is only a virtual landmark but does represent the design intent of the original design. The building was designed as an exhibition pavilion and not as a permanent structure.

Technology and design intent

The architects of the Modern Movement and their successors placed great stock in technology to help change the social and architectural face of the world. Like 'Pip', the hero in Charles Dickens' *Great Expectations* they had 'expectations' and 'prospects' and were full of hope that technology was going to make a better life for all. This promise came with a price: the demise of traditional craftsmanship as the core value for architecture and design and indirectly with an effect on the long-term durability of the buildings created. Earlier building technology was more concerned with the economic use and saving of costly and durable materials and less with the quality or the cost of labour. With the rising cost of labour and the increased demand from a growing and affluent middle class not only the expense of the building material became a concern but also the volume and speed of construction. References to mass-produced products such as automobiles are common and indicative of those changes and the related expectations.

With this emphasis on building technology comes the use of new and often experimental technologies and materials. Because of a lack of understanding of and experience with a particular material or system, those very same materials and systems once so promising may perform unsatisfactorily or may fail altogether today. This raises a series of important philosophical and ultimately technical questions that go well beyond our earlier experiences in scope. Where the system or its materials are unsatisfactory or failing should the entire assembly be replaced because of the integral nature of the system? Can this still be called preservation? What if in-kind replacement, the goal of earlier philosophies, is not feasible or desirable if the earlier system has failed? Does this mean that the use of redesigned systems or substitute materials are a given, particularly if the primary interest is in the preservation and enhancement of the original design intent?

Although these issues may generate important philosophical and financial discussions, there is one significant and undesirable side-effect. Wholesale refurbishment or replacement provides the opportunity to 'modernise' the appearance of the building and a re-positioning of the real estate asset in the market place which may possibly result in the elimination of additional significant and important portions of the original building. For instance, simply suggesting the replacement of sections of an original curtain wall that is failing may not be without its own pitfalls. This will result in the loss of a substantial part of the traditional authenticity of the building. In many instances, this may be unavoidable if a safe, sound and watertight condition is to be maintained. However, it is to be hoped that the argument can be made that maintaining the overall visual intent is, after securing safe and sound conditions, the primary goal to be accomplished in the preservation and conservation of important modern architecture.

While the above considerations may apply also to the preservation of any modern building, several issues, peculiar to the United States, that affect preservation need to be considered at this time. Building in America grew considerably during the period from 1880 to 1930 both in the number of buildings erected as well as the scale and size of the individual structures. The economic growth and expansion that fostered the development of the skyscraper, also saw the growth of other American institutions: corporations and financial institutions. As a result many buildings that deserve preservation are historically identified with (and formerly owned by) these American giants. The oeuvres of such practices as Skidmore, Owings and Merrill, Edward Durell Stone and Eero Saarinen show that development clearly. These buildings express as much the individual talents of their architects as the prowess and power of their owners.

However, the economic climate and corporate thinking have changed. Changed fortunes, lack of willingness, ability to spend the appropriate funds or the (often erroneously perceived) reduced functionality has begun to affect and potentially endanger the survival of many of these unique and idiosyncratic buildings. In addition there has always been a lack of any public funding, subsidy or significant tax considerations. This frequently requires a combination of public pressure, innovative financing and unique public and private partnerships to enable preservation.

Aside from the lack of public funding, there are also few or no statutory or regulatory powers to enforce designation or listing. The deeply engrained principle of (more or less absolute) property rights makes any regulatory intervention difficult because of challenges to their constitutionality. The limited controls that do exist are under considerable pressure because of the changed political climate and rise of the so-called property rights movement.

To illustrate more specifically the issues of technology and design intent, two buildings, some thirty years apart, have been selected: the Woolworth Building and Lever House.

The Woolworth Building is a good example of that divergence of style and technology. Once the tallest structure in the world (it probably still ranks as the highest (high) Gothic building) the structure was completed for the F. W. Woolworth Company in 1913 after the designs of the architect Cass Gilbert at a cost of $13 million. The structure consists of a riveted structural steel portal frame clad with a gothic exterior made of architectural terra cotta that is carried directly on the structural steel. This type of construction, which is essentially load bearing masonry inserted into a structural frame, was widely used at the time because it allowed a great deal of (repetitive) ornament.

The building is still largely occupied by the original company and represents, as an office building, the layout typical of the period. With the elevator located in the tower the remainder of the building is laid out in double loaded corridors with offices at either side. The overriding concern at the time for natural light and ventilation could be accom-modated in that manner. In spite of the less than efficient layouts and the differences with more contemporary buildings as far as mechanical and other systems are concerned, the distinctive nature of the architecture and fame of the building has ensured that the structure has largely survived intact.

The exterior of the building demonstrates the great expectations when new structural forms are combined with old technologies resulting in a technical solution that is not entirely resolved. In essence the structural principles and architectural details of eighteenth and nineteenth-century load bearing construction were inserted into a steel frame. In other words an eighteenth-century brick house from Virginia was stuck up in the sky. In the restoration of some years ago many of these issues needed to be addressed and resolved.

Substantial sections of terracotta were found to be dangerously broken and were removed. The terracotta fractured not only because of the corrosion of the structural steel anchoring and support systems but also because of excessive compressive stresses in the material. When tested with strain relief gauges, stresses from 1,500 to 4,000 psi were recorded, well in excess of acceptable safety standards. Moisture caused the volumetric expansion of the terracotta, and re-hydration of the fired clay (which was tightly restrained by the existing wall construction) and pressure built up. This is another example where the combination of technologies led to some unforeseen interface problems. Cutting every other horizontal joint to the full depth of the terracotta block, some four inches, was found to be the best method of reducing the pressure to acceptable levels and minimising damage to the masonry. Where replacement units were necessary, high quality cast stone blocks were used which accurately simulated the original colour and detail.

The decision to choose a cast stone as replacement material rather than terracotta is the type of decision that will become more frequent in the restoration of a modern building where the economic obsolescence of a material is likely to be as critical as its physical condition. Cast stone was selected for economic, technical and logistical reasons. With no large production facility for terracotta available at the time (thousands of replacement units were required) quality, turnaround and delivery time became critical. While obtaining a replacement unit in terracotta was expected to take as much as six months, a cast stone block could be delivered in two weeks and at lesser cost.

The repair of the tourelles (a French term used on the Cass Gilbert drawings) or small towers, which extend along the four corners of the main tower from the forty-seventh to the fifty-second floor, are examples of 'creative restoration' (Figure 10.4). While one tourelle was a usable chimney at one time, the other three were decorative. With separate steel frames attached to the main structure and clad in terracotta, the tourelles were in poor condition because of severe exposure and their inaccessibility for maintenance.

After considerable study of various alternatives which ranged from complete elimination to complete rebuilding in kind, a modified replacement system that evoked the original design was selected. After repairing the structural steel and filling the masonry voids where necessary, a new aluminum panel system was designed to enclose the entire tourelle. Because the metal fabrication process allowed only for bending shapes and applying minimal detail, all original architectural detail had to be simplified and compressed to its visual essentials in such a manner that the overall architectural articulation and appearance was maintained. Colours for the baked finishes of the aluminium were not just used to match the original detail but, like the original design, enhanced the articulation of the design with its profiles and mouldings.

On close observation the differences between the new and the old is very apparent but when moving further away the distinction becomes less and less obvious. When seen from the ground or when comparing with a photograph taken directly after completion of the original construction, the change is hardly noticeable. A concern that the new surfaces would become more noticeable over time because of their smoother finish has proved to be unwarranted (Figure 10.5).

The cladding of these tourelles was by no means an inexpensive alternative. While the uniqueness of the original architectural composition and detail was recognised, it could hardly be observed from the ground, fifty-four storeys below, or from further away. Once it was determined that the primary significance of these tourelles was in the overall silhouette of the building, a solution or a 'creative restoration' was found. The simplification of form supported the overall appearance and silhouette – in other words the design intent of the original architecture.

Because the large majority of pre-World War Two high-rise buildings use traditional masonry supported on a structural steel frame, repair and replacement can follow mostly traditional methods. After the war with the changes in construction methodologies more pronounced, and the predominant use of metal and glass and the elimination of the so-called wet trades (that is the masonry trades), the problems change and overall performance of the building system becomes more critical. Much of the experience and understanding is gained over shorter periods of time with little opportunity between different projects to improve performance.

While Lever House (Figure 10.6) is generally seen as one of the first curtain wall buildings, some experience was acquired in the construction of the UN Secretariat Building, built between 1947 and 1950. The wall sections were partially modified during construction. The excessive wind and water pressures generated during a hurricane exposed several inadequacies in the original design and led to the addition of gaskets and weep holes.

To achieve sufficient rigidity, carbon steel channels were incorporated into the early curtain walls. While this became a standard solution for the first decade, it also resulted in a fundamental problem because of corrosion caused by water infiltration or condensation. The corrosion forced sections apart allowing additional water to enter, and the process accelerated.

The visual impact of these early skyscrapers is not easily appreciated today because the surroundings have so drastically changed. For example, the Woolworth Building was once the tallest building in the world but now seems dwarfed by the twin towers of the World Trade Center. Lever House is now surrounded by many curtain-walled office buildings but, when constructed, Park Avenue was lined with large residential buildings dating from the beginning of the twentieth century. These Beaux-Arts style masonry buildings stood in sharp and dramatic contrast to the gleaming and shiny glass box of a soap company.

Designed by Gordon Bunshaft of Skidmore, Owings and Merrill and built between 1950 and 1952 the building is an example of the 'corporate' post-World War Two architecture. The structural steel framing and floor system was separated completely from the glass and metal curtain wall, in essence establishing the concept of core and shell. The separation went as far as moving all structural

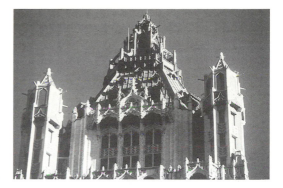

Figure 10.4 Woolworth Building, New York City. Architect: Cass Gilbert, 1913. Exterior detail. Photograph by Theodore H.M. Prudon, 1981. The complexity of the historic design and the condition of the original architectural fabric (terracotta) necessitated the replacement of the four 'tourelles' of the Woolworth Building some 700 feet above the ground. Rather than seeking a literal replacement (whether in design or in materials) the new tourelles were a new visual interpretation of the original design intent

Figure 10.5 Woolworth Building, New York City. Architect: Cass Gilbert, 1913. Exterior view. Photograph by Theodore H.M. Prudon, 1981. While the contrast between old and new is rather evident from relatively close distance, further away the design intent of the original tourelles is fully met by the new tourelles. The overall appearance of the tower remains intact without the need for historic refabrication

Figure 10.6 Lever House, Park Avenue, New York City. Architect: Gordon Bunshaft, Skidmore Owings and Merrill, 1952. Photograph by Theodore Prudon 1996. The successive failure of original spandrel glazing and related sections has resulted in a gradual replacement. The overall effect is a diminishing of the visual consistency of the design intent. The repair and replacement necessary and presently contemplated will ultimately result in an appearance that visualises the expectations of the original design intent but with only a very small portion of the original fabric remaining

supports out of the outer wall and eliminating any distinction between primary and secondary mullions. To stiffen the wall, vertical structural steel U-channels were attached to the horizontal spandrel beams. Horizontal glazing angles were attached to the sides of the verticals. The glazing was placed in the rabbits and secured against the horizontals and verticals with carbon steel glazing stops. The assemblies were covered with stainless steel covers. The wall had no operable sections – one of the first of its kind – and was wet glazed. A system of flashing and weep holes allowed any water that entered to drain out.

While remarkable in its simplicity the stick build curtain wall of the Lever House is still a hybrid technology and very reminiscent of the earlier masonry walls with its system of flashing and weep holes. Where the Woolworth Building may be described as an assembly of eighteenth century brick houses in a steel frame, the curtain wall of Lever House can be characterised as a series of early storefronts in the sky.

At the location of the spandrel, a concrete block wall was maintained as a fire stop as required by the building code at the time. A small section of block was more or less suspended below the slab while the remainder was placed on top of the slab. The front of the block wall was parged and painted and served as a 'shadow box' for the tinted and wired vision glass that was used at the spandrel level.

The wall began to show problems very quickly after completion. The limited life span of the early caulking and sealant compounds undoubtedly had something to do with the need to reseal. By the 1960s the corrosion of the carbon steel glass stops and rabbits as well as the wire embedded in the spandrel glass was sufficiently advanced that glass breakage became a common occurrence. The corrosion also forced the screw-mounted stainless steel covers to open further allowing even more water to enter. While an on-going programme of glass replacement was instituted, it was not easy to match the original glass consistently resulting in the wide variety of colours existing in the spandrels today.

These on-going and progressively worsening conditions led to a re-examination of the curtain wall and the development of a repair and replacement strategy. The underlying philosophical approach essentially accepted the need to maintain the overall visual appearance and design intent of the curtain wall, but identified the necessity to use contemporary technology and materials to achieve a better performing solution.

Over a period of time it was necessary to replace all ferrous glass stops and rabbits with non-ferrous sections. The main vertical structural steel channels, which were found to be in a reasonable condition, will remain but have to be cleaned and painted. For different reasons, all vision glass, spandrel glass and stainless steel covers will be replaced. While the wire glass will be replaced because of its unsatisfactory performance, the vision glass will not be salvaged because it would require extraordinary effort to minimise breakage. Because the existing stainless steel covers have been severely damaged and bent, new covers will be installed to restore the machine-like precision that is such an integral part of the design intent of the original building.

The result of this curtain wall repair and replacement project, once completed, will be an elevation that closely resembles the original in appearance. However, the amount of original material that remains in the exterior wall will be minimal. In the context of traditional preservation philosophy the authenticity of the wall could be questioned and most likely would have to be described as a reconstruction.

To rely, for the preservation of modern architecture, on current preservation principles and philosophies presents a fundamental dilemma. Developed during an era concerned with saving the art and craft of building in the face of the onslaught of the Industrial Revolution, these principles are not suited for safeguarding contemporary buildings designed to celebrate the very advancements of that revolution. The emphasis on traditional technologies, the intimate relationship between the architect and the artisan – whether expressed or implied – as opposed to the use of machine-made materials, more economic substitutes or labour-saving techniques, are likely to be irreconcilable.

A new and appropriate preservation philosophy has to be based, therefore, on the very ideals that have given these buildings their meaning and form. That is to say that the significance will not be in the intricacy of its stone carvings or the mastery of its repoussé copper but in the principles of the new design, the sleekness of the forms and the transparency of its architecture. Therefore the authenticity of the original design ideas has taken on an additional significance. If preserving historic architecture thus far was about saving the intrinsic value of the design and the craftsmanship, then for the architecture of the Modern Movement in particular it must be first and foremost about safeguarding the intrinsic value of the original

design. In other words the preservation of the design intent must be one of the central tenets for any new preservation philosophy.

Making the design intent an important aspect of the new preservation philosophy offers also new and intriguing opportunities for the design of adaptive and continued uses. Here also is a unique chance to reconcile the antagonism and separation between design and preservation. Design for and in historic buildings and districts, certainly in American practice, has been characterised, for decades now, by a contextual temerity. The very desire not to offend the historical context – or the preservation community for that matter – will detract from the strength of the original design. These stylistic adaptations or re-interpretations result in the very eclecticism to which the Modern Movement objected. Design therefore must be a true partner in the preservation of the modern monument and working together to enhance the design intent is the true opportunity for architects and preservationists. This new cooperation could lead to 'creative restorations'. These 'creative restorations' will not be in the style of Viollet-le-Duc who added historically correct elements that should have been there but never were, or in the fanciful manner of Disney, but truly creative solutions that enhance the qualities and strengths of the original design and its intent.

The principles to guide and, to some extent, the language to describe the safeguarding of the architecture of the more recent past cannot be the same as for earlier and more traditional architecture. New attitudes and concepts must be established that reflect our economic realities as much as the ideology of the original architecture. The architecture of the Modern Movement and many of its precursors broke the rules of eclecticism to forge a new aesthetic. The new preservation philosophy must also break with earlier precedent to be able to save the architecture of the twentieth century for the future. It is time to have once again 'Great Expectations'.

11 The House of Culture, Helsinki (Alvar Aalto)

Tapani Mustonen

The House of Culture was Aalto's third project for a big public building in Helsinki (Figure 11.1), the first two being the Rautatalo (the Iron House) and the headquarters of the National Pensions Institute. The House of Culture was designed as a meeting place and cultural venue for workers (Figure 11.2). The first sketches were drawn in 1952, but actual detailed planning overlapped with the building's construction between 1955 and 1958. The building work was an example of the workers' solidarity of its day: one third of all labour was given, voluntarily, as unpaid hours. The first and most extensive phase of the restoration of the House of Culture, which began in 1989, was done by Alvar Aalto & Co. with Mrs. Elissa Aalto as head of the project.

The listing process

During the 1980s the use of the building drifted more and more towards commercial purposes, being rented out as a venue for concerts, seminars and so on. At this time no major renovations had taken place since the completion of the building, only some minor repair work, some of which was architecturally unsympathetic to the whole (Figure 11.3). However, at the end of the 1980s the situation came to a head: the basic services of the building were in need of updating, there was substantial wear and tear to all the main spaces, service systems were insufficient by modern standards and in part out of order. In addition, the interior circulation needed alteration. Architecturally the building was in need of protection and in some places in need of restoration to its original state. The owners of the

building successfully applied for protection of the building under the terms of the Building Protection Act. The protection meant obligations in managing the building, but it also made public funding available for its restoration. The House of Culture was designated as 'protected' in 1991; it was the youngest building to be protected by law in Finland at the time.

The assessment of the building

Working together with the National Board of Antiquities a 'Protection Classification' was formed for the House of Culture. This process divided spaces into four categories based on both their architectural value and condition. First, spaces which were on the whole well kept were to be preserved without physical or technical changes. Second, office spaces and meeting rooms were to be permitted some technical changes as well as some changes of function depending on their location. Third, badly defaced spaces (the café, the cinema) were to be permitted restorative changes, based on the character of each space (Figure 11.4). Fourth, the basement of the building was to be permitted larger changes with technical requirements and services in mind.

The aims

The aim of the restoration was to revive the original expression and atmosphere of the building which had faded over the years and to combine necessary new technical requirements and functions with the

Figure 11.1 The House of Culture, (Alvar Aalto 1955–58) Helsinki. Photograph by Allen Cunningham

original. Original materials and working methods were to be used as much as possible – taking into account the 'protection classification' of each space. A greater aim was to keep the restoration as gentle and low-key as possible. The offices involved in the design and the construction of the original building in the 1950s were also employed for the restoration. This was a natural decision as it meant that original documents and plans as well as a large amount of personal recollection about the building was still available. Recollection was important because the amount of voluntary work done meant that many details were decided on site and were not recorded.

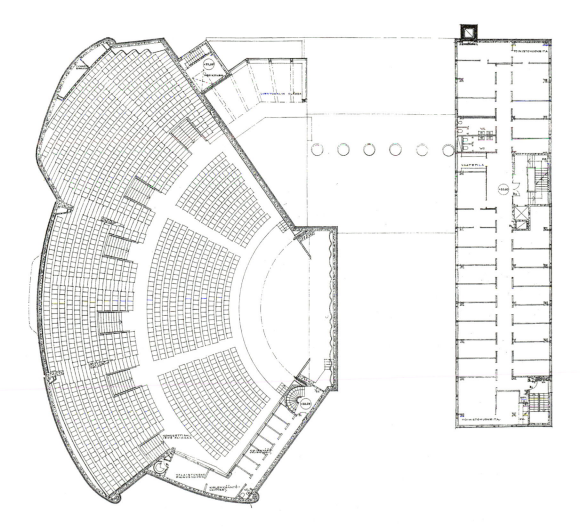

Figure 11.2 Plan at auditorium level, showing its urban form
Source: Courtesy of the Alvar Aalto Foundation

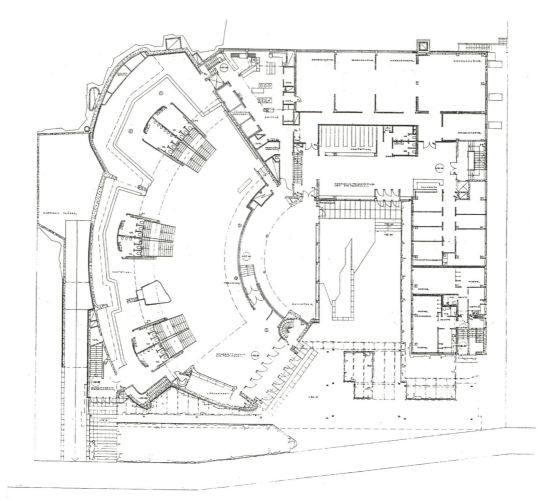

Figure 11.3 Ground floor plan, early 1960s
Source: Courtesy of the Alvar Aalto Foundation

The restoration stages

The actual restoration work was divided into three stages owing to shortage of money. The first two stages were ready in the autumn of 1991. The technical work was greatly increased because of this staging process. The renovation of the services in the concert hall (air conditioning, wiring), which had been placed in the last stage of the building work, had to be done during the earlier stages, in order to avoid having to pull down rebuilt structures later on. After 1991 the building changed owners twice, but it has been maintained continuously, with the biggest effort so far being the restoration of the original windows in 1997.

Luckily almost all the original building materials used were still available. The House of Culture had large amounts of floor tiling and architraves in its own stores. The plastic flooring of the office and meeting rooms was removed and relaid with linoleum, the original material. Internal doors were renovated and rehung in other parts of the building as the building work proceeded. The heavy oak-surfaced doors were partly re-veneered and re-trimmed. The copper surfaces of the office facades and the purpose-designed-brick exterior of the auditorium have not needed renovation.

Case-study: the old cinema 'Alppisali'

The restoration of the House of Culture is a collection of many different methods of renovation. Some spaces and details were retained in their present state, others, like the café and the cinema,

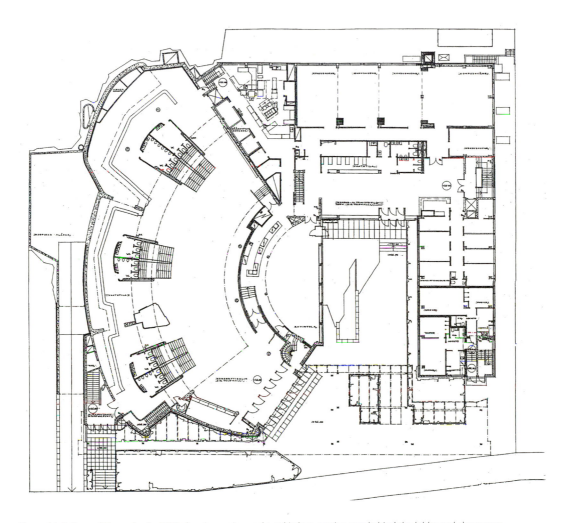

Figure 11.4 Ground Floor plan in 1993 showing major works at kitchen, service area behind the lobby and classrooms
Source: Courtesy of the Alvar Aalto Foundation

were returned as closely as possible to their original condition. New interventions such as staircases were made, and so on. To make the interaction of these various aspects at the House of Culture more tangible it is simplest to observe one complete space: in this instance the cinema, which over the years had suffered severely, its last use being as a discotheque with a flat floor.

The entrance and lobby of the cinema were reasonably well preserved, so it was sufficient just to patch and paint the walls. The restricted toilet areas at the ticket booth level were increased in size by taking space from the old projector room, which also created an area for overcoats. Showing films through the old hatches is still possible however.

The flat floor of the cinema itself was removed and its original slope restored (Figure 11.5). Dirt was cleaned away and the nails and screws left from the disco period were removed from the elegant wood panelled walls and ceiling. The ventilation system which operated through grilles was kept. The lighting of the cinema needed to be brighter than it had originally been but the new lamps were placed in the old lighting areas. The room was completely rewired; the new wiring being either under the floor or behind the new front wall of the stage. Two interpreters' booths and a service space were added underneath the old projection box at the back of the room. New seating was designed, as the old tube-framed seating which was designed for the sloping

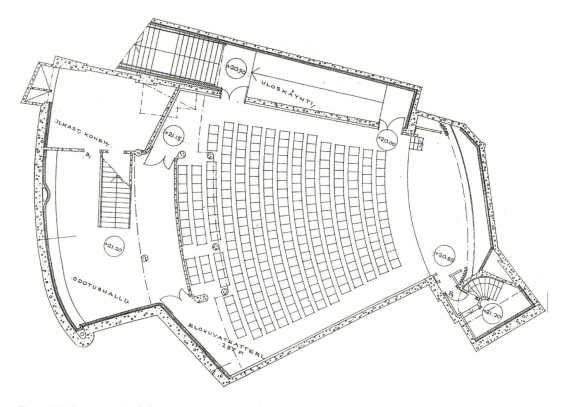

Figure 11.5 Cinema – original plan
Source: Courtesy of the Alvar Aalto Foundation

floor, had been altered at some stage to match the flat floor (Figure 11.6).

After the restoration the auditorium was used for about a year as a conference facility for about 200 people, since when it has been a 'student stage' of the Theatre Academy of Finland which is housed in the House of Culture for the time being. As a result of lessons learned from earlier changes of use the room was prepared for this purpose: the valuable wall panelling was protected by covering it with plywood boards, the seating was removed and stored elsewhere, and the stage was covered with a protective surface (see Figure 11.6). The Theatre Academy will have a building of its own some time after the turn of the century and that is when the cinema, the '*Alppisali*', will be restored to the state it was in at the completion of the renovation in 1991.

Ventilation problems

During the alteration works it was particularly important to minimise visual disturbance owing to changes in the ventilation system, to keep the original appearance of the structures whilst bringing their performance up to current norms. Problems of renovating the ventilation system of the House of Culture were caused by restricted services spaces, small vertical ventilation shafts and the staged construction programme. The false ceilings have been kept intact in the protected areas to allow air circulation to operate in the way it was originally designed to. An example of this is in the café where the original system of fresh air blowing directly through small openings in the ceiling was restored. It was also important to retain all the components which contribute to the architectural whole such as the grilles and air vents. To achieve this it was vital for the architects and other planners to work in constant cooperation, both off and on site. Indeed, this cooperation was not restricted just to ventilation but extended to all other technical matters.

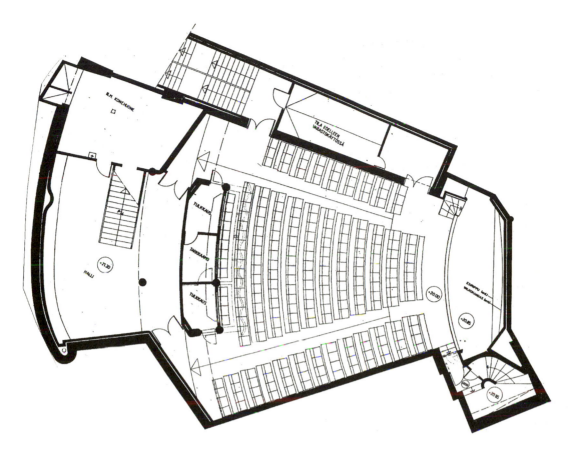

Figure 11.6 Auditorium (former cinema) 1991; recording studio elements from the 1960s were removed
Source: Courtesy of the Alvar Aalto Foundation

Abstract electricity

Although the building was completed less than forty years ago, and although it is still in roughly the same use, the demands on its electrical systems have increased greatly. Present demands and standards for light intensity, sound systems and security electronics, to name but a few, demanded drawn-out planning and negotiations between the designers and the authorities.

The original lighting of the main spaces was repaired, technically updated where needed, and painted. The storage rooms of the House of Culture yielded old lamps which were re-used after having been repaired. New café lights were manufactured using the old lamps as models.

Furnishing the building

Some of the original furnishings and fittings were still in use and possible to repair (Figure 11.7). Whenever possible, they were cleaned, recovered or refinished. However over the years the fittings of many of the spaces had been destroyed. This was the case in the café for instance, where the serving counter had been completely redesigned. The movable furniture of the building was a mixed bag and few rooms had had purpose-built furniture designed for them in the first place. Original period furniture was found for the café elsewhere in Helsinki. It was also possible to manufacture a new series of chairs for the café based on the old model. The most important spaces were refurnished with Artek furniture, and Ilmari Tapiovaara's classic wooden chair, still in production, was chosen as the basic chair for all the meeting rooms.

The original colouring of the building was a clear,

Figure 11.7 New doors to the apartment 1991. Photograph by Tapani Mustonen

Figure 11.8 Auditorium (former cinema) after restoration in 1991. Photograph by Tapani Mustonen

Theatre, music, teaching and changing owners

The first stages of the renovation were completed in the autumn of 1991. The Finnish Radio Symphony Orchestra used the building for rehearsals and recordings, and in 1992 the Theatre Academy moved in as well. During the throes of the recession of the early 1990s and after various changes in ownership the House of Culture was finally bought in 1994 by Arsenal, a state-owned company in charge of property acquired by the state through bankruptcies. Arsenal is also not in a rush to sell the building, as it is in profitable, busy use and it has been able to finance the renovation project in a controlled manner.

Architect Elissa Aalto died in the spring of 1994 and the Aalto office closed down at the end of the same year. Elissa Aalto had sustained the heritage of Alvar Aalto and Finnish Modernism since the death of Alvar Aalto in 1976. Since the closure of the office, this task has lain with the Alvar Aalto Foundation, which was set up in the 1960s and which now operates from the atelier in Munkkiniemi, Helsinki, which Alvar Aalto designed for his practice. Since 1995 the restoration architects for the House of Culture has been Iivanainen & Mustonen Architects.

simple off-white. The only exception to this was the cinema (Figure 11.8). The auditorium was a dark grey-blue, the lobby a light cream and light grey. These colours were also kept during the renovation even though the new use of the auditorium could have supported lighter colours.

12 Sant'Elia Infant School, Como (Guiseppe Terragni)

Maristella Casciato and Cristiana Marcosano Dell'Erba
translated by James Madge

Nationally and internationally, the work of restoration which has been carried out at the Sant'Elia Infant School in Como, an outstanding work by Giuseppe Terragni built in Como between 1934 and 1937, has been a significant event with wide-ranging implications for the continuing debate concerning the future of the icons of modern architecture (Figure 12.1).

This work was carried out from 1982 to 1984, under the direction of Carlo and Emilio Terragni, nephews of the architect, who approached their task fully conscious that they were dealing with a recognised landmark of modern architecture and that their intervention must achieve two distinct, and possibly conflicting objectives: on the one hand, a monument, faithful to its – albeit unfinished – 'historical' form and, on the other, a building renovated so as to maintain its value in use.[1] The scope of the restoration included the making good of deficiencies in the original execution, the correction of incongruities resulting from a previous restoration and, above all, a solution to the issue of incompleteness due to the omission in the realised building of certain parts of the original design. The chosen course was to reconstruct the building as it was at its opening in 1937, to preserve all the parts and finishes which could be 'repaired' and to employ contemporary materials and techniques which, while meeting up-to-date specifications of performance, were compatible with those used originally.

Beyond the exemplary nature of the methodology and the solutions adopted in this particular case by the Terragnis, is their concern to establish a precise attitude towards the general issue of the restoration of recent architecture.

The project of Giuseppe Terragni

From its inception in September 1934 to the inauguration of the Sant'Elia school in October 1937 (Figure 12.2), the evolution of the design was beset with problems; the original idea went through four major revisions and many aspects of the design had to be amended, not least the whole of the building's vertical dimensions.[2] The client for the work was a charitable institution, prompted by the need to build a new infant school in the Sant'Elia district following the sale of a previous building to the provincial administration. In all probability the commission was initially entrusted to Attilio Terragni, Giuseppe's brother, who was already consultant to the institution for the maintenance of infant schools, but it was, in reality, Giuseppe alone who worked on the project from the start. In a letter dated February 1936, Attilio states that he has put the whole thing into the hands of his brother 'with a sincere desire to endow the city with an infant school on the most rational architectural principles.'

The land acquired was situated between Via dei Mille and Via Alciato. The first design studies appear to have concentrated on issues of the building programme, questions of planning and ministerial standards for educational buildings. The building was placed close to the existing structures so as to leave the greatest area free for the garden, onto which, facing south-east, opened the refectory, play area and the classrooms. The south-east orientation

Figure 12.1 South-east façade with the classrooms and fabric canopies, following restoration

of the classrooms was retained in successive schemes as was the C-shaped plan form, considered the best answer to the requirements of the programme (Figure 12.3).

Although revised instructions and the need to bring costs within the available budget called for a further revision, Terragni was, nevertheless, progressing towards the final state of the project; a case in point is the canopy closing the courtyard which, in this new version, is joined to a free-standing canopy placed in front of the classrooms and to a pergola on the side of the garden, these objects taking on an autonomous role within the composition (Figure 12.4). The definitive scheme which resulted from this process was publicly presented, along with a cost estimate, on 10 March 1936.

Several amendments to the programme further modified the building's eventual form: the exclusion of the kitchen block; the elimination of the entrance canopy, of the basement level and of the access-ramp to the terraces; the use of cheaper finishing materials than those originally planned and, finally,

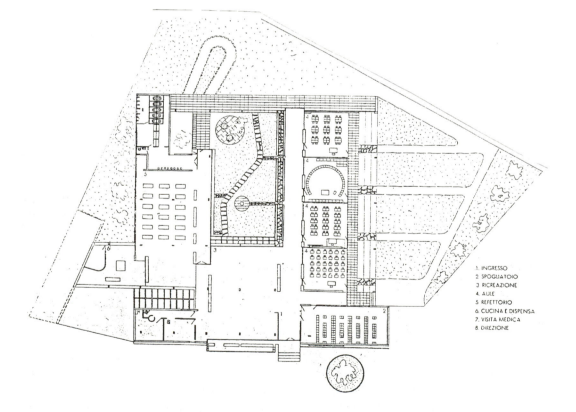

1. INGRESSO
2. SPOGLIATOIO
3. RICREAZIONE
4. AULE
5. REFETTORIO
6. CUCINA E DISPENSA
7. VISITA MEDICA
8. DIREZIONE

Figure 12.2 Ground level plan – final version
Source: Tecnica ed Organizzazione January–March 1940

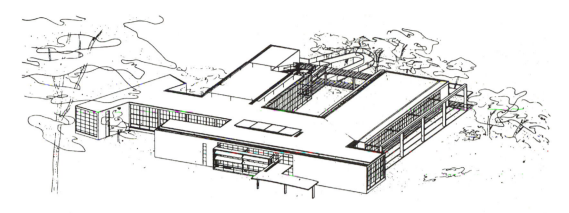

Figure 12.3 Isometric view of the project

the reduction by one-third of the area of concrete and glass construction. Problems of a structural order arose during the year (June 1936–June 1937) that construction was carried out, calling for urgent revisions. Excavations prior to pouring the foundations revealed the swampy character of the subsoil which, together with about 3 m of fill from an earlier period, made it necessary to consolidate the ground with groups of piles, to enlarge the foundation pads and to lay a 50-cm bed of crushed stone. Construction was also hindered by problems, common to all building work carried out on the eve of the war, of securing a supply of steel as well as a general instability of prices. The final inspection, however, which took place in June 1939, confirmed the proper execution of the work and its conformity with the approved design.

A final analysis of this protracted design process highlights the extent to which the evolution of the idea was not just tied to functional or distributive issues but represents a process of transformation in the expressive strategy of the architect, of the elements and the rules of composition (Figure 12.5). On the basis of an initial *schema*, which was never abandoned, there unfolds a process of metamorphosis tending, on the one hand, towards simplification, the definition, that is to say, of a system of rules – the column grid, the double register of heights, the reduction of openings to just three types – and on the other towards an increasingly subtle complexity in the characterisation of primary compositional elements (Figure 12.6).

Giuseppe Pagano, for all that he had criticised the *Casa del Fascio* at Como for its 'literary striving to be

Figure 12.4 Classroom façade (archival photograph)

Figure 12.5 View of the corner between the via Alciato and the outside garden – in the foreground the volume which houses the changing room (archival photograph)

different' and for a 'propensity for the rhetoric of restless form', presents the Sant'Elia Infant School as a landmark in the modern architecture of Fascist Italy: 'A beautiful school, bright, luminous and spotlessly clean, will foster in the child a natural feeling for hygiene, a spontaneous disposition for order and cleanliness, the true mark of civilization.' Using the accepted language of international

Figure 12.6 View of the refectory – on the right the glass façade towards the play area

functionalism, he can find in the 'relaxed freedom of the plan' and the 'plastic invention' of this architecture an exemplary instance of 'social art' (Costruzioni-Casabella, 1940).

The restoration

Restoration was necessary because of the serious disrepair into which the infant school had fallen at the end of the 1970s. This was in spite of a major refurbishment, only ten years earlier (1968), which was intended to rectify an almost identical situation brought about through total neglect because of the forced suspension of maintenance during the war. Despite some carelessness in specification and a certain crudity in its execution, this timely intervention, in which all the finishes were replaced, the roof re-covered and the mechanical plant reconstructed, at least assured the preservation of Terragni's masterpiece which, otherwise, 'probably would have disintegrated, leaving nothing but the structural frame so that any subsequent attempt at

reconstruction would have been difficult if not impossible'.[3] The replacement of some 800 square metres of steel-framed glazing with metal box sections would, today, seem particularly careless and the relocation of the kitchen in the end bay of the refectory so as to make space for a caretaker's flat is clearly open to criticism – although this last alteration, carried out with light-weight partitions, was easily reversible.[4]

After an interval of ten years, however, it was specifically those parts which had been subject to the most extensive treatment which most required attention: the roof had developed numerous leaks and the window-frames were seriously attacked by rust. These circumstances led to the restoration, during the 1980s, by the Studio Terragni. The final measured cost of the project was approximately a billion lire. The scheme drawn up in 1982 had three principal objectives: to reinstate the original plan, to bring the building technically up to date and to secure the structure.

The work of restoration was preceded by a lengthy period of study in which the architects examined the documentation conserved in the archive of the Terragni Studio and that held by the building's owners, the Infant School Body. Analysis of drawings, photographs and documents relating to the design and its realisation, as well as accounts and correspondence between the architect and client, provided evidence indispensable for an intimate knowledge of the building's construction, but it also threw light upon the realities of the relationships and the cohesive aspirations operative in Como during the years that Terragni was working there.

From the documentary evidence – now conserved partly at the Terragni Foundation and partly in the Communal Archive – the designers could check the disparities between the original project and its realisation as well as those between the latter and the situation which they now confronted, the legacy, that is to say, of the 1968 restoration. On this basis, they determined their course of action. Their choice was to reconstruct the building as it had emerged from the construction site in 1937. The parts which were omitted, even if they were present in the penultimate draft of the design, were not regarded as amputations. In their view, the realised building is not to be regarded as a truncated version of the original but should be accepted as an architectural fact in its own right whose image today is more authentically recognisable than would be any hypothetical completion of the original design. In this way, the incomplete condition of the restoration has acquired its own value of permanence.

The missing parts – the kitchen block, the entrance canopy and the pedestrian ramp leading to the roof – those elements of the design which would have established the iron discipline of the square are properly left 'hanging', free to enter our thoughts without needing to take on a material reality.

Rejecting as arbitrary the notion of completing Terragni's original project by adding his intended kitchen block on the north-west boundary, the designers decided to put the kitchen back in its original position. The spatial integrity of the refectory was thus restored. It was also possible to block an outside service door to the kitchen and to reinstate the ribbon window on the north elevation.

The technical enhancement of the building was concerned with the windows, floor-finishes, painting and decoration. As already noted, the previous intervention had not achieved a lasting solution besides which, as a study of the photographic documentation makes clear, it had compromised the external appearance of the original in which very fine metal frames had created a highly rarefied effect. The substituted frames were, in fact, of larger section than the originals.

This time, the glazing system (Figure 12.7) has achieved a character very close to the original. The Saferrot system, using rubber gaskets, is also effective in preventing draughts and the use of Visarm clear glazing, 5+/+5 mm thick, has greatly improved the thermal efficiency of the system.

It was decided to return to Terragni's original specification for the floors which had been altered in the course of construction, that is, to use linoleum throughout. This material, which was only used in the classrooms, had been replaced in the greater part of the building with marble chip tiles. The flooring used in the restoration is 'Linodur' in 20 cm squares, 4 mm thick, a type of linoleum which has come back into production in Italy in recent years and is of distinctly higher quality than earlier versions of the product. Tiles of single-fired 'Klinker' are used in the kitchen and toilets.

The heating installation was entirely renewed in all its parts, boiler, pumps, expansion tank, burner, pipework and radiators; similarly, the whole of the sanitary system was replaced and the electrical

Figure 12.7 Detail of the metal window frames to the classrooms, and the external canopy which serves as a brise-soleil

installation brought up to current safety standards.

Due to moisture penetration from the roof and round the windows, the plaster and paintwork had to be completely renewed. A considerable improvement in the internal environment was achieved through the elimination of rising damp which had been present from the start on account of a variable water-table close to the surface upon which the school was built. Since the floors had to be completely replaced, it was decided not to reconstruct the under-floor void of the original but to provide a ventilated floor made from an array of concrete tubes covering the whole area below the building.

With respect to structural repairs, the non-loadbearing walls on Via Alciato, which were independent of the main reinforced concrete structure, needed to be underpinned with piling. Although, in the previous refurbishment, these same walls had been taken down and rebuilt on wider foundations, continuing settlement had led to further failure. Of equal gravity was the state of the roof in which, also, many fissures had opened up, causing breaks in the waterproofing. This was replaced with a layer of PVC sheets laid over polystyrene insulation panels, a package which should guarantee a permanent solution to problems of leakage as well as an effective thermal barrier.

The external landscaping, hard and soft, was also carefully reinstated. Tree-pruning has had the further effect of eliminating one of the causes of failure in the roof.

How, finally, should one judge 800 square metres of glazing renewed, almost exactly, like the original? Does it simply reproduce what was there before, or is it something new? A casual observer might see in the restoration no more than a faithful and correct rendering of the text. But there is a difference in the reflective quality of the glazing which, on closer inspection, betrays its substitution. There is no denying the powerful contrast between this new element and the opaque surfaces of the rendered walls, themselves renewed, but to which a gentle patina of time has given a sense of authenticity.

In terms of its on-going maintenance, the Sant'Elia Infant School is directly comparable with buildings such as Villa Savoye, which has already required more than one major restoration. The artistic value which we place upon these architectural icons is inseparable from their image of perfect integrity as artefacts and this, in turn, is dependent upon the most fragile of material and constructional detail. From top to bottom of their delicate plaster skins, their great areas of glass held in the slenderest of metal frames, their un-protected planar facades, the traces of human life and the work of the elements are immediately visible (Figure 12.8).

The only alternative to such a precarious cycle, in which the flawlessly gleaming image of the new must always give way to the desolation of structural decay, can be nothing less than a continual programme of maintenance, sustaining the work in a permanent condition of its intrinsic 'newness'.

Notes

1   This building is not only a perennial subject for celebration by architectural critics: it has been identified as belonging to the cultural heritage of Italian architecture of this century and brought within the scope of the law 1089 [1939] which protects the aesthetic quality of the country's architecture and environment. The relevant archives are held in the Terragni Foundation, in the Communal Archive and the Terragni Studio Archive, all in Como.

2   The reason for the reduction in the overall height, brought to light in the preliminary researches of the Terragni for the restoration, was not the result of an over-estimate in the scope of Giuseppe Terragni's original design, but a situation which arose at an advanced stage in the design when the Infant School Body, having to complete the purchase of the site in order to reduce their obligation to the administration of Como, were obliged to reduce the budget cost. For a thorough analysis of the phases of the design, see also *L'Asilo Sant'Elia, Como 1934–37*, compiled by C. Baglione, *Giuseppe Terragni, Opera completa*, Electa, Milan 1996.

3   Terragni, E. & C., *Relazione generale Asilo Sant'Elia*, Como 1982. Terragni, E., 'Restoration of the Sant'Elia School in Como (Guiseppe Terragni, 1936–37),' DOCOMOMO Conference Proceedings, Eindhoven, 1991.

4   The frames were replaced, not on account of their decay but because of their poor resistance to draughts. The possibility of realising the north-western block proposed by Terragni as a space for the kitchen was also considered but set aside.

Figure 12.8 Façade and window details

Bibliography

F. Columbo, *L'Asilo sant'Elia a Como. Un edificio bellissimo per educare i bambini,* (*Recuperare* no. 34, 1988)

A. Ferrari, *Quell'asilo è monumento,* (*Construire,* no. 60, 1988)

A. Fattori, G. Salustri, (*Giuseppe Terragni, Asilo Sant'Elia a Como (1936–37),* (*Frames,* gennaio 1993)

A. Marciano, *Restauro perfetto di un edificio perfetto,* (*L'architettura Cronache e storia,* no. 373, 1986)

G. Pagano, *'L'Asilo infantile di Como'* (*Construzioni-Casabella* no. 150, 1940)

A. Sartoris, *'Un Asilo infantile a Como'* (*Il Ventro* no. 9, 1939)

E. Terragni, *Restoration of the Sant'Elia school in Como* (*Giuseppe Terragni, 1936–37,* DOCOMOMO Conference proceedings, Eindhoven, 1991)

E. and C. Terragni, '*Relazione generale Asilo Sant'Elia* Como, 1982

D.G. Vitale, *'Asilo Sant'Elia'* (*Rassegna* no. 11, 1982)

L'Asilo Sant'Elia, Como 1934–37 scheda a cura di C. Baglione, *Giuseppe Terragni, Opera completa,* (*Electa* Milan 1996)

D.G. Vitale, *Giuseppe Terragni, AsiloSant'Elia, Como 1935–37* (*Architecture Mouvement Continuité,* no. 9, 1985)

13 Bellerive-Plage Baths, Lausanne (Marc Piccard)

Patrick Devanthéry and Inès Lamunière
Translated by Allen Cunningham

Introduction

'Restore the Bellerive-Plage Baths!' The announce-ment of this task in the summer of 1990, rang out like a wager associated with the memories of youth, the clanking of metal lockers to which generations of Lausanne citizens contributed, real emotion at the recollection of an inherited, rational, modern architecture (Figure 13.1).

We outline three of the qualities to be retained in particular as illustration of the priorities guiding the restoration. There is first, the functional organisation of the building as an entity with its controlling geometries; the long, curved horizontal form containing two floors of cubicles for men and women capped with a continuous solarium, are anchored by the vertical form of the entrance rotunda (Figure 13.2). Second, is the restoration of concrete and steel, to expose their expressive, plastic qualities. There are, finally, characteristics arising from the employment of unskilled labour during the original construction, the effects of which are still to be found in the building fabric. The restoration work of the baths has been preoccupied constantly with these three conditions.

Thus, it is the functional organisation and the generating geometries which have determined a new distribution of rooms for personnel and for the restaurant and self-service, preservation of the main staircase leading to the beach, retaining the circulation system for the changing rooms and sanitary facilities on the floor of the building containing the cubicles (Figure 13.3), restoration of the solarium and siting the new family cabins at the end of the composition, in an extension of the curved geometry generated by the complex.

The reason for exposing the 'raw' materials may be explained by examination of the sections of the rotunda and the building containing the cubicles. These are classic examples of the heroic expression associated with reinforced concrete. The employ-ment of large cantilevers allows the façade to be conceived as an independent structure; this expresses the horizontality and together with the imprint of the formwork gives expression to the resolution of static forces. The minimum profiles of the structure declare loyalty to economy of means, and bring to light inherent qualities which result in an expression of rare elegance. It is imperative that homage is paid to this achievement by preserving these characteristics. The employment of standard hardware and the inventiveness displayed in the conception of the sheets of glass which slide down vertically like a guillotine, operated by hydraulic jacks driven by electric motors below and activated by a starting handle, impose a respect for the original concept which will ensure their repair and continuing 'magical' operation.

The building site of 1936 to 1937 was the occasion when a significant number of unskilled labourers contributed their efforts to construction of the baths where the hand of the worker, without benefit of mechanical aids, is immediately apparent. Taking account of this situation led to the degree of respect to be accorded to the technical solutions adopted like, for example, rendering taking the form of a mortar thrown with a trowel

Figure 13.1 Bellerive-Plage [Marc Piccard 1936–7]. Restoration by Patrick Devanthéry and Inès Lamunière

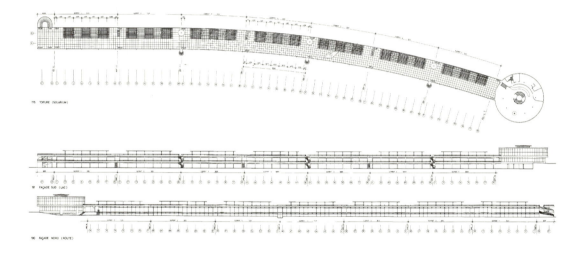

Figure 13.2 Plan at roof [solarium] level – north and south elevations

through a ribbed trellis, the apertures between being no greater than 3 to 5 cm. To restore the qualities thus produced requires understanding the actions of these men.

The restoration project

The point of departure adopted for the restoration of the baths at Bellerive-Plage rests upon certain postulates. These are backed up by the development of the theories and practice of modern restoration, that associated with ancient monuments and with the inheritance of contemporary architecture.[1]

It is imperative to select the means which require the least imposition consistent with the nature of the building, not only during the process of restoration but also when the effect of the works have faded. The adopted solutions will be based upon a maximum simplicity and reversibility, and it is the essence of the building which must determine the nature of intervention. In so far as an archeological artefact is not an object with which to play, it is necessary to establish a rapport between the spatial organisation and its everyday use, between technical problems at formal and constructional levels and the isolated and often contradictory demands. The

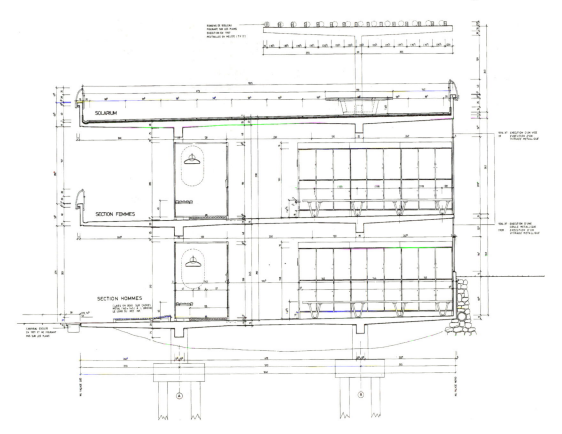

Figure 13.3 Transverse section through the building containing the cubicles. Here the crucial work is to restore the concrete. The visible deterioration is due to a series of factors. First, in common with all reinforced concrete which has so preoccupied our generation, the profiles are too thin. It was this characteristic which so interested our forebears and produced such elegance. Consequently, the reinforcement has inadequate cover and natural carbonation of the concrete has lead to corrosion of the steel. Second, resulting from building faults, the waterproofing to the roof of the solarium did not fulfil its role over a period of years and a cycle of freezing temperatures de-laminated the concrete paving slabs

design in general of the restoration project is, in this manner, sketched out.

It is proposed to:

- maintain all integral elements which are conservable;
- repair elements which are threatening to fall off or are broken (see Figures 13.4 and 13.5);
- reconstitute elements which have disappeared or those which threaten the survival of the building;
- transform those parts which are redundant relating to social purposes, those which compromise the general configuration or, more positively, transformations which provide revelations.

Method

Familiarity with, and understanding of the object, given its general context and unique characteristics, provide the only secure basis when making choices and determining the hypotheses governing intervention. Given this, the methodology for investigation developed within such a conceptual strategy, implies three areas of work:

- research into the history and chronology in order to establish on site from day to day, Piccard's intentions, and the successive transformations of the building, traced year by year from 1937 to the present day;[2]
- the architectural accounting which orders the synthesis of the condition of the complex, by diagnostic examination of the state of the

Figure 13.4 Solarium column during restoration. Photograph by Philippe Pache

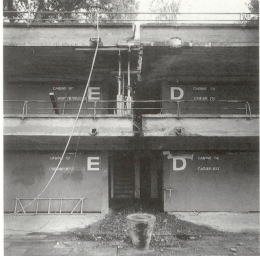

Figure 13.6 South façade at expansion joint during restoration. Photograph by Philippe Pache

Figure 13.5 Solarium column and pergola after restoration

Figure 13.7 Expansion joint at roof level during restoration. At the base of the cantilevers on the south side, in particular at the location of the expansion joint, there was no remaining reliable concrete. On the significant surfaces only 4 to 6 centimetres of compact concrete of the original 12 centimetres remained. In the end there was a constructional error which originates damage which it is impossible to remedy without changing the fundamental nature of the building; the 31-metre distance between the expansion joints is too great and the induced stresses have caused constant cracking of the parapets and paving slabs. The different exposure to the sun on the north and south sides exacerbates this problem. Photograph by Philippe Pache

Figure 13.8 View of the restored waterproofing and solarium paving tiles. The thickness of the tiles has been reproduced, cast on a bed of gravel, instead of the original sand, which channels the water for drainage purposes; the old bitumen joints which inflate in the heat of the sun have been replaced with an elastic polymer. Where the paving slabs have been destroyed by freezing at the expansion joint and there are visible holes at the lower level, reconstruction is mandatory. The boundaries of the deterioration were indicated by a grindstone cut, the formwork consisted of wooden planks and the reinforcement sits on the rough surface of the in-situ concrete. Where the slabs are only 4–6 centimetres thick the cantilever has been reinforced with metal plates concealed in the concrete

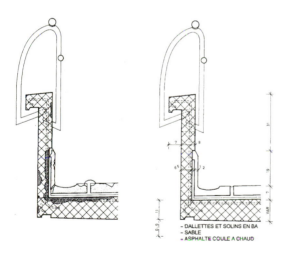

Figure 13.9 Details of the parapets on the south side of the solarium in 1990 and in 1937 as constructed

Figure 13.10 Parapet condition in 1990. The concrete parapets are between 6 and 8 centimetres thick, cast into irregularly placed large scale planks, the texture is porous, the aggregate often visible, and the impression is rough. All the sealing, fixing of ironwork and gargoyles was implemented with mortar which has, from the start, been visible as patchwork. In 1990 it was discovered the concrete was carbonated and a large number of eruptions were visible due to oxidation of the reinforcement. It is probable that the concrete was consolidated around only one layer of reinforcement rendering the exterior skin of the parapets only quasi-intact. It was possible to confine restoration to the interior face of the parapets thus preserving much of the original material

laboratory, which determines and validates the priorities; each assumption is verified systematically during the reconstruction process with constant reference to source material.

Historical analysis as operating instrument

An understanding of the building resulting from detailed historical research becomes an operating instrument to facilitate analysis of the non-destructive deterioration resulting from the construction methods (see Figures 13.6–13.8).

For example, thanks to the photographic record and the architectural and engineering archive, it is possible, without recourse to sophisticated techniques, to trace the reinforcement in concrete elements and to assess the seriousness of degradation (Figure 13.9).

building, all in the context of the vital functions and the nature of those functions; predicting the future use of the building is, equally, one of the 'givens' which influence the choice and hierarchy of any interventions;

• finally, it is the building site, treated as a

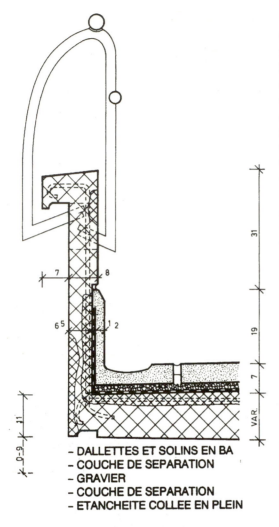

- DALLETTES ET SOLINS EN BA
- COUCHE DE SEPARATION
- GRAVIER
- COUCHE DE SEPARATION
- ETANCHEITE COLLEE EN PLEIN

Figure 13.11 Detail of the restored parapet. The repair has been implemented in the end, to preserve as far as possible the existing concrete and the texture: the rusted steel was extracted by hand [cut out as structural integrity allowed], then sandblasted and protected with an epoxy covered with quartz to provide key for a binding mortar. The finishing has been achieved employing a mortar containing identical aggregates to the original thus simulating the character and colour. Light sandblasting with sand and water at very low pressure was followed by the application of an acrylic paint delicately cement tinted, which provided a unified aspect for the whole building a protection which will need to be repeated every five to seven years. This task was carried out by one mason who worked over the whole building

Given the original documents and the publicity accorded in contemporary journals, the materials employed, the paint specification, the finishes and the chosen techniques may be recalled with a degree of certainty (see Figures 13.10–13.12).

The timing of successive interventions has been traced, their precise locations and the nature of the modifications, sometimes to correct the faults typical in new buildings, sometimes to enhance the degree of comfort. Thus, the question of the 'primitive conditions in the changing rooms' was repeated again and again until the installation, in 1942, of mullioned glazing on the north facade. Resulting from this, the building has proved to be inadequately ventilated thus imposing certain requirements on the restoration programme.

The record of maintenance and alterations is, equally, a fundamental source for understanding the nature and degree of the works undertaken during the life of the building; the repairs often ignore the cause by concealing a fault or deterioration and avoiding implementing a lasting remedy. The change in the roof covering of the rotunda is a good example; instead of analysing the reasons for leaks [apparent soon after completion], the 'repairs' consisted in hanging a suspended ceiling inside and enhancement of the roofing consisting of raised sheets of aluminium; waterproofing was thus assured, but the proportions of interior spaces and external appearance of the rotunda were destroyed.

The programme as project

The richness of source material has enabled a high level of aspiration to be achieved in understanding the three-dimensional organisation of the building (Figure 13.13). Four successive layers corresponding to the same number of building sequences can be identified.

The first, emanating from the archeology of the project, refers to the working drawings made in Marc Piccard's office from 1935 to 1936. These, together with progress photographs taken on site, enable a reliable reconstruction, without casting any shadow on the state of the building at the completion of construction.

The second stage sheds light on the first alterations made under the direction of the architect from 1938 until, probably, just up to 1942. The sources for this programme are those from various management reports on the Plage and quotations and proposals from Marc Piccard. It is not always possible to check the precise dates and the exact nature of these interventions.

The third layer concerns the condition of the interventions carried out between 1963 and 1965

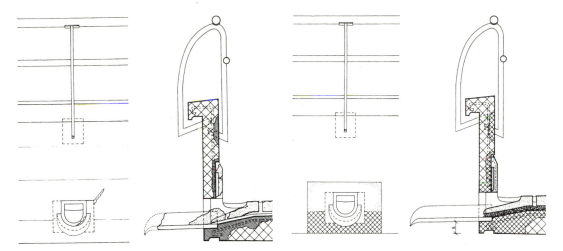

Figure 13.12 Detail of gargoyle before (left) and after (right) restoration

Figure 13.13 Partial view of restored façade showing gargoyles. Broken and covered in saltpetre, the whole assembly has been reconstructed. Prefabricated, as in 1936, in very refined moulds made like cabinet work and composed of fine strips, the gargoyles were replaced in their original locations set into cut, rectangular depressions

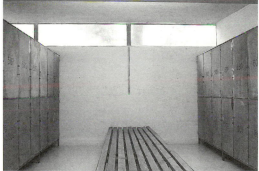

Figure 13.14 View of cubicles following restoration. Here, it was necessary to be convinced of the value of continuing to utilise galvanised steel boxes [the material and its form of details, in particular the punched out numbering system formed by holes which also provide ventilation for the lockers]. The floor finish had to guarantee good hygiene. The lower sections of walls were painted yellow to warm the atmosphere and the lighting levels were enhanced for comfort and security

when the major works, an extension to the Plage in the image of Expo '64, witnessed Bellerive-Plage alter in scale. Here, the proposals and estimates recovered from the archive provided a means of verifying the observations made on the spot. The final layer represents the survey we conducted during the autumn of 1990.

Diagnosis as hypothesis

The diagnostic technique consists of a series of

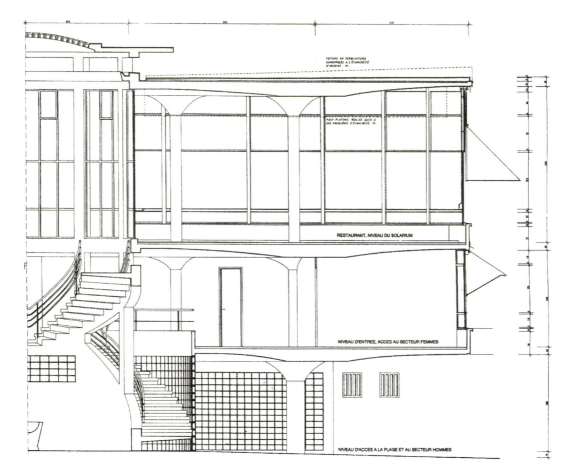

Figure 13.15 Transverse section through the rotunda (the annotations refer to the various interventions relating to the 1936–7 original). It was necessary to recreate the big void of the cupola and the access between the restaurant and the beach as the central pivot. This required cleaning the floor, repairing the concrete cupola, disassembling the handrail and reinstating the yellow nickel which time had eroded and successive layers of aluminium paint had obscured. It was necessary to resist placing an escalator in this void; restoration sometimes imposes the necessity to resist unwelcome intrusions

Figure 13.16 View of the restaurant in the rotunda in 1990

expert investigations, to analyse the carbonation of the concrete or to analyse the chromatography, and through the state of deterioration of the building, section by section, of which the photographic documents and the records provide the evidence. A functional diagnosis recorded the actual use of the baths (Figures 13.15–13.17). The potential for the building emanates from the preoccupations of the users. From these two elements may be deduced the measures which constitute an effective programme providing the line of approach for the project. The state of decay of the building was serious relating to waterproofing, the carbonated surfaces of the

Figure 13.17 View of the restaurant space in the rotunda after restoration. To sense the volume of the circular restaurant , open to the panoramic view of the lake, it was imperative to liberate it from the self-service paraphanalia which has, like octopus tentacles, infiltrated three quarters of the space. The 'free flow' of the old kitchen has been restored behind the glazed screen which has been rediscovered.The waterproofing of the roof has enabled the removal of the suspended ceiling which had hidden the upper volume of the space and now reveals the mushroom headed columns and restored their proper proportions. On the columns, countless layers of paint had hidden the original standard finish, a surface of stainless steel which may have served as permanent formwork or been applied later

Figure 13.19 The rotunda façade after restoration – partial view. Restoring ironwork is a bit of a lottery. The rusty conditions of the standard sections, especially at the bottom of the glazing, condemned them from the outset. Given the real test where the thermal conditions of the building, especially in summer, do not impose additional constraints, it is possible to retain the existing sections provided the work is done on site to substitute the lower elements and then sandblast, protecting the profiles, before applying the final coat of paint

concrete and the ironwork of the rotunda (Figures 13.18 and 13.19), each acting like a series of unhappy transformations which conceal the true image.

The building site as measure

Conservation sites are more concerned with material which already exists and will remain in place, than with plans which determine the means of procedure (Figure 13.20). All the available knowledge [historical, intentions, diagnoses, project material]

Figure 13.18 The appearance of the rotunda roof profile and window sections during restoration

Figure 13.20 View of the metal elements and concrete at the base of the rotunda during restoration

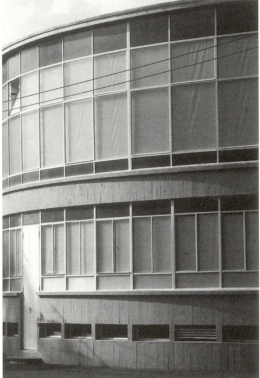

Figure 13.21 View of the restored façade showing board-marked concrete. The scouring of the concrete parapets of the rotunda revealed traces of oil from the hydraulic window mechanism, which staining originates from the opening of the Plage in 1937. These splashes justified, at the time, a coating of white paint. Since then at least twelve successive coats of paint, without any cleaning off, destroyed the texture provided by the narrow vertical planks of the formwork. The concrete broken by the anchors for the storage boxes has been repaired, but this required the application of transparent, semi-porous, acrylic paint, after the metal armatures had been treated

define the objectives of which the site is the focus. Reference to examples and the training of workers, particularly the 'hand' of the masons responsible for the repair of concrete surfaces, is a dominant preoccupation. It is as often necessary to re-discover a technique which in less than sixty years has been lost as to invent one which employs modern methods and modern materials on an inherited structure, but without altering it.

On site project

Apart from the principles, the ambitions of the project are very precise, very simple. Quiet voices whisper the leitmotif: 'do as little as possible', 'respect the implications of the building', 'be guided by what it [the building] says', 'suppress inherited solutions', 'maintain, repair, no more . . .', 'recover the spatial qualities and those of its use', 'transform the building in order to reinforce Piccard's intentions', 'respect the patina and textures however basic' . . . all-encompassing ambitions where one confronts all-knowing critical expectations, where the limits of our abilities are defined as inadequate to

Figure 13.22 View of the rotunda main entrance in use in the 1930s

Figure 13.23 View of the rotunda main entrance before restoration (1990)

Figure 13.24 View of rotunda after restoration. Restoring the original roof profile and ensuring water tightness brought with it some surprises leading us to shed preconceptions. The roof had probably not been watertight for thirty years and the additional aluminium roof raised above the original by 50 centimetres on a wooden substructure allowed water to infiltrate around the edges of the roof slab. In addition, the false ceiling concealed and blocked the pipes ventilating the roofing surface. All these conditions combined to reduce the concrete around the edges of the slab to powder, requiring extensive reconstruction. In order to achieve a façade having due dignity it was simply a question of studying the very first photographs. It was necessary to free the façade of the neon, reconstruct the sign over the entrance and restore the curved security grille which, every morning in the summer, disappears into the ground as if by magic

satisfy all that one might wish, where the final, chosen solution will have maximum integrity (Figures 13.21–13.25).

Notes

1 See Alberto Grimoldi 'Restauration, conservation: deux réalités antithétiques?' *FACES*, No 9, Summer 1988, p. 24.
2 See Martine Jacquet, *Bellerive-Plage, Chronologie,* ITHA, Lausanne, December 1990.

Figure 13.25 Bellerive-Plage restored. Photograph by Sergio Cavero

14 Villa Noailles, Hyères: Villa Cavrois, Lille (Rob Mallet-Stevens)

Aline Leroy, Cécile Briolle and Jacques Repiquet

Introduction

There are two characteristic sides to the Modern Movement's research into residential architecture; the social, collective residential unit and the detached family house. The aim of the first was numbers; a minimal, standardised, economic housing unit, produced using industrialised methods. The second, denying methods and designed for financially better-off clients, expressed an architecture of quality, an experimental research as a response to new needs, with its radical redefinition of traditional design elements. Some twenty years after Christian Gimonet's project for transforming the La Roche and Jeanneret houses into the Corbusier Foundation, the recent restoration of the Noailles house and the deplorable condition of the Cavrois house have put new fuel onto the fire in France, restarting the debate about how to re-use modern residential architecture and about the urgency and conscious restoration projects in this field.

In 1923 a celebrated patron of the arts, Viscount Noailles, commissioned the young Parisian architect Rob Mallet Stevens (1886–1945) to build his holiday home at Hyères, on the Côte d'Azur (Figure 14.1). In 1932, the same architect built a luxurious house for a rich family of textile industrialists in Croix, in France's industrial northern region. These are the two most important examples of Mallet-Stevens' residential architecture, comparison of which has been provoked by a succession of recent events.

For a decade or so, the Noailles house was the scene of the most important moments of French society and intellectual life, an irreplaceable witness to the Roaring Twenties and to the survey of the artists of the international avant-garde, one of the key sites of the history of twentieth century taste. The Noailles family received famous guests there (the Giacometti brothers, Henri Laurens, Darius Milhaud, Francis Poulenc, Igor Markevitch, . . .) encouraging meetings and the development of international artistic expression. In 1926, Man Ray used it as a location for shooting his film *The Mysteries of the Castle Dé*, while Luis Buñuel studied the script of *The Golden Age* there (Figure 14.2). The quality of the heritage of cultural life that took place in the villa between the wars is doubtless one of the reasons for the restoration of the house.

Contradictions

The Noailles house has always been attributed a minor role in the history of modern architecture, so an in-depth historical reinterpretation is necessary, both in order to add elements of critical knowledge and to establish the foundations of the project for restoring and utilising the house. In fact the villa is considered more as a starting point in Mallet-Stevens' brief career, more as one of the examples of elegant, refined architecture of the 1920s and 1930s, than a neo-plastic masterpiece in the history of contemporary architecture. As the architecture of transition, it is also true that the building carries a sizable number of contradictions with it. The villa is set at a distance from any form of theoretical exemplification. Its central nucleus is the expression of traditional functions, without any attempt to

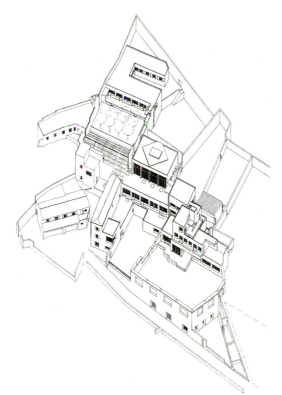

Figure 14.1 Axonometric view of the Villa Noailles

Figure 14.2 Villa Noailles July 1928. Photograph by Thérèse Bonney

describe the typology of the layout. 'Because of his programmatic neutrality, Mallet-Stevens moved away from the intellectual avant-garde of the purist and neo-plastic movement', as Kenneth Frampton has quite correctly written. It is a heterogeneous project, marked by a proliferation of spaces (on a floor plan of more than 2,000 square metres), built

in stages between 1924 and 1933, but only controlled by Mallet-Stevens during the first period (after the construction of the central nucleus, the Viscount's study, called the pink drawing room, the small house, the swimming pool, the gymnasium, the squash court, the pavilion, the cubist garden by Guévrékian, . . .). The house is an object that grew in layers, from its origin through its developments. From the beginning Mallet-Stevens tended to refuse to give the house the appearance of an autonomous object. More than a villa, he gave the complex the aspect of a small village (Figure 14.3); he restored existing buildings and doubled the possible levels of interpretation of the perspectives and volumes as though multiplying them (Figure 14.4). The way he treated the screen wall around the garden-cum-piazza as a façade is a typical example.

His attitude towards the landscape is one of

Figure 14.3 Villa Noailles c. 1930, from a contemporary postcard

Figure 14.4 Villa Noailles 1992. Photograph by Jacques Repiquet

camouflage, without any attempt at ostentation or even differentiation: the paint colours blend with the colours of the earth, the base of the building is ample and broad, well rooted to the ground. The house establishes a respectful relationship of dialogue with the surroundings as they existed before it came to the scene: it approaches the ruins without demolishing them, re-uses the large vaulted cellars of an ancient Cistercian monastery as an integral part of the house, transforming them into a large reception room, it re-uses old farm houses on the property as guest houses for the villa.

Fruit of disagreements

The design also highlights Mallet-Stevens' total indifference towards modern innovative construction techniques; his formal choices are completely independent of the technique he used to translate them into being (Figure 14.5). His research of materials is more aimed at finishes than structural parts. The mechanisation of certain fittings and the presence of particular pieces of equipment (foldaway fixtures, hygrometers, barometers, an astrolabe, a sextant, . . .) are the only signs of confidence in twentieth-century progress. But the choice of these gadgets can also be interpreted easily as a simple sign of sensitivity to the aesthetics of machinery.

The Noailles house is a joint rather than an individual achievement, the fruit of strong disagreements between the client and the architect, between the declared needs of modernity, 'of utility and profitability' of the former and the latter's architectural obsessions. The result is a design full of contradictions, mirroring a period when criteria and lifestyles were on the change. We find ourselves wondering whether the only thing that was missing between the Viscount's ideas and Mallet-Stevens' architectural design was a written programme, an analysis of the client's requirements, or quite simply the experience of modern country house living.

In conclusion, this house is a fragmentary achievement, where Mallet-Stevens created interiors with a relatively neutral, unreal architectural structure to act as a support for the complementary work of craftsmen, artists and interior designers: the 'small flower room', by Theo van Doesburg, the open air room with a suspended bed, by Pierre Chareau, the glazing in the study and the staircase by the glass master Louis Barillet, the bas-relief by Henri Laurens, clocks by Francis Jourdain, the furnishings by Djo Bourgeois, the guest room by Sybold van Ravesteyn and also outdoors, the garden by Guévrékian, the sculpture by Jacques Lipchitz, and so on.

Decay

The Viscontess Noailles often lived in the house until she died, after which it was sold to the town of Hyères in 1973. But while the well-maintained gardens were open to the public, economic and cultural interest was dormant until 1989, despite the fact that its facades and roofs were listed in the Supplementary Inventory of Historical Monuments in 1975, later complemented with the interiors in 1987.

In 1985, architects Cécile Briolle, Claude Marro and Jacques Repiquet drew up a project for utilising the villa as an 'International Centre for Meetings and Creation'. The proposal did not come from the owners, but from the architects themselves, as their conclusion to a study, where an analysis of the spaces and their layout demonstrated the need for a programme of complementary activities around a common theme that would bring the site back to its original vocation. The specific characteristics of the inhabitable spaces make any passage to a new use very complex: only a light, multifaceted programme can blend in with the typology of the habitat.

Figure 14.5 Villa Noailles during construction c. 1925

Pragmatic approach

The reutilisation project, which provides for meeting rooms, study spaces, a restaurant, a museum and spaces for temporary exhibitions, is based upon two types of work: restoring the central buildings to their original condition and a global restructuring of the service spaces, adding some new volumes in the remaining spaces. The heterogeneous nature of the spaces is used as a design element. In the 'quality' spaces, the aim of the architectural design is to 'transmit culture': time is immobilised and the main house is to be kept and transformed into a museum, open to the public. On the other hand the plan is to make some radical changes in the service spaces, to adapt them to new requirements and a new life. Altogether the project does not descend from specific theories of restoration, but is regulated by selective criteria based on in-depth historical study of the architectural body as a whole.

Because of the state of decay of the villa when they began their labours, the careful work of Briolle, Répiquet and Marro in the first section, covering the central part of the house, is almost more of a 'superficial' reconstruction than preservation work. They have restored the fixtures in wood and iron, the ingenious mechanisms of the windows, the heaters, sanitary fixtures and taps. They had to replace the sliding windows in the open air room by Pierre Chareau, the glazed ceiling in the pink drawing room (Figure 14.6), Jourdain's clocks and the brass door handles that Mallet-Stevens designed. They consolidated the under-sills of the windows, replaced the waterproofing in the roof terraces and redid the outer paint work.

Interior reconstruction

The badly damaged floors (made in Terrazzolith, a coloured material in a cement paste), cast in-situ and very popular during the 1920s because of its qualities (easy maintenance, hygienic, acoustic absorbence, . . .), have been recast identical to the original on the basis of samples taken from the site and analysed. In the park behind the villa, the beautiful cubist garden designed by Guévrékian has been laid out anew (Figure 14.7), using the gardeners' recollections, photographs, original drawings and measurements made on site as a basis. This reconstruction is crucial for gardening culture,

Figure 14.6 Glazed ceiling in the pink drawing room

Figure 14.7 'Cubist' garden by Guévrékian after restoration

as this vegetable miniature is one of the extremely rare cubist gardens that was the model for many copies all over the world.

The conclusion of the work was marked by a cultural event set in the old vaulted rooms of the basement floor; a small exhibition about 1930s style furnishing, entitled 'Noailles et les modernes – les traces d'un style' [Noailles and the modernists – the traces of a style], a symbolic event for the reopening ceremony of the Noailles house after more than fifteen years of abandonment.

Cavrois house

Built in 1931 to 1932 in Croix, in the suburbs of Lille, the Cavrois house is an ambitious residence in the grand European tradition of bourgeois residential architecture. With its outer appearance and cladding in light coloured brickwork inspired by Dudok's Town Hall in Hilversum, the Netherlands, the Cavrois house is the work of maturity par excellence, the positive synthesis of Mallet-Stevens' experience in the all-encompassing Hyères and Mésy, where architecture, interiors and landscapes were all designed by Mallet-Stevens. Inhabited until the mid-1980s, then stripped of its furnishings, which were sold at Sotheby's in 1987, the house was later sold as part of a much broader development plan intended to take place on the Cavrois land, its demolition was planned. Now, despite rather late administrative protection measures, the villa is a pitiful ruin, deprived of all its finishes. Thus its fate is by no means clear, although the house is actually already in an irreversible state of decay.

Restore and rebuild

Noailles and Cavrois: these two examples are particularly significant, as their dramatic story is shared by the majority of modern architecture. 'Dynastic' diatribes only worsen the fact that these homes are unsuitable for contemporary lifestyles, that they are very expensive to maintain and that they gradually lose value. Until they are eventually sold and later abandoned, gradual decay attacks the integrity of these architectural works. It is high time we take notice of this situation, as the protection of the twentieth century architectural heritage also depends on these circumstances. Faced with the ruins of the Modern Movement, we no longer have the option that the authenticity of the original will be protected. The only thing we can do now is to restore and rebuild.

CAVROIS, NOAILLES: THE PRESENT STATE OF TWO MALLET-STEVENS VILLAS

Cécile Briolle and Jacques Repiquet (translated by Allen Cunningham)

The parallel established by Aline Leroy in her 1991 essay between the two villas representing the Modern Movement in France somewhat conceals the reality. The singular destinies of these two buildings which, in the 1980s were in similar states of disrepair, evolved quite differently.

The villa Noailles in Hyères and the villa Cavrois in Croix, 'modern châteaux', represent extremes in the evolution of Mallet-Stevens' work, two interpretations of domestic space separated by time. The first exploration at the villa Noailles was an improvisation, full of hesitation and discovery through trial and error which resulted in complex forms, poorly controlled, and exhibiting contradictions between form and structure whereas at Croix, successfully applied logic and perfectly controlled execution resulted in a coherent image, a monolithic building dominating its park.

Many elements of the villa Cavrois architectural programme appear to have been inspired by the experiments at Hyères, in particular the importance attached to the equipment (sanitary fixtures, plumbing, heating and vacuum cleaning and the clocks to be found in every room), the comfort of the occupants and the integration of the sporting facilities with the habitable spaces. Particular interior design details and decoration such as the flush light fittings and the clocks to be found in every room operated from a central control, emanate from Hyères.

In Lille the period of abandonment and havoc was halted by the classification of the building as a Monument Historique. However, the fencing in and other minimal safeguarding procedures put in place by the state were not followed up with restoration or plans for re-utilisation. Given the general disposition and the scale of the villa Cavrois, the generosity of the circulation and the halls favoured its continued life as a public building.

The fact that the building is in private ownership hinders all attempts at its rescue. The public, while opposed to its destruction, have not been forthcoming with a coherent alternative; public agencies are not prepared to co-operate in a project for its satisfactory re-utilisation given the significant expense of the works including the cost of acquisition which is enough to discourage the commune, the département, the region or, indeed, the state to go it alone. Only an association will control the confusion surrounding the situation, organise opinion and propose solutions. Remember that at Hyères it was in this way the situation was unblocked. . . . The rescue and rehabilitation of the villa Noailles had made steady progress since 1991 (Figure 14.8).

The restoration project has proceeded in phases to provide the town of Noailles with a Centre Culturel de Rencontres [Conference Centre for Culture], dedicated to architecture.

Effectively integrated into the international network of the Centres Culturels de Rencontres, a line of reference was established which progressed towards themes dedicated to twentieth century architecture and the conditions for the conservation and restoration of our recent inheritance – in liaison with DOCOMOMO – and also a focus for debate, a platform for international exchange around the creation of an architecture of our times.

The organisation of the building into distinct units allows for the disposition of rooms to satisfy three requirements:

- exhibition space and documents (temporary exhibitions, an archive, a library specialising in built examples in the south-east, an area for contact with the public);
- seminars, conferences and meetings (in the largest rooms concentrated around the swimming pool and accessible by means of new vertical circulation);
- social spaces and residential accommodation (spaces for research and discussion – five rooms for study and meeting, twenty bedrooms, service and technical equipment, meeting and eating spaces, a restaurant).

Independent from the realisation of the cultural project was a succession of phased work programmes – tuned to the available funds – the logic based upon the urgency of safeguarding the fabric without forgetting the functional objectives.

The work programme to rescue the buildings was launched in 1997. Concentrated in the first place upon enclosing the buildings, this operation allowed for the repair of buildings of incontestable, historic, architectural significance, to take action on those

Figure 14.8 Partial view of the villa in 1992. Photograph by Jacques Repiquet

buildings neglected since the 1990 restoration. The swimming pool, sports hall, guest rooms and extended circulation spaces close to ruin were restored to their original appearance, albeit only on the exterior.

The building covering the swimming pool, in particular, posed significant technical problems (Figure 14.9). In addition to the repair and reinforcement of the masonry and the meticulous restoration of the steel supports and mechanisms of the large sliding-folding bays which constitute the south facade, it was necessary to restore the translucent canopy over this volume (Figure 14.10). The assembly consisting of thin slabs (60mm) of reinforced concrete and glass blocks solidly attached to the beams never allowed for expansion and contraction. The glass paving imploded and during the first years following completion, lost their transparency. It was necessary to contrive an arrangement which, while respecting the conditions for adequate water-proofing, separated the slabs and provided expansion joints coinciding with the pattern of beams. To execute this arrangement required particularly rigorous methods of execution in order to respect the original geometry (Figure 14.11).

The next stage concerns restoration of the interiors of the same elements of the building, given that the service spaces – communal building, old kitchens, the domestic quarters, garage – will at a future stage be repaired and adapted to accommodate the new functions directed towards the public and the visits of researchers. It will be these last stages of the building works that the

Figure 14.9 Swimming pool in 1985. Photograph by Etienne Revault

Figure 14.11 Villa Noailles. Roof of swimming pool following restoration. Photograph by Jacques Repiquet

Figure 14.10 Swimming pool in 1928. Photograph by Therèse Bonney

spaces devoted to welcoming and providing information, the restaurant, the specialised documentation centre and the room for information and communication will be arranged.

The 'grand' spaces which will be restored to their original condition conceal, as a result of their 'double skin' the bulk of restoration, the enhancement of services, bringing security and levels of comfort up to present expectations. The visible vertical and horizontal partitions are, in this building, separated from the structural elements; cupboards and false ceilings accommodate the spaces for services necessary to the rehabilitation including new ducts, plumbing, and other equipment contributing to comfort.

The destiny of these two examples of twentieth century buildings demonstrate how, without being monumental, they exhibit a powerful architecture recalling a valuable social inheritance which it is possible to rescue from material decay and public indifference through the expression of a clear political will which is translated, through direct action, into recognition and protection as a Monument Historique.

15 De La Warr Pavilion, Bexhill (Mendelsohn and Chermayeff)

John McAslan

Background

The history of the De La Warr Pavilion and its commissioning is well documented. The project started out as a tentative town council motion to erect an entertainments building in the redbrick seaside town of Bexhill in 1930. The town's dynamic socialist mayor, the ninth Earl De La Warr, took control of the project and initiated an open competition in 1933 for its design with the modernist architect Thomas Tate as its senior assessor. The winning entry, designed by Erich Mendelsohn and Serge Chermayeff, engineered by the pioneering Felix Samuely with quantity surveying by Cyril Sweet, shocked and delighted the town's local residents when it opened in 1935 (Figure 15.1).

Mendelsohn, one of Europe's leading modernist architects, had arrived recently from Berlin. Like many German émigrés, he spent some time in England before moving to the United States. His greatest achievement during his five-year stay in England was the De La Warr Pavilion – a steel and concrete construction with striking white rendered surfaces reminiscent of his finest work in Germany. However, Mendelsohn was not to witness the building's completion, as he left for Jerusalem prior to finishing the project and Chermayeff was left to supervise the latter stages of its construction. Despite the building's active use in the years immediately following its completion it was eventually to suffer from insensitive alterations. By the early 1980s (when interest in the Pavilion began to re-emerge) it had become neglected and decayed.

Listing and phased renovation

In 1986, following an extensive campaign for its restoration, the Pavilion achieved a Grade I listing status (saving it from further insensitive alteration), and in 1989 the locally run Pavilion Trust was established to enhance the building's opportunities for protection, repair and increased usage. These steps paved the way for the Pavilion's restoration and adaptation.

The first stage of this began in 1992 when John McAslan & Partners were appointed to produce a strategy for the Pavilion's long-term use, endorsed by the building's owners, Rother District Council. The practice felt strongly that the identification of substantial and sustainable future uses should form the basis of any programme for the conservation of the building. Phase One of the project, the repair of its external fabric, began in 1993, followed by the preparation of a maintenance plan for future repair cycles supported by a substantial English Heritage grant, and a financial commitment from the District Council to the building's future.

In 1994 the practice was invited to extend its appointment into a series of phased design and construction packages. From this emerged a strategy for the Pavilion's internal and external adaptation and restoration (Figure 15.2). The first stage of this process, Phase Two of the works, comprising the renovation of the first floor conference hall, bar and gallery (including the former library), was completed in 1997. The majority of funding for this came from grants, notably a substantial award from the European Community. Funding for future phases is now being secured through a staged £10million Arts Council Lottery Award for the ground floor café and entrance renovation (Phase Three), renewed services and environmental controls (Phase Four), external landscaping enhancement (Phase Five), and Phase Six is to consist of a linear extension to the north of the east wing (similar to Maxwell Fry's 1963 proposal), housing arts, education and office accommodation on its upper floor and an enlarged kitchen at ground level. Clearly a major proposal of this nature, which has been generated by a perceived need for new facilities and which involves significant change to the building's existing configuration, has required careful consideration to produce sensitive interventions which will complement the form of the building's landmark listed structure.

The strategic planned approach adopted by the architects, supported by the District Council, English Heritage and the Arts Council, is beginning to produce benefits. The external repairs and renovated and enhanced interiors are taking shape, while the Pavilion has transformed its events programme with a focused arts strategy which has recently included exhibitions on the work of artists such as Leger, Le Corbusier and Gris. One can begin to appreciate the delights of this classic modern structure, and its dynamic new uses, and look forward in anticipation to its phased renovation.

Technical specification

Critical to the repair and restorative elements of the works has been the development of specifications for each fabric repair and replacement element, namely external walls, terraces, balconies, glazing, fixtures and fittings.

External walls

Original construction   (Figure 15.3) The walls were rendered in a 20 mm three coat render. On top was a scrape self-finish coat designed to sparkle. Under that was a coat of 1 : 3 Portland cement : sand on top of an undercoat of 1 : 3 water-repellent cement : sand, all on reinforced concrete wall panels hung off a concrete-encased steel frame of 410 mm x 150 mm RSJ columns and vierendeel trusses. The internal walls were constructed in 65 mm breeze blocks restrained by the steel frame.

Figure 15.1 View of the restored De La Warr Pavilion south balcony and staircase enclosure. Photograph by Peter Cook

Condition   Water had permeated the render and freeze/thaw action had caused it to 'blow' – this had in turn caused corrosion of the steel reinforcement. The self-finishing render had been painted and had subsequently been stained. The ground level kitchen-extension boundary wall was built without copings and the condition of the render to the wall had deteriorated. The west elevation annexe had been partly rebuilt in block work and its render was in decay.

Restoration   Walls were redecorated with one coat of bonding primer and two coats of high-polymer-based masonry paint. In instances where render was 'blown', it was cut back to reach adhered render and repaired with a maximum 20 mm three-coat render on a 3 mm spatterdash of 1 : 2 cement : water which included an acrylic emulsion bonding agent. Where reinforcement was shown to be corroded it was cut back to steel, blast-cleaned and painted with epoxy corrosion-inhibiting paint. The wall to the kitchen extension was reformed with a damp proof course, coping stones and the original render rebate detail, featured elsewhere, introduced using stainless steel stop beads. The 80 mm 'blown' render to the two-storey west elevation was cut back and replaced with a primer coat and a thick coat of high-build polymer modified cementitious repair mortar and finished with a 1 : 0.5 : 4 cement : lime : sand final coat.

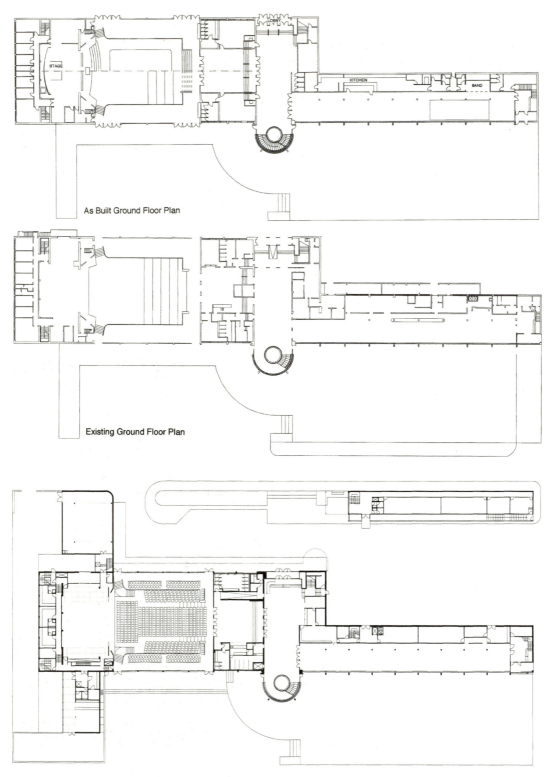

As Built Ground Floor Plan

Existing Ground Floor Plan

Figure 15.2 Plans at first floor level: original (top) as altered (middle) and as proposed with the disengaged north east extension by John McAslan & Partners (bottom)

Columns

Original construction   The external balcony columns were constructed out of steel flats welded into a box section. A rainwater pipe was fixed to the fronts of the columns and the assembly encased in concrete. Columns were finished in 305 mm x 75 mm buff vitreous tiles.

Condition   (Figure 15.4) Partial corrosion had taken place to the steel, leading to concrete expansion. The original tiles had spalled away and been replaced with mosaic tiling.

Restoration   The column concrete was stripped back and the steel box sections wet-blasted to SA 2.5 to remove the deposits of soluble salts. The steel was painted with Sika Isosit Poxicolour primer to 150 microns thickness. Steel reinforcement was shot-blasted to the front of the columns to form the bullnose profile. The steel boxes were then drilled and filled with Sika Top 77 to provide fire resistance to the columns. The whole surface of the column was coated in Sikandur 32 and a 15 mm render coat of Sika Top 77, providing a cementitious base upon which new 305 mm x 75 mm x 25 mm faience tiles were fixed.

Terraces

Original construction   Originally it was intended to lay 920 mm x 460 mm cast-stone paving slabs, but this proved too expensive and the terraces were subsequently finished in 230 mm x 230 mm x 25 mm concrete tiles with an exposed aggregate, laid in a two-by-eight grid with 20 mm longitudinal joints and 6 mm latitudinal joints. Steps were finished with in-situ cast concrete matching the finish of the tiles. The margins of the terraces to the building were finished in terrazzo with ebonite dividing strips.

Condition   Many of the original tiles were broken and the levels had become uneven due to settlement. In front of the bandstand on the south terrace, the original paving was removed and replaced with smooth black paving tiles to provide a suitable surface for dancing. Much in-situ concrete paving had become cracked.

Restoration   The north terraces were re-paved using original, preserved paving tiles. The south terrace

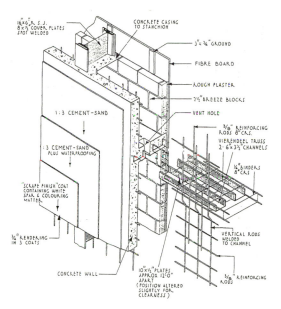

Figure 15.3 Original construction drawing of external wall

Figure 15.4 Column during reconstruction

was entirely re-paved using 230 mm x 230 mm x 25 mm precast vibrated concrete paving tiles with an exposed granite/red felspar aggregate matching the original tiles and laid on a 25 mm sand:cement screed to the original grid. The in-situ terrazzo margins have been re-formed with black PVC-U dividing strips.

Balconies

Original construction (Figure 15.5) The balconies were constructed in a welded steel frame encased in a reinforced concrete sandwich construction laid to falls towards the gullies at the foot of the columns.

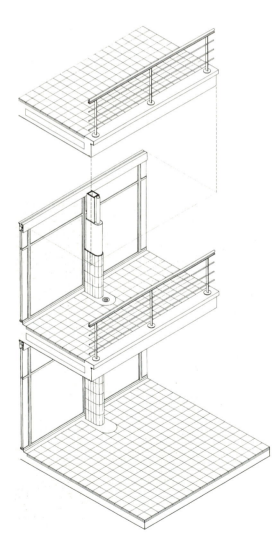

Figure 15.5 Isometric view of balcony construction (John McAslan & Partners)

Parapets were formed in 230 mm x 5 mm cast stone. Bitumen damp proof courses, lapped and bedded in 1:1 mortar, were laid over the concrete. The balconies were finished on the top face with 230 mm x 230 mm x 25 mm concrete paving tiles with an exposed aggregate laid in a two-by-eight block grid with 20 mm longitudinal joints and 6 mm latitudinal joints.

Condition (Figure 15.6) Major cracks had appeared in the concrete due to apparent corrosive expansion of the reinforcement. Many of the paving tiles were cracked and the balconies were structurally unsafe.

Restoration (Figure 15.7) Concrete was stripped off the original frame and the existing welded RSJs were wet-blasted to SA 2.5 to remove the soluble salts. The steel was painted with 450 microns isocyanate pitch. The tops of the steel sections were also finished with Sikadur 32 waterproofing compound. The steel was encased in a reinforced concrete sandwich construction laid to falls and incorporating a cast-in drip to the leading edge. A three-layer performance membrane was torched onto the top face in 228 mm x 228 mm x 25 mm precast vibrated concrete pavers with an exposed granite/red felspar aggregate on sand:cement screed laid in a two-by-eight block grid. The inner upstands to the balconies and the margins were finished in in-situ cast terrazzo with black PVC-U dividing strips. The parapets, concrete fascias and balcony soffit were finished in a skim-coat cementitious water and chloride resistant coating.

Balustrades

Original construction (Figure 15.8) Handrails were supported on continuous T-sections. The intermediary rails were formed in galvanised steel. All external metalwork was primed with anodite followed by two coats of oil primer.

Condition The low-grade steel balustrades were corroded and did not satisfy criteria to resist lateral loads.

Restoration New balustrades were fabricated using galvanised high-yield Grade 50 steel with pocket fixings cast into the concrete. All welded joints were filled with metal putty filler and the assembly was primed with zinc phosphate and finished with two

Figure 15.6 View of curved balcony during reconstruction

undercoats and a gloss overcoat. The handrail to the inner balustrade on the curved balconies was formed in polished aluminium. Stainless steel kicking rails are planned to be installed at low-level set back from the balustrades. This element will be clearly identifiable as separate from the original design.

Glazing

Original construction (Figure 15.9) The café, library and first floor bar were originally constructed with W20 steel section sliding openable glazing in 2 m 690 mm panels hung from steel channels. Weatherproofing was provided by phosphor bronze draught excluders. There was no upstand between the external and internal areas. Elsewhere all the windows were glazed in steel sections. The north and south stair were glazed in a curved steel-section curtain-wall system. On the south stair the glass is supported by mullions carrying horizontal rails. Glazing was supplied by Crittall.

Condition The slim steel sections to the sliding glazing on the south elevation were corroded. These

Figure 15.7 View of curved balcony and south staircase enclosure following restoration. Photograph by Peter Cook

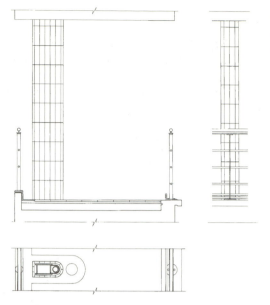

Figure 15.8 Section through balcony showing handrail assembly drawing John McAslan & Partners)

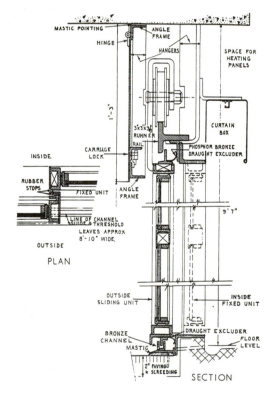

Figure 15.9 Original glazing assembly

were replaced with fixed timber-section windows destroying the relationship between internal and external areas. The glazing to the stair enclosures is consistent with the original design, although the glass and some sections have been replaced. Elsewhere the majority of the windows have been replaced with timber-section glazing.

Restoration   The sliding steel section 'walk-through' glazing will be re-introduced to the south elevation giving full access to the balcony terrace. A high-grade galvanised W20 steel-toughened glazing system will be sealed with Finseal weathering strips and neoprene buffers. It has been proposed to introduce a recessed heating channel to reduce condensation to the glazing and to reinstate the fabric blinds to the balconies.

Fixtures and fittings

Original construction – fixtures and furnishings designed by the architect included a rigid 7-metre pendant light in the centre of the south stair with six levels of 1 metre fluorescent tubes fixed to a chromed brass tube between matching discs, a steel flagpole fixed to the north stair glazing and two roundels of 4 m 270 mm and 2 m 135 mm diameters fixed to the south and east elevations.

Condition – the pendant light had been altered, the chrome discs painted dark blue and the tube re-drilled to accept new fittings. The flagpole was re-located to the roof of the north stair and the two roundels had been lost. Many of the chairs had been replaced although a few remained in storage, painted red.

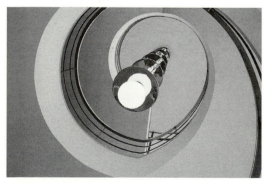

Figure 15.10 Restored 7-metre pendant lighting fitting in south staircase. Photograph by Allen Cunningham

Restoration – the pendant light has been restored (Figure 15.10). All discs and, where possible, the original tubes have been retained and re-chromed. Slimmer fluorescent tube lamps have been fitted and a concealed 180 degree coupling joint fabricated within the top disc so that the light can be turned to enable replacement of the lamps while reinstating the rigid joints at each level. A galvanised, powder-coated 10m flagpole has been fabricated and reinstated on the north stair enclosure (Figure 15.11) and the roundels reinstated. A number of the original chairs have been restored, and the original library shelving will be reinstated (Figure 15.12).

Conclusion

With the £10 million Arts Lottery Award in place, work is now underway to complete the building's restoration, adaptation and extension by the millennium. Planning approval and listed building consent applications are in place and significant support for the proposals has been secured from both the Royal Fine Art Commission and English Heritage.

Figure 15.12 Library and Reading Room as built

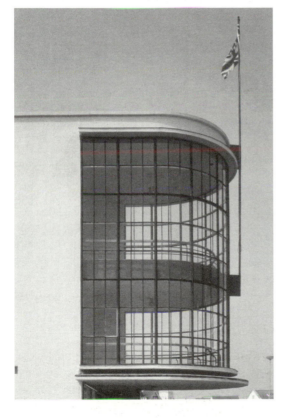

Figure 15.11 Restored flagpole on north staircase enclosure.

16   Aluminaire House, USA (Kocher and Frey)

Neil Jackson

Introduction

Kocher and Frey's Aluminaire House was built for exhibition in New York in 1931. A. Lawrence Kocher was the managing editor of *The Architectural Record* and the facilitator. Albert Frey, a Swiss who had arrived in America only the previous year having recently been working for Le Corbusier, was the designer. And the Aluminaire House was novel, innovative and widely broadcast. Framed with aluminium pipe columns, decked with steel and clad in profiled aluminium sheeting, it promoted a lightweight, prefabricated construction process which allowed for flexibility and multiple application. As a house type the Aluminaire House drew heavily upon Corbusian precedents, evoking the Maisons Citrohan and the Esprit Nouveau Pavilion in its section, and the Maison Cook in its plan.

Since its first building, the Aluminaire House has been relocated three times and is currently framed-up but awaiting completion on the campus of the New York Institute of Technology at Central Islip, Long Island. This last move was funded by the New York State Office of Parks, Recreation and Historic Preservation: this shows an awareness of the Aluminaire House's importance and a recognition that Modern Movement architecture has assumed the age and status of historic building.

The Aluminaire House

The conservation and/or preservation of Kocher and Frey's Aluminaire House presents, on the surface, some philosophical problems. Writing in the

DOCOMOMO International Journal in 1994, the late H. Ward Jendl[1] summarised these quite well:

> The house was designed to be exhibited indoors – in fact, as initially exhibited its walls were incomplete, cut away to show construction detailing. Its structure was lightweight and somewhat flimsy. Finally, the house has been greatly altered, and moved not once but twice in its short history.[2]

Nevertheless the New York State Office of Parks, Recreation and Historic Preservation provided funds for its rescue and the New York Institute of Technology gave it a site.[3] The only other Modernist exhibition buildings of similar date which have been built and rebuilt, and still command attention, are Le Corbusier's Esprit Nouveau Pavilion from Paris, and Mies van der Rohe's German Pavilion from Barcelona.[4] Kocher and Frey's Aluminaire House, therefore, must be quite significant.

The Aluminaire House was built for the 1931 Allied Arts and Building Products Exhibition, held jointly with the annual Architectural League Exhibition at the Grand Central Palace, adjacent to Grand Central Station in New York.[5] This was a big event, for it celebrated the fiftieth anniversary of the Architectural League. Yet it was hardly innovatory, one critic writing:

> It is almost all old stuff . . . an accurate cross-section of prevailing standards in American architecture – these irrelevant sentimental sculptures and reliefs, these cornices and false facades, and dwelling houses which

superimpose upon their functionalist interiors fitted with electric refrigerators and incinerators any style which the owner happens to fancy.[6]

There was even a *Salon des Refuses* organised by Philip Johnson and promoted with the message 'See Really Modern Architecture, Rejected by the League, at 903 Seventh Street'.[7] So how did the Aluminaire House get through the League's selection process? It was displayed as an industrial exhibit.

Although credited to Kocher and Frey, the Aluminaire House was largely the work of Albert Frey, a young Swiss then aged 27, who had arrived in the United States only the previous year.[8] Lawrence Kocher (1885–1969), who was to offer him a job soon after his arrival, was already established as a Modernist: he was managing editor of *The Architectural Record* and the designer in 1929, with his associate Gerhard Ziegler, of a poured concrete courtyard-plan house for the author Rex Stout, located in Connecticut, just across the state line from Brewster, New York. This was the first such structure on the east coast.[9] Frey came with good credentials and Kocher, who had recently lost Ziegler back to Europe, must have thought himself fortunate. For between October 1928 and July 1929 Frey had sat alongside Jose Louis Sert and Charlotte Perriand in the Paris office of Le Corbusier and Pierre Jeanneret. Here he had worked on the Centrosoyus Administration Building, building the model and preparing presentation drawings; on the Villa Savoye, for which he did construction drawings and, with Pierre Jeanneret, developed design details; and on the Maisons Loucheur, in which he was involved, with Le Corbusier, from the outset. He also helped prepare construction drawings for the curious Cité de Refuge barge conversion.[10]

But working for Lawrence Kocher could hardly have been more different to Frey's experience in the progressive, cosmopolitan atmosphere of Le Corbusier's office. Yet what became a partnership with Kocher was to be a perfectly balanced affair. Philip Johnson recalls that 'Frey was the designer and Kocher was the writer and the front man',[11] and the pair operated from Kocher's house at Forest Hills, Long Island. It was Kocher, of course, who obtained the invitation to design the centrepiece for the Allied Arts and Building Products Exhibition, but in the way of that office it was Frey who designed it.

Yet to say that the Aluminaire House was all Frey's

doing would be wrong. 'It had aluminum in it, you know', Frey later explained, 'and it was very airy. And also luminaire means light'.[12] Kocher was certainly interested in the design implications of sunlight and natural ventilation, and of healthy living, as his articles in *The Architectural Record* show.[13] In March 1929 he had published, with Gerhard Ziegler, 'Sunlight Towers', a design for high-rise apartments which gained 'fuller advantage from sunlight by turning rooms to an angle of 45°', giving the street elevations a saw-tooth effect (Figure 16.1).[14] Like the later Aluminaire House, these apartments were to have steel-framed windows with 'violet-ray glass' and a sun room, gymnasium and swimming pool were to be provided at roof level.[15] Kocher's interest in daylighting is further evidenced by an article he wrote with Frey on 'Windows' in 1931.[16] Here in *The Architectural Record* they stated: 'Good architecture is not dependant upon window shapes. Windows should be given sizes and proportions that are suitable to daylight needs.'[17]

The strict design provenance of the Aluminaire House is best found, nevertheless, with Le Corbusier, although unlike his masonry designs, this building was metal. Structurally, the closest thing Le Corbusier designed to the Aluminaire House were the Maisons Loucheur, small workers-houses on steel legs strengthened with wire cross-bracing. But they

Figure 16.1 Sunlight Towers, sun chambers on roof
Source: *The Architectural Record*, March 1929, p. 307. © British Architectural Library, RIBA, London

remained unbuilt. Unbuilt too were the Maisons Citrohan of 1920 and 1922, yet they also contributed something to the sectional arrangement of the Aluminaire House, as did the two exhibition houses Le Corbusier built in, respectively, 1925 and 1927: the Esprit Nouveau Pavilion at the Exposition Internationale des Arts Décoratifs in Paris, and the single house at the Weissenhofsiedlung in Stuttgart. The Aluminaire House was, as Frey said, 'very much like the Stuttgart house, with the open porch below and the roof garden. And it has a two-storey living room. I was influenced by that.'[18] Frey had visited the exhibition and had been particularly impressed with Le Corbusier's designs 'because they all included the outdoors . . . I was not much impressed with Mies van der Rohe's apartment block,' he added. 'It was not very imaginative compared to Corbusier's work. It [i.e., Le Corbusier's] has so much more imagination to it.'[19]

In its adaptation of Le Corbusier's prototypical house-types, the Aluminaire House was a three-storey building, the lower and upper storeys being cut away, as the frame allowed, to provide a covered entrance below and a sun terrace above (Figure 16.2). In this arrangement it conformed to Le Corbusier's 'Cinque Points'.[20] Only the middle floor enclosed the full footprint of the building. Here the main activities were contained: the living and dining room, the kitchen, and the bedroom and en suite bathroom. Yet they were not distinct from the floor above for the living room was a double-height space, in the manner of the Maisons Citrohan, with

stairs rising to a library gallery above the dining room. This in turn opened onto a roof terrace, with a lawn and roof planting. The library actually doubled as a second bedroom and was provided with its own compact toilet and shower room which rather daringly overhung, from the centre of the gallery, the living room below. All the service spaces – the garage, furnace and storage – were located on the ground floor, adding to the impression that living in a modern residence was something best experienced only from an elevated position.

Although the Esprit Nouveau Pavilion affords comparisons to the Aluminaire House in both its section and in the duality of its plan, the one Corbusier house which offers the most striking parallels is the Maison Cook, built in 1926 at Boulogne-sur-Seine. For here the arrangement of the plan, if not the exact configuration of the rooms, provides a serious precedent. The similarities are most noticeable on the ground floor, where a long, bull-nosed central hallway and stairs separates the drive-through garage from the covered entrance; and on the top floor, where the library, roof terrace and the void, upper space of the living room are all that are found. The two middle floors of the Maison Cook are fused into one at the Aluminaire House, the stairs still acting as the separator, with the double-height living room and gallery to one side, and the kitchen, bathroom and bedroom to the other. Although the whiplash curves of Le Corbusier's plan are done away with, some of his idiosyncrasies are repeated: the close positioning of

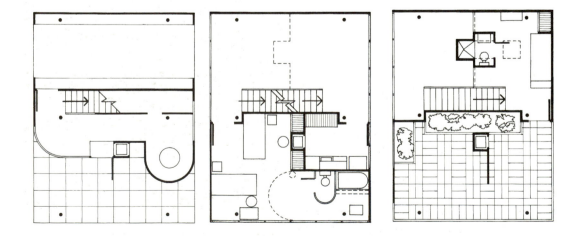

Figure 16.2 The Aluminaire House, floor plans. Left to right: ground level, first floor, second floor/roof

column and wall, for example, and the use of a bullet-shaped cubicle to enclose the WC. And, as at the Maison Cook, a dumb-waiter runs through all the floors from the entrance hall to the rooftop.

The Aluminaire House was one of just two built American houses included in Philip Johnson and Henry-Russell Hitchcock's *International Exhibition of Modern Architecture* at the Museum of Modern Art in February and March 1932. Although the house was not shown in the catalogue, *Modern Architecture*, it was noted therein that 'A. Lawrence Kocher, editor of the *Architectural Record*, has built with Frey an experimental alumimum house', and Frey himself was cited as one 'of the younger men just beginning to build . . . who have received their training chiefly in the offices of the leading Modern architects of Europe'.[21] The other built American house Johnson and Hitchcock exhibited, interestingly, was also designed by a European – Richard Neutra's Lovell Health House – and similarly suggested, and strongly, a European provenance. The Aluminaire House was, however, included in Hitchcock and Johnson's book *The International Style: Architecture Since 1922*, but, like most of the other buildings, only as a photograph and plans. Although not mentioned by name in the main text, references was made to the illustration,[22] but here the caption was neither encouraging nor particularly edifying:

> An experimental house with a skeleton of aluminium and with walls thinner than are permitted by urban building laws. Corrugated aluminium sheathing reflects the surroundings agreeably.[23]

For an exhibition house which was designed acontextually, this last comment is not particularly insightful.

The other important English language book of the time, F.S.R. Yorke's *The Modern House* (first published 1934), did not include the Aluminaire House until its fourth edition in 1943, when it took in several American buildings for the first time. Yet the photograph included in that book, like the one in Hitchcock and Johnson's, showed the house in its second incarnation.[24]

As the principal exhibit at the Grand Central Palace, the Aluminaire House was very successful. As Frey remembers, 'there was lots of publicity about it in the newspapers.'[25] The *New York Herald Tribune*

claimed that 'Aluminum house at architects' show marks new building . . . Model structure designed to harmonise with the modern mechanical progress'.[26] Elswehere a cartoon showed a burglar with a large pair of tin snips in his hands. Beneath the headline 'Architecture visited by 1000', another newspaper reported:

> Throughout the exposition the metal house has been one of the chief points of interest. Yesterday afternoon visitors were waiting in line to enter and explore its interior. . . . A. Lawrence Kocher who with Albert Frey designed the building said yesterday that after the close of the exhibition the house would be reconstructed outdoors and its practicability thoroughly tested. The site for the house has not yet been decided upon.[27]

In the event, the New York architect Wallace K. Harrison bought the Aluminaire House for $1,000 during the exhibition and, the day after the show

Figure 16.3 The Aluminaire House as re-erected on Wallace Harrison's Long Island estate, 1931. © British Architectural Library, RIBA, London

closed, had the house disassembled. Although this took just six hours, its reassembly the next month on Harrison's Huntington, Long Island, estate was more protracted:[28] it took ten days (Figure 16.3).[29] Not only was this second version more complete than the first, the structure once exposed for exhibition was now hidden behind new cladding panels, but, as Mrs Wallace Harrison later told Joseph Rosa, a heavy rainstorm had washed away the chalked-on numbers which should have guided the reassembly.[30] Nevertheless, Harrison re-erected the house without any guidance from either Kocher or Frey: 'He did not engage me in any way,' Frey said. 'I just went there at weekends when I had time because I was interested in how it went.'[31] The result, as Rosa notes, was that the structural rigidity was compromised. It might have been for this reason that soon afterwards Harrison added two single-storey side-wings to the building.[32] These wings, apparently, bore no relationship to the house and a decade later the Aluminaire House was relocated by Harrison once again, this time apparently being slid down the hillside to its new site. The discovery, when the house was dismantled for its final relocation, of 1931 newsprint used within the walling as insulation, does suggest that the house was moved bodily from one location to the next by Harrison. This time it was cut into a hillside with an entrance pushed through into the middle storey, the lower floor becoming a basement and the open top floor, which was to house a piano for Mrs Harrison, being enclosed. Thus it remained, decaying, until it was 'discovered' by Joseph Rosa while researching his book on Albert Frey. Rosa found that the tenant had been evicted and that the house was to be demolished to make way for development. A vociferous campaign, taken up by the New York Times and the Huntington Historical Society, eventually secured the building when, in 1987, the New York Institute of Technology obtained funding from the New York State Office of Parks, Recreation and Historic Preservation to enable the relocation of the house to its Central Islip site on Long Island. There was an added benefit for the owner: the removal of the house was not only to be paid for by somebody else, but would also provide a tax write-off. Rebuilding, under the direction of Michael Schwarting, has been necessarily slow, as funding is restricted. But by 1994, when an awards dinner was held, the frame had been reassembled and was on

show. Joseph Rosa remembers it looking uncannily like the Maison Domino.[33] Thus in its rebirth it returns to its source.

In the late 1920s The Architectural Record was very responsive to new ideas. In October 1929 it had run an editorial article by Robert L. Davidson which promoted the possibility of building with new materials:[34]

> The modern architect is aware of changed conditions which demand economy and truthful expression in present-day buildings. The spirit of the age, which is clearly dominated by the machine and mass production, makes necessary the adoption of machine-made products, considered in the light of their aesthetic effects, steel, copper, aluminum and alloys . . . [and] glass with health-giving qualities. All are added to the architect's palette.[35]

So for the magazine's managing editor, Lawrence Kocher, to design an exhibition house of machine-made products, particularly aluminium, was understandable. The house, of course, was not all aluminium: indeed, the windows (which used ultra-violet glass) were steel-framed, the doors were steel-faced and steel-framed, and the stairs was steel too. Albert Frey had built a quarter-inch-to-the-foot model of the house to help him solicit building materials from manufacturers. 'It was about this big,' he said, gesticulating with his hands, 'and you could have it in a box so it was easy to take around'.[36] He was successful, for over thirty manufacturers rose to the bait.[37] ALCOA provided the aluminium pipe columns for the principal structure; Truscon the steel floor deck, the steel windows and the steel stairs; and coloured flourescent tubes to simulate daylight values were provided by Claude Neon Lights Inc. of New York. The tight schedule and the disparate nature of the suppliers meant that the house could not be pre-assembled, but had to be erected for the first time in the exhibition hall. 'The idea,' Frey later explained, 'was to stimulate manufacturers to prefabricate and so on.'[38]

The Aluminaire House was supported on a grid of six 125 mm (5 in) diameter aluminium pipe-columns set approximately 4.2 m (14 ft) apart. Aluminium and steel channel-girders, attached to the columns, supported light-weight steel beams upon which was laid pressed-steel floor decking covered with linoleum and cork. It was, as H. Ward Jendl has noted, the first house in the United States to use steel decking for floors (Figure 16.4).[39] The structural frame meant that the walls needed to be only self-supporting and, as a result, were very thin: a nominal 75 mm (3 in) sandwich construction of two 12.5 mm (1/2 in) insulation boards separated by 50 mm (2 in) square studs supported on steel angles, and clad externally with building paper and panels of 1.2 by 1.5 m (4 by 5 ft) aluminium sheeting (Figure 16.5). These panels were corrugated for rigidity and fixed with aluminium screws and washers. The interior finish, except in the bathroom, was something called 'Fabrikoid', a nylon lining, manufactured by Dupont, which was subsequently painted: the bathroom was finished in black Vitrolite.

Like other contemporary innovatory buildings, such as Richard Neutra's Lovell Health House (Los Angeles, 1929) and Leendert van der Vlugt's van der Leeuw House (Rotterdam, 1929) the Aluminaire House made much use of both recent technology and health-promoting features. Electrically-operated overhead doors were fitted at each end of the drive-through garage, while on the floor above, located between the main bedroom and bathroom, was an exercise room. Natural daylight was simulated indoors by recessed neon tubes and reflectors, and ultra-violet light aided sun-tanning. This treatment was consistent with the position taken in Kocher and Frey's contemporaneous article on 'Windows' where they state that 'physicians and illuminations engineers have consistently called attention to the value of daylight, particularly of sunlight.'[40] Throughout the design there were built-in cabinets and closets, and fold-away fixtures and fittings. And even the en-suite toilet was contained in its own plastic compartment made of a translucent material called Lumarith. It is clear, then, that, although the Aluminiare House was not, as the name might suggest, an all-aluminium building, the image and appearance of the house was of something new and airy, something light-weight and modern, and this was perfectly reflected in the name.

As with Le Corbusier's prototypical house-types, the Aluminaire House was not necessarily intended to stand alone, but rather to be part of a multiple housing development. Arrangements of what were called 'unit houses' were published by Kocher and Frey in *The Architectural Record* in April 1931, the

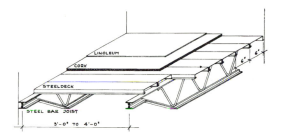

Figure 16.4 The Aluminaire House, lightweight roof and floor construction
Source: The Architectural Record, April 1933, p. 282. © British Architectural Library, RIBA, London

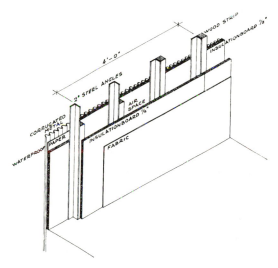

Figure 16.5 The Aluminaire House, wall systems
Source: The Architectural Record, April 1933, p. 284. © British Architectural Library, RIBA, London

very month the Aluminaire House was on show at the Grand Central Palace.[41] One configuration had the houses set in a large, hollow rectangle in the manner of a Berlin city block, just as Le Corbusier had done with his hanging garden scheme for Freehold Maisonettes (Immeubles-villas) of 1922, a development of the Esprit Nouveau Pavilion.[42] 'Standardization', wrote Le Corbusier, 'here comes into its own. The maisonettes represent a type of house-arrangement which is rational and sensible. . . . Mass-production is even more essential than anywhere else in great enterprises of this kind.'[43] Another configuration had the units arranged singly, in pairs, or strung out in a terraced form, reflecting most closely the housing scheme for

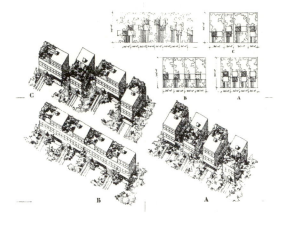

Figure 16.6 Airplane view of three combinations of same house-unit
Source: *The Architectural Record*, April 1931, p. 327. © British Architectural Library, RIBA, London

Bordeaux-Pessac, some of which was built in 1924–6 (Figure 16.6). Here, wrote Le Corbusier, 'the primary elements have been minutely fixed and are multiplied with endless variations. This,' he added significantly, 'is a genuine industrialization of the Builders' Yard.'[44] The published plans of Kocher and Frey's unit house do not show the same room configuration as the Aluminaire House exhibit, but nevertheless represent three-storey structures, supported on a grid of six columns, and with the lower and upper floors exposed to provide, respectively, a porch and a roof terrace.

There was, apparently, no statement or manifesto attached to the Aluminaire House. As an exhibit, albeit an 'industrial' one, it was intended to stand alone. Exactly two years after the Allied Arts and Building Products/Architectural League Exhibition at the Grand Central Palace, *The Architectural Record* published an article by Kocher and Frey which neatly summarised the intention of the Aluminaire House. It was called 'New Materials and Improved Construction Methods.'[45] The article began by observing that 'the more important new materials and methods of construction are derived from efforts to reduce labor on the job, to lighten weight of construction and transportation and incidentally to lower cost', and then gave a check-list of twenty-seven 'ideals' which assisted towards this goal. Not all applied to the Aluminaire House – it was not, for example, lightning-proof and fireproof throughout –

but the majority certainly did. The article concentrated upon lightweight roof and floor construction, and upon walling systems, using the Aluminaire House as an example in each category. Even if some of the 'ideals' would now appear to be unattainable in the materials chosen for the Aluminaire House, the broader notions have lasted, and are here worth repeating:[46]

- Dry construction
- Lightweight
- Parts capable of replacement and addition
- Wall units of uniform size to permit interchange of parts
- Erection and installation of units by unskilled labour
- Possibilities for demolition and re-erection on new site
- Economical use of space because of thickness of walls
- Interior partitions flexible and capable of varied arrangements
- Closets, cabinets and equipments as units
- Minimum cost of construction and upkeep

What these ten 'ideals' demonstrate is an attitude towards house manufacture which promoted off-site prefabrication, modular planning and unit-construction. Within ten years this had become, as part of the war effort, a necessity. Within twenty years, through the promotional efforts of John Entenza's magazine *Arts and Architecture* and the Case Study House Program, and the built work of Californian architects like Raphael Soriano and Charles and Ray Eames, Lawrence Kocher and Albert Frey's vision had become a domestic reality. This, perhaps, is why the Aluminaire House is so significant.

As both Joseph Rosa and H. Ward Jendl have observed, the treatment of a temporary, pre-fabricated, exhibition house as if it was a static structure of historic significance by, say, Neutra or Howe and Lescaze, raises philosophical problems. Yet in recognising the significance of the Aluminaire House in terms of, and for what it is – a temporary, prefabricated, exhibition house – shows a considerable understanding, on the part of the New York State Office of Parks, Recreation and Historic Preservation, of its nature as well as an appreciation of its importance. The placing of the Aluminaire House, in its own right, on the National Register of Historic Places would be a triumph.[47] Such insight, if demonstrated by other statutory authorities, would make the work of DOCOMOMO that much easier. The situation is analogous to that experienced in Britain in the later 1950s when the Victorian Society, founded in 1957, fought to save buildings apparently so despised by an inter-war generation which took gentility and perhaps even itself so seriously. Time and education made the change, and although the pendulum of taste and acceptability have swung to almost the other extreme, and William Morris and themed Victoriana surround us, a battle for good sense and architectural understanding has been won. The strange story of the Aluminaire House might just suggest that the same could soon be said for Modernism.

Acknowledgement

I am grateful to Joseph Rosa for sharing his knowledge of the Aluminaire House, and to Allen Cunningham and A. Peter Fawcett for their insights into the work of Le Corbusier. But most of all I am grateful to Albert Frey, for the time he spent with me.

Notes

1 H. Ward Jendl, who died recently, was Deputy Chief of the Preservation Assistance Division of the National Parks Service.
2 H. Ward Jendl, 'With heritage so shiny: the Aluminaire, America's first all aluminum house', *DOCOMOMO International Journal*, 12 November 1994, p. 42.
3 A grant of $131,750.00 was awarded in 1987.
4 Le Corbusier's Esprit Nouveau Pavilion from the 1925 Exposition Internationale des Arts Décoratifs in Paris was rebuilt in Bologna (1977). Mies van der Rohe's 1929 Barcelona Pavilion was rebuilt on the original site (1987). Neither, strictly speaking, were reassemblies of the original parts, which was the case with the Aluminaire House.
5 The exhibition lasted from 18 to 25 April 1931.
6 Helen Appleton Read writing in the *Brooklyn Eagle*, quoted in Robert A.M. Stern, Gregory Gilmartin, Thomas Mellins, *New York 1930, Architecture and Urbanism Between The Two World Wars*, (New York, Rizzoli International Publications,1987) p. 343.
7 Ibid.
8 Albert Frey moved to Palm Springs, California in 1939 and lives there in a house of his own design.
9 See 'Houses built with new construction methods', *The Architectural Record*, April 1933, p. 288.
10 Frey's time in Le Corbusier's office is well documented in Joseph Rosa, *Albert Frey, Architect* (New York, Rizzoli International Publications, 1990) pp. 16–17.

11 Philip Johnson, interviewed in 1987 and quoted in Joseph Rosa, *Albert Frey, Architect* op. cit. p. 26.
12 Albert Frey interviewed by Neil Jackson, Palm Springs, California, 24 September 1991.
13 See A. Lawrence Kocher and Robert L. Davidson, 'Swimming Pools (Standards for Design and Construction)', *The Architectural Record*, January 1929, pp. 68–87, and also A. Lawrence Kocher and Gerhard Ziegler, Architects 'Sunlight Towers', *The Architectural Record*, March 1929, pp. 307–10.
14 A. Lawrence Kocher and Gerhard Ziegler, Architects 'Sunlight Towers', *The Architectural Record*, March 1929, p. 307.
15 Ibid. p. 310.
16 A. Lawrence Kocher and Albert Frey, 'Windows', *The Architectural Record*, February 1931, pp. 126–37.
17 Ibid. p. 127.
18 Albert Frey interviewed by Neil Jackson, Palm Springs, California, 24 September 1991.
19 Ibid.
20 Le Corbusier's 'Cinque Points' are: the use of piloti, the open plan, the free facade, the strip window, and the roof garden. He stated in *Oeuvre Complete, Vol. 1, 1910–1929*, (Paris, 1929, pp. 128–9) that he identified these points in 1926, although they are as early as the Domino House of 1914. The Cinque Points actually appear, apparently for the first time in print, in *Precisions sur un état présent de l'architecture et de l'urbanisme. Une maison, une palais* (Paris, 1928).
21 Philip Johnson and Henry-Russell Hitchcock Jnr., 'The Extent of Modern Architecture' in Philip Johnson and Henry-Russell Hitchcock Jnr. *et al., Modern Architecture International Exhibition* (New York, Museum of Modern Art, 1932), p. 22.
22 Henry-Russell Hitchcock and Philip Johnson, *The International Style: Architecture Since 1922* (New York, Norton & Co, 1996, first edition 1932) pp. 65, 84.
23 Ibid. p. 69.
24 F.R.S. Yorke, *The Modern House*, (Cheam, Architectural Press, 1943, fourth edition) p. 205.
25 Albert Frey interviewed by Neil Jackson, Palm Springs, California, 24 September 1991.
26 From a newspaper cutting in the collection of Albert Frey. Date unknown.
27 From a newspaper cutting in the collection of Albert Frey. Source unknown.
28 In *The International Style*, Henry-Russell Hitchcock and Philip Johnson give the location as Syoset, Long Island. This is because Harrison's 85-acre estate stretched from Huntington to Syoset. Huntington is the preferred and correct location. Joseph Rosa, telephone conversation with Neil Jackson, 29 October 1997.
29 This is the figure given by Joseph Rosa. In her monograph on Wallace Harrison, Victoria Newhouse says that 'instead of the eighteen days stipulated by Kocher and Frey for erection, the job took several months'. This, presumably, includes the levelling of the land, the building of a concrete base and the making of an approach road. See Victoria Newhouse, *Wallace K. Harrison, Architect* (New York, Rizzoli International Publications, 1989) p. 60.

30 Joseph Rosa, *Albert Frey, Architect* (New York, Rizzoli International Publications, 1990), p. 28.

31 Albert Frey interviewed by Neil Jackson, Palm Springs, California, 24 September 1991.

32 It was, according to Joseph Rosa, always Harrison's intention to extend the building: he had a wife, a baby daughter, a nanny and a chauffeur to accommodate. The nature of the extension, nevertheless, might have been a response to the structural instability of the building. Joseph Rosa, telephone conversation with Neil Jackson, 29 October 1997.

33 Joseph Rosa, telephone conversation with Neil Jackson, 29 October 1997.

34 Robert L. Davidson, 'New Construction Methods', *The Architectural Record*, October 1929, pp. 362–85.

35 Ibid. p. 384.

36 Albert Frey interviewed by Neil Jackson, Palm Springs, California, 24 September 1991.

37 Frey suggested that 'maybe fifty' firms made contributions. 'They were all interested in promoting sales, you know, because it was during the Depression.' Albert Frey interviewed by Neil Jackson, Palm Springs, California, 24 September 1991

38 Albert Frey interviewed by Neil Jackson, Palm Springs, California, 24 September 1991.

39 For a description of the construction, see H. Ward Jendl, 'With heritage so shiny: the Aluminaire, America's first all aluminum house', *DOCOMOMO International Journal*, 12 November 1994, pp. 42–3.

40 A. Lawrence Kocher and Albert Frey, 'Windows', *The Architectural Record*, February 1931, p. 127.

41 A. Lawrence Kocher and Albert Frey, 'Real Estate Subdivisions for Low-cost Housing', *The Architectural Record*, April 1931, pp. 323–7.

42 Le Corbusier (trans. Frederick Etchells), *Towards a New Architecture*, (London and New York, Architectural Press, 1946) pp. 228–9.

43 Ibid. p. 231.

44 Ibid. p. 234.

45 A. Lawrence Kocher and Albert Frey, 'New Materials and Improved Construction Methods', *The Architectural Record*, April 1933, pp. 281–7.

46 These ten items are selected from the list given in A. Lawrence Kocher and Albert Frey, 'New Materials and Improved Construction Methods', *The Architectural Record*, April 1933, p. 281.

47 As part of the Wallace Harrison estate, the Aluminaire House was listed on the National Register of Historic Places prior to its removal to Central Islip.

17 Maison Prouvé, Nancy

Agnès Cailliau

Built in 1954 in only a few weeks, Jean Prouvé's private house (Figure 17.1) is set on a very steep slope on one of the hills surrounding Nancy, on land he acquired at a very low price because it was considered non-constructible.

The house results from the optimisation of:

- adaptation to this beautiful wooded south-facing spot, overlooking Nancy centre. A platform had to be dug, almost as wide as the vertical retaining wall which resulted from the excavation process;
- the recuperation of some products from his Maxeville workshops located close to his property, which had been recently abandoned. ('Le comble est que j'ai dû construire ma maison, principalement avec des éléments de récupération dans le stock à détruire des ateliers');
- Prouvé's revolutionary idea of construction, based on the combination of a light structure and envelope, which was particularly well adapted in this situation.

Prouvé built the house himself with his son and a few friends. His aim was to build a very cheap house, which was designed to last for only a few years. In 1984 the property, which was about to be torn down, was bought by the City of Nancy. The city was pressured by the French Minister of Cultural Affairs who was aware of this heritage as the house had already been registered on the List of Historical Monuments.

Consequently, this 'temporary' house had to last as long as possible in the 'interests of history, art and archaeology . . .' – Prouvé's friends smile when contemplating this contradiction and continue to observe that, once again, he was not understood by the French administration.

Since the imposition of the preservation order, the house had been left empty, more or less neglected; it was occasionally visited by architects and architecture students coming from all around the world, guided by Catherine Coley from the Association A.M.A.L. (Archives Modernes de l'Architecture Lorraine), protector of Jean Prouvé's work.

The structure of the house is quite simple:[1]

- on the north-facing façade, 60 cm away from the high earth wall which is retained with iron rails as employed by the army, stands a double frame of metal profiles counter-braced with a timber filling (Figure 17.2). It supports and protects a 27-m line of cupboards along the entire length of the house. This structure is lined with aluminium on the exterior;
- on the west side, a large pivoting window opens the living room onto a small terrace (Figure 17.3);
- on the south front, three different types of panel enclose the space:
  1 high glass, fixed panels which illuminate the large living room of the house (Figure 17.4);
  2 aluminium panels, perforated with rows of round windows lighting the service rooms, the kitchen, bathroom and main entrance doors of the house (Figure 17.4);
  3 other panels protect the four bedrooms; these include windows, their shutters functioning like 'guillotines' with counterbalance mechanisms being hidden behind the wooden spandrels which allow

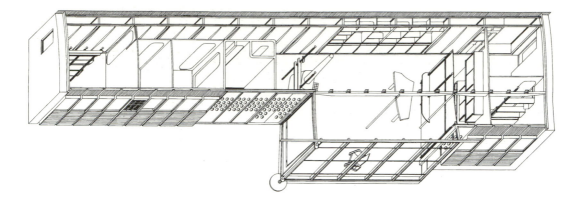

Figure 17.1 Axonometric of la Maison Prouvé showing layout and structure, drawn by Isabelle da Costa
Source: Archives Famille Prouvé, AMAL, Inventaire Général de Lorraine, SPADEM

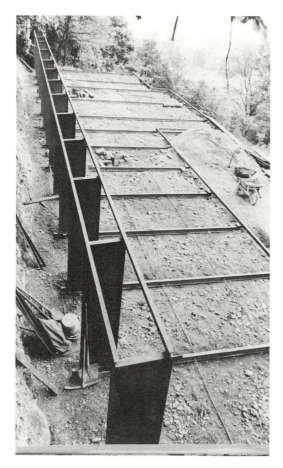

Figure 17.2 North façade double frames of metal profiles on the retained, excavated platform
Source: Archives Famille Prouvé, AMAL, Inventaire Général de Lorraine, SPADEM

Figure 17.3 Large pivoting window and fixed glass panels to the living room
Source: Archives Famille Prouvé, AMAL, Inventaire Général de Lorraine, SPADEM

them to be moved easily up and down;
- the two gable ends of the house are built of masonry. The western pinion is constructed of stone and the eastern one is concrete.

Also in concrete, the floor which incorporates the heating water pipes, was cast directly on the natural ground.

Spanning the external envelope, a curved timber 'vault' made up of linked panels has been constructed (Figure 17.5). These are made from three thin, crossed layers of pine, stuck together. The width of the panel module (1 m) determines the size of each room. On the eastern, larger part of the house (living and dining-room, kitchen and office) the wooden panels are hooked onto an intermediate metal beam, creating an elegant counter-curve in the ceiling. A light aluminium panelled roof covers the house and protrudes significantly on the south front.

Inside, the layout is very simple: a concrete 'nucleus' encloses the bathroom. Elsewhere the internal partitions are made of pine panels. The doors are cut straight out of the material. In order to enable continuous sawing, the four corners of each opening have been rounded, which, associated with the narrow corridor, gives an impression of being on a boat (Figure 17.6). This corridor leads to the bedrooms, just large enough to accommodate a minimum amount of furniture, like small cells, and opens onto the living room, the real heart of the house. There, the northern line of cupboards is reduced in height because they are surmounted with wooden and sheet-iron shelves which feature increases the perceived depth of the living-room.

A concrete free standing fire-place is isolated on the entrance side of the room, decorated with bright coloured ceramics on its front.

To live in this house, hidden in a big garden, would be an incredible opportunity a lot of architects might dream of. The Nancy city administration and Jean Prouvé's friends and family wanted it to 'live' again, after thirteen years of emptiness. They would be happier to see it being occupied by an architect (a specialist in heritage preservation) who would maintain this ephemeral construction in its original function than to preserve an empty nest prone to deterioration and undesirable visits (Figure 17.7).

The 'studio' (Figure 17.8), built by Prouvé further down in the garden, has deteriorated more seriously. It appears to have rusted and a small part of its structure has fractured.

However, the genius of Prouvé (Figure 17.9) is still clearly felt after all these years in many of the houses and gardens which are well preserved, standing in a lovely part of France (Lorraine and Vosges), remote from the busy world.

Figure 17.4 Perforated aluminium panels to service rooms and window panels to the bedrooms
Source: Archives Famille Prouvé, AMAL, Inventaire Général de Lorraine, SPADEM

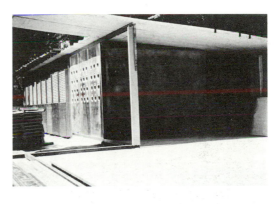

Figure 17.5 Timber roof structure
Source: Archives Famille Prouvé, AMAL, Inventaire Général de Lorraine, SPADEM

Note

1 'In the slatted timber panels can be recognised the Pavillon Démontable, and in the perforated steel doors, perhaps the Maison Métropole. The fact that these elements and others could also be found in his own temporary holiday cabin . . . at Carnac, Morbihan (1946), in the Maison Tropicale (1949), and in the Mame printing works at Tours (1950) shows the flexibility and versatility of this system.' (Part 3 Chapter 1 'Europe and Australia in the 1950s' p. 128 *The Modern Steel House*, Neil Jackson (E. & F.N. Spon 1996).)

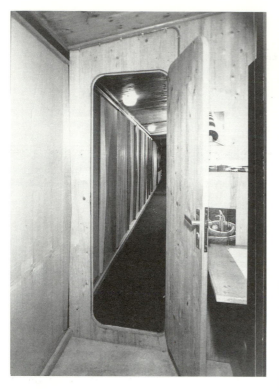

Figure 17.6 Corridor with cupboards
Source: Archives Famille Prouvé, AMAL, Inventaire Général de Lorraine, SPADEM

Figure 17.8 Prouvé's studio
Source: Archives Famille Prouvé, AMAL, Inventaire Général de Lorraine, SPADEM

Figure 17.7 Entrance doors
Source: Archives Famille Prouvé, AMAL, Inventaire Général de Lorraine, SPADEM

Figure 17.9 Jean Prouvé in 1954
Source: Archives Famille Prouvé, AMAL, Inventaire Général de Lorraine, SPADEM

18 Zonnestraal Sanatorium, Hilversum (Jan Duiker)

Wessel de Jonge

Introduction

The conservation and repair of reinforced concrete is one of the many challenges that must be addressed in the preservation of Modern Movement architecture. Distress is common to the minimalist concrete work in many modern buildings and poses great problems, that are now being mastered in technical terms. At the same time, conceptual questions about longstanding principles of material and design authenticity that arise when dealing with such buildings are still under forceful debate among the professions. Jan Duiker's Zonnestraal Sanatorium of 1926–28 for Hilversum, the Netherlands, provides a striking illustration of this dilemma.

Modern Movement: function and time

In the Machine Age, building traditions underwent unprecedented changes. The onset of industrialisation triggered a demand for new types of building exhibiting particular features. The introduction of new materials and developments in construction technology allowed engineers and architects to fulfil these needs to an ever-growing extent.

During the Industrial Revolution the functional programmes became increasingly diverse, more specific and, therefore, short-lived. So did the buildings that were created to respond to such demands. These developments ultimately led to the pioneering works and revolutionary ideas of the Modern Movement.

By the end of the nineteenth century it was mainly the engineers who started to recognise the dimension of time and the transitoriness of architecture. By 1920 architects had become more successful in establishing direct links between user requirements, the design of a building, and its technical lifespan. The consequent translation of these ideas into practice produced the specific architecture of the Modern Movement. Jan Duiker (1890–1935) was among the protagonists of this movement in the Netherlands. In the architectural periodical *de 8 en Opbouw*, the main mouthpiece of the Dutch het Nieuwe Bouwen in the late 1920s and early 1930s, he wrote:

> Why is it that one refuses to view form as the materialisation of the functions demanded from the organism. . . . Here, the question can be put bluntly and clearly, since the shape of the requirements, given the materials and knowledge of our time, leaves only one appropriate form, the functional one. . . . This form . . ., is nothing more than an answer that matches the requirements most directly: the most economic solution.[1]

Duiker clearly considered architecture as a matter of reason rather than style, as illustrated through his many excellent buildings. He regarded buildings as utilities with a limited lifespan by definition, and loved to compare his works with automobiles and aircraft.[2] With Zonnestraal – a sanatorium that was established in the conviction that tuberculosis would be exterminated within thirty to fifty years – he produced the first and arguably most direct response to a shortlived functional programme of his professional life.[3] Thus the transitoriness of modern movement architecture can, in some cases, be understood as part of a design intention. It is obvious that the restoration of such buildings calls for a re-evaluation of traditional preservation doctrines, such as the those included in the Venice Charter and the Operational Guidelines to the World Heritage Convention.[4] Buildings from the Industrial Age require different techniques for conservation and repair. More importantly it is necessary to arrive at a new conceptual approach that will allow us to foster the spirit of modernity. If the characteristics of transitoriness are concealed by advanced restoration techniques for eternity, an artificial memento is all that will be left behind.

Concrete

The concrete structural frame of Auguste Perret's rue Franklin flats in Paris of 1903 heralded one of the most important features in the architecture of the twentieth century. His idea paved the way to the 'Plan Libre', a conception that developed into a major principle and a prime expressive quality of modern architecture in the hands of his one-time apprentice Le Corbusier.

However, many building engineers had already designed structures which anticipated Le Corbusier's theoretical writings even before being widely published. For instance, the Dutch engineer Jan Gerko Wiebenga (1880–1974) designed a remarkably modern Technical School in Groningen as early as 1923, with a full concrete structural frame, light infills, and steel framed windows arranged in horizontal bands. It was the same year that Le Corbusier canonised the free plan in his publication 'Towards a New Architecture', and just three years before Duiker invited Wiebenga to help him work on the Sanatorium.[5]

The structural frame was a precondition for the spatial concepts to accommodate modern life. Concrete was new, versatile, and liberating, but also efficient, hygienic and fire-proof. The visual impact of Modern Movement architecture largely depended upon the impression of lightness, thinness and the minimalist aesthetic that was attainable in fresh concrete.[6]

Despite the long-term practical experience of structural engineers with this 'miracle material', concrete was experimental in its architectural applications.[7] The idea that reinforced concrete constructions would withstand the ravages of time and require no maintenance has proven to be a myth, and today, historic concrete structures are a main concern for the preservation professions.

Duiker

Duiker's entire work reflects a desire to create a clearly comprehensible structure, both in terms of construction and functional/spatial organisation. With the elimination of decorative elements and the often naive manner in which new materials were introduced, this led to a specific image of his architecture. Indeed, the facade of the Zonnestraal Sanatorium was nothing more than a membrane of steel and glass.

To materialise his ideas concerning functional building, Duiker followed a rigorous distinction between loadbearing structure and infill. Related to the idea of varied lifespans was the introduction of prefabrication for building components. Prefabricated parts were mounted on to the structural frame rather than constructed in situ, which allowed for easy replacement in the future. The prefabricated concrete spandrel panels of the Sanatorium were the first to be used in Holland. Directly linked to Duiker's architectural ideas on open plans and rationalisation of construction, are a series of technological innovations. His inventions range from Zonnestraal's pre-cast panels to heating systems such as the radiation ceiling panels of his Open Air School in Amsterdam (1927–8), and his patented hot-air system for the Gooiland Hotel in Hilversum (1934), (which never, unfortunately worked properly).

Like most of Duiker's works, Zonnestraal does not excel in its detailing, and often fails to meet present-day construction standards. Though many assume that such constructions resulted from professional ignorance, research suggests that Duiker, and many likeminded colleagues, were well aware of what they were doing.[8] Apparently, other motives entered into it as well, such as the acceptance of a limited technical lifespan, in line with the functional life expectancy of the sanatorium.

Spiritual economy

Duiker designed his buildings to be as light as possible, with minimum amounts of material being used. The dimensions of the concrete members at Zonnestraal closely follow the moment diagram, and beams are haunched at their supports to take up the shear forces. The necessarily complicated carpentry for formwork was not uneconomic in a period having cheap labour and relatively expensive materials. The aim for optimal construction is referred to by Duiker as 'spiritual economy' which, as he wrote in 1932, 'leads to the ultimate construction, depending on the applied material, and develops towards the immaterial, the spiritual.' [9] The principle of 'spiritual economy' provided the basis for a design process that pairs an artist's inspiration with an engineer's knowledge, an 'engineer's-art'. The 'art' of architecture was to be found in technology itself. Duiker himself compared this with the construction of medieval cathedrals, the bright composition of Bach's fugues and the 'horrifying magnitude' of Einstein's theories.[10]

Back on Mother Earth, optimisation was often a bare necessity, due to the continuous shortage of funds experienced by many of Duiker's clients. He again needed all his 'engineers-art' to make the actual construction of Zonnestraal possible, albeit in two stages. The economy building and a first pavilion for patients were finished in 1928, together with the concrete frame for a second pavilion. The Dresselhuys Pavilion could only be completed in 1931. The complex was to have had two further pavillions to the south, which were never built.

Zonnestraal

The Sanatorium (Figure 18.1) was part of a larger aftercare colony for tubercular patients, that was based on British examples and founded and financed by the National Union of Diamond Workers. Since money was extremely short, a cheap construction method was required. Although the reason for not adopting a timber frame, eminently suitable for sanatoria in Holland at the time, is still unknown, it is obvious that the function benefited from the slender and open construction. The pavilions clearly illustrate how Duiker, with his associate Bernard Bijvoet (1889–1979) and structural engineer Wiebenga, assimilated the

Figure 18.1 Zonnestraal Sanatorium on the edge of the woods, overlooking the moors near Hilversum, shortly after completion of the second pavilion in 1931. Photograph by KLM Aerocarto

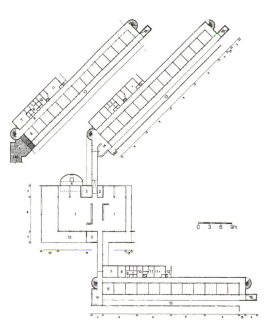

Figure 18.2 Plan of the Dresselhuys Pavilion as completed in 1931. Drawing by the author

concrete frame with the architectural layout that is tailored around the required functions.

Each pavilion consists of two wings linked by a lounge (Figure 18.2). The two-storeyed wings are set at 45° to each other, allowing unhampered views and admitting plenty of daylight. The wings feature parallel girders set off at 3 m, creating a zone for individual patient rooms (Figure 18.3). The

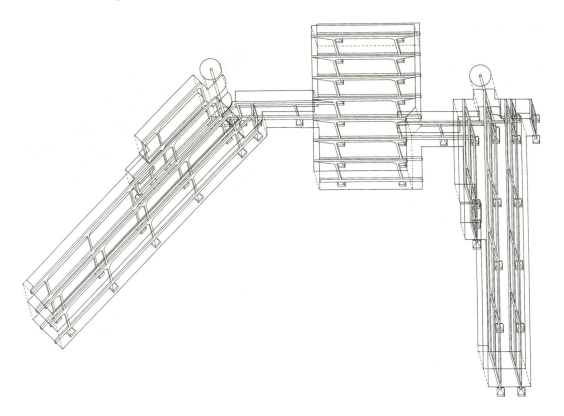

Figure 18.3 Structural frame of the first pavilion. Drawing by the author

cantilevers of the floorslabs provide terraces on the sunward side and a corridor to the north that connects the rooms and links the stairs at both ends. Across the corridor is a small section for services and facilities. One end of each corridor turns a corner to lead to the lounge, the angle of rotation thus being assimilated in both wings. The point of rotation is supplied by the spiral concrete staircase, which provides access to the upper floor and the roof terrace. The structure of all three buildings is entirely based on a 3 m module, from layout to detail. In the structural frame, the girders and beams span typically 9 m with a 3 m cantilever (Figure 18.3). The floor slabs span 3 m from girder to girder, with a 1.50 m cantilever to both sides. In the pavilions even the floor height comes up to the module, consti-tuting a three-dimensional grid. The patient rooms between the girders are 3 × 3 × 3 metres on centres.

The origin of this module appeared to be based not so much on a systematic functional analysis but rather on the Dutch 1918 Concrete Regulations. According to these, the formwork of floors with a span up to 3 m may be removed after a week. With larger spans, a curing period of four weeks had to be allowed. This was a crucial condition in view of the strict six months construction schedule for Zonnestraal.[11]

Concrete technology

In line with Duiker's architectural approach, the frame of the sanatorium buildings has been designed with minimum profiles (Figure 18.5). If the diagram of static moments for the girders is considered, the combination of 9 m spans with a 3 m cantilever seems rather optimal. It allowed minimalisation of structural members, thereby saving precious concrete and creating a minimalist architectural expression. For floor slabs, the combination of 3 m spans with 1.50 m cantilevers seems less economic in static terms. Yet it allowed the use of slabs 12 cm thick at their supports, that taper to a mere 8 cm in the middle of spans and at the cantilevers' perimeter. Even these thin floors have a top and a bottom layer of reinforcement, plus light orthogonal reinforcement to spread tension forces. It is clear that there can hardly be any concrete covering the reinforcement in such cases. It is only in this respect that the concrete frame does not come up to the 1918 requirements. Archival research suggests, however, that the lack of covering arose as much from poor control during construction rather than from design failure.[12] Yet, to expect proper execution with four layers of reinforcement in a 80 mm thick slab, as Wiebenga did, must at least partly be attributed to wishful thinking.

To fill the narrow and complicated formwork, the concrete was watered down to make it more fluid. The high water-to-cement ratio together with the nonhomogeneous mixture of the concrete resulted in an extreme low compression strength in some locations; in some columns similar to that of wet sand (9,4 N/mm²). In addition, concentrations of coarse aggregate have been found, particularly near areas of dense reinforcement. The extreme porosity of the concrete caused the carbonation of the material to reach beyond the reinforcement in most

Figure 18.4 Structural frame of the first pavilion in 1928

cases, depassivating the basic environment of the steel. Finally, chlorides were found in the upper floorslabs of at least the Dresselhuys Pavilion which were partly added to advance curing in winter.

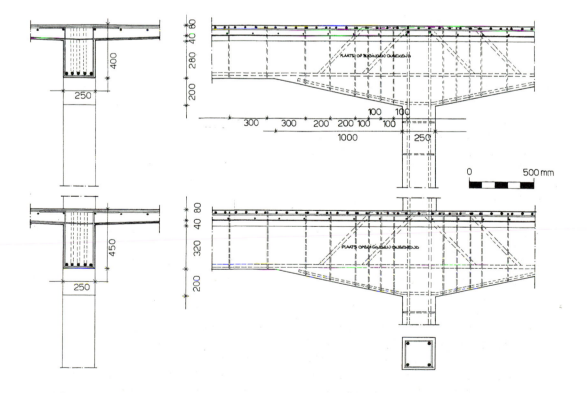

Figure 18.5 Concrete details of the Dresselhuys Pavilion. Drawing by the author

Obsolete

After the Sanatorium was transformed into a general hospital in 1957, numerous extensions were added, mainly to the north of the economy building (Figures 18.6 and 18.7). A series of wooden barracks were

Figure 18.6 The economy building in 1928 (estimate). The glazed façades expose the 'intestines' of the boiler house. Photograph by Eva Besnyö
Source: DOCOMOMO Archives

Figure 18.7 South elevation of the economy building showing the spiral stair to the dining hall on the second floor
Source: DOCOMOMO Archives

scattered all over the estate, compromising the serene clarity of the original layout.

The oldest pavilion was completely refurbished in 1955–8 and stands unrecognisable today. The main building was refurbished around 1976, and the interior arrangements completely changed, partition walls removed and the slender steel-framed windows replaced by aluminium ones.

The Dresselhuys Pavilion was largely left unchanged. After 1973, when the south wing was abandoned, the remaining part of the building served administrative functions for another ten years. Since the early 1980s, the pavilion has stood obsolete as a victim of the elements and local hooligans. Most windows are broken and the concrete is fully exposed to the climate. The damage caused by corroding reinforcement is enormous and parts of this pavilion are today unsafe. Control calculations indicate that, theoretically, the pavilion has collapsed. The frame is supported by the light separation walls which were, of course, never designed to serve this purpose. Fortunately, the other two buildings are in a much better technical condition.

Preservation challenge

Similar to the way the preservation of modern architecture inspires a conceptual debate, so the technical background of these pioneering buildings now presents particular problems to the preservationist. One practical problem is the often poor material quality. In the drive for formal clarity, traditional details such as copings, sills and overhangs, weathering falls and surface relief generally were omitted.[13] Many modern buildings weather very inelegantly and, in contrast to many older structures, a patina on their immaculate envelope rarely suits them. The minimalist aesthetic together with a degree of professional naivety in applying young technologies poses great technical challenges for the preservation profession today. By taking full advantage of material properties, buildings were designed with extreme sensitivity concerning building physics, notably with respect to thermal performance and condensation. Modern architects in the prewar period obviously lacked certain knowledge compared to what we know today. Conceptually speaking, however, a greater problem is that we do not yet know sufficiently what exactly was the extent of their knowledge. Without such relevant information, the relationship between the construction and the original design intentions is hard to evaluate, and we lack a solid basis from which to determine what type of interventions are historically respectful and therefore responsible.

In the mid-1980s, research to identify technical options for the restoration of Zonnestraal suggested two principle and conflicting approaches.[14] If preservation of the architectural ideas is the goal, the deteriorated Dresselhuys Pavilion (Figure 18.8) could be demolished and reconstructed, employing advanced techniques to match the original design. The appearance of such an exact replica would allow us to understand the original design approach, but almost all the materials would have to be renewed. In the Venice Charter and the World Heritage guidelines, however, material authenticity is a key feature. Since the Netherlands Ministry of Culture intends to nominate Zonnestraal for the World Heritage List, reconstruction would probably not be acceptable.

Another option is to repair and reinforce the existing structural frame, again using state of the art contemporary techniques. Although such a restoration would be more expensive than reconstruction, it would be more respectful in terms of the building's material authenticity. However, it might involve fundamental, visible changes to the building, such as the increased dimensions of its beams and columns. This would compromise its design authenticity, in particular Duiker's basic concept of 'spiritual economy'. The conflict between the underlying ideas of the Modern Movement and longstanding preservation principles is evident.

Restoration project

With the aim of preserving the original buildings, several attempts to find a new use for Zonnestraal were undertaken in the last decades. Proper exploitation provides the best opportunities for any building to survive. When compatible, an appropriate new use will also allow for the preservation of the Zonnestraal buildings in their original state.

For some years, the Hilversum General Hospital – the heir and lessee of the buildings – has been searching for a solution. A new set-up as a health care centre has recently been developed into an

Figure 18.8 The Desselhuys Pavilion in 1997 illustrating the ongoing decay. Photograph by Wim Kluvers

integral plan for restoration and extension of the ensemble by the architects Hubert-Jan Henket and Wessel de Jonge. It was found to be a viable proposal in November 1997, after the Netherlands Ministry of Culture decided to raise an earlier promised subsidy to 11 milion Dutch guilders.[15] The proposed new function is close to the original use, and sufficiently compatible with the existing, tailor-made structures.

The centre involves preventive and curative health care, mainly for heart patients, orthopaedic treatment and after-care. Both pavilions will serve as an accommodation for curative patients. The economy building will again be used as the main entrance and reception, along with some general services. The three buildings will be carefully adapted for their new use and restored according to the original, though to varying degrees.

Functions that are unsuitable for the historic buildings – due to their size, layout or technical specifications – will be accommodated in an extension to the north of the economy building, so as not to obstruct the view of the open landscape to the south. The new building will feature additional medical functions, baths and sauna, sports facilities, and accommodation for those who come to Zonnestraal for a three to five-day preventive health care programme. It connects to the economy building through an underground corridor with paramedic functions.

Non-original buildings will be demolished and the natural environment around the original ensemble will be restored. In the future Zonnestraal will again be perceived as the 'Ship on the Moors', as it was originally nicknamed. The works are planned to start with the Dresselhuys Pavilion and the economy building by the end of 1998. When this first stage is finished by the year 2000, the restoration of the third building will follow within a few years.

Various approaches

In order to capture Zonnestraal's spirit of modernity, the original state of the 1931 ensemble has been taken as a reference in terms of layout, function, and architectural and technical solutions (Figure 18.9). The varying condition of the three original buildings suggests a different restoration approach for each of them. The third building was put to its new use in 1995, in anticipation of future restoration. Since it features few original characteristics, the restoration will primarily aim to recreate the balance between the three fragile white pavilions of the original ensemble. The extended structure will be cut back to its original volume. The original façades, which were lost during earlier renovations, will be replaced by similar ones with double glazing to reduce energy consumption. The exterior of the economy building is intended to be reconstructed according to the original. A faithful reconstruction is possible due to the discovery of one original façade when an earlier extension to the building was being demolished in the summer of 1997. The original interior layout is known quite precisely and appeared largely compatible with the new functions required. A sophisticated heating and cooling system has been designed to control draughts and condensation, and to master solar gain in the dining hall on the second floor, without disturbing the original space and details.

The Dresselhuys Pavilion presented the most principled decision of all three buildings. It represents the original to the maximum extent, and needs to be carefully restored. Recent developments now allow us to balance to some extent the two approaches defined in the 1980s. Although the roof slab and the balcony cantilevers will have to be fully rebuilt, advanced concrete repair techniques now allow for two-thirds of the structural frame to be repaired with only marginal visible effects. The concrete covering on the exterior can be increased by replacing the 15 mm layer of plaster by levelled, high performance shotcrete, thereby also slightly increasing the compression strength of the columns. The girders will be additionally supported by the façade substructure, after the foundations have been extended so as to support directly some of the steel posts. A similar solution will be adopted for internal girders, with slender steel columns integrated into the plastered walls between the rooms and the corridor.

Some of the steel framed windows (Figure 18.10) can still be repaired in the work shop, while others will be replaced by windows produced from similar profiles (Figure 18.11). The number of authentic elements and materials compels respect for the original detailing with single pane glazing. A restrained heating system, produced in Britain, is designed to reduce excessive draughts and condensation. A major part of the interior partitions and finishings will be repaired. The remaining original fixtures such as lamps, heating radiators, furniture, washbasins and sinks will be repaired and reinstalled in a few rooms which will be furnished according to the original.

The proposed restoration works for the Dresselhuys Pavilion are expected to respect the material authenticity of the building, without, however, compromising its design integrity.

Conclusion

The value of Modern Movement buildings in particular, must be based on more than their appearance. Understanding the original design approach is critical to the conservation process. In the case of Duiker's works, the bare structures are vital to the original concept (Figure 18.12). His

Figure 18.9 Model of the proposals by Hubert-Jan Henket and Wessel de Jonge. Photograph by Fas Keuzekamp

technological innovations are directly linked to his ideas about the free plan and rationalisation of construction. Even if some of them failed, we must be aware that the experiments of modern engineers and architects represent a historic significance of their own.

The absolute value of materials and construction as applied in modern architecture must not, on the other hand, be overestimated. In view of the limited functional lifespan, most building materials employed in modern structures are shortlived, so that the authenticity of materials is difficult, if not often impossible to maintain.

When speaking about an architectural ideal that pursued industrial building methods and the assembly of machine produced components, one could successfully argue that indeed the very materials are not the essence. The authenticity of appearance, form, detail and spatial qualities is sure to be of more significance. The core of modernity in architecture, however, remains the idea, the conceptual starting points of the original architect.

Notes

1 J. Duiker, 'De nieuwe Fordfabriek te Amsterdam', *De 8 en Opbouw*, 1933, pp. 113–118.
2 J. Duiker, contribution to a brochure on the occasion of the opening of the Cineac newsreel cinema in Amsterdam, 'Handelsblad/Cineac: een gebeurtenis' (an event), 2 November 1932.
3 During the preparatory meetings for the planning of the sanatorium the Board of Zonnestraal indicated a life expectancy of thirty years. The minutes of these meetings are today in the International Institute for Social History in Amsterdam.
4 In 1992, DOCOMOMO was invited by ICOMOS to recommend a revision of the Operational Guidelines to the World Heritage Convention for the inclusion of modern architecture and urbanism in the World Heritage List. ICOMOS, the International Council for Monuments and Sites, is an NGO and the professional advisor to UNESCO's World Heritage Committee. The DOCOMOMO recommendation, *The Modern Movement and the World Heritage List*, was submitted to the Committee in December 1997.
5 Wiebenga left to work in the United States soon after the schools were finished in 1923. After his return in 1926 he published a series of articles that reflect his fascination with a variety of professional issues ranging from rational planning and construction, to functional building and material properties. His involvement in the planning of Zonnestraal and several other key modern buildings in The Netherlands reached far beyond the average professional

Figure 18.10 Present condition of balcony doors in Dresselhuys Pavilion

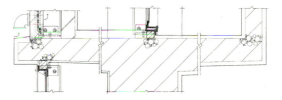

Figure 18.11 The Dresselhuys Pavilion showing thin profiles and façade details. Drawing by the author

involvement of a structural engineer. He advised Duiker on many issues, among others about the finishings to be applied in Zonnestraal, and revised the specifications, which was unusual in The Netherlands. See Bibliography.
6 See J. Allan, (Bibliography) p. 151.
7 O. Wedebrunn, 'A Miracle Material. The Abstract Expression of Concrete', *DOCOMOMO Journal*, 17 (1997), pp. 32–7.
8 See H.A.J. Henket and W. de Jonge, (Bibliography) p. 20.
9 J. Duiker, 'Dr. Berlage en de "Nieuwe Zakelijkheid"', *de 8 en Opbouw*, 5 (1932), pp. 43–51.
10 Ibid. p. 49.
11 See H.A.J. Henket and W. de Jonge, (Bibliography) p. 36, 37.
12 The clerk of the works suffered from a long illness and a young and then still inexperienced technician filled his place most of the time.
13 See J. Allan, (Bibliography) p. 151.
14 The research by H.A.J. Henket and W. de Jonge resulted in a report, that was later summarised and extended with an English summary, (see Bibliography).
15 A subsidy of 6 million Dutch guilders was promised by the Netherlands Ministry of Culture in 1994, with another 2.5 million provided by a private fund, adding up to 8.5 million

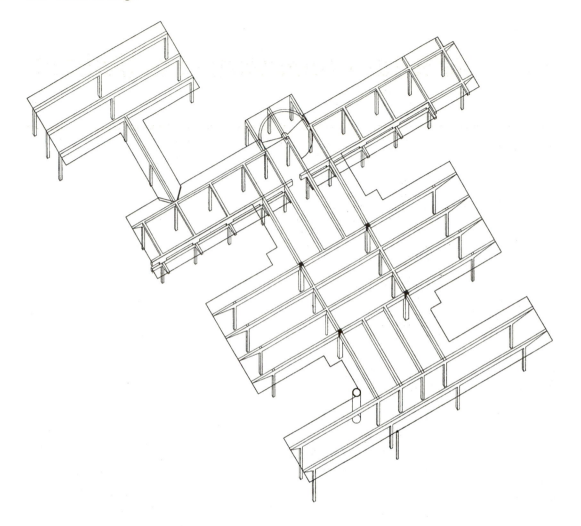

Figure 18.12 The slender structural frame of the main building

guilders. In 1997, the Ministry promised another 2.5 million, thereby increasing the total amount of grants to 11 million. The cost for the restoration and extension are estimated to total 45 million guilders.

Bibliography

J. Allan, 'The Conservation of Modern Buildings', in E. Mills (ed.), *Building Maintenance & Preservation. A guide to design and management* (Oxford, Butterworth Architecture, 2nd revised edition, 1994), pp. 140–80.

W. de Jonge, 'Contemporary Requirements and the Conservation of Typical Technology of the Modern Movement' in H.A.J. Henket and W. de Jonge (eds), *First DOCOMOMO Conference Proceedings* (Eindhoven, DOCOMOMO International, 1991), pp. 84–9.

W. de Jonge (ed.) 'Exposed Concrete', *DOCOMOMO Journal*, 17 (1997).

W. de Jonge (ed.) *The Fair Face of Concrete* (London, Routledge, 1998).

DOCOMOMO International Specialist Committee in Registers, *The Modern Movement and the World Heritage List* (Eindhoven, DOCOMOMO International, 1997).

H.A.J. Henket and W. de Jonge, *Het Nieuwe Bouwen en Restaureren. Het bepalen van de gevolgen van restauratiemogelijkheden* (Zeist/Den Haag, Rijksdienst voor de Monumentenzorg/Staatuitgeverij, 1990); Dutch text with English summary, pp. 96–100.

J. Molema and P. Bak (eds), *Jan Gerko Wiebenga. Apostel van het Nieuwe Bouwen* (Rotterdam, 010 Publishers, 1987); Dutch text.

J. Molema and W. de Jonge, 'Johannes Duiker', *The Architectural Review*, 1055 (1985), pp. 49–55.

J. Molema, *Ir. J. Duiker* (Barcelona, Gili, 1989); English/Spanish text.

19 Villa E-1027 Roquebrune digitalised

Stefan Hecker and Christian F. Müller

The Design of E-1027: Maison en Bord de Mer

The house was built for a 'person who likes work, sports, and likes receiving friends'. With these words Eileen Gray described the purpose of the Maison en Bord de Mer in a special edition of *Architecture Vivante*.[1] She spent the building period 1926 to 1929 almost exclusively at the site in Roquebrune on the French Côte d'Azur. She designed everything herself, from the architecture through the furniture to the smallest details of the interior decoration. The small villa contains the *salle*, two bedrooms, a servant's room and utility rooms. The *salle* was partitioned with screen furniture serving as a living room, dining area, wardrobe, shower or as an alcove for guests if required. The E-1027 was a laboratory for experiments. Gray herself appraised the Maison en Bord de Mer: it 'should not be considered a perfect house where all problems are resolved. It is only an attempt, a moment in a more general research'.

The outstanding quality of the design lies mainly in the close interweaving of the interior and exterior, which were conceived together right from the start. It is the combination of architectural envelope, furniture and the details of the furnishing that provides a strong impression of space.

Eileen Gray learned the metier of architecture in the mid-1920s by herself. Until that time, she had no experience at all of building and so drew upon the support of her friend Jean Badovici, editor of *Architecture Vivante*. This explains the rather strange sounding name, E-1027: E for E(ileen), 10 for Jean (J is the tenth letter in the alphabet), 2 for B(adovici) and 7 for G(ray). Badovici is considered to be the co-

designer of E-1027. Nowadays it is difficult to find out how much Badovici took part in the design process of the house. However, his role may have been mostly that of critic and advisor.

Virtual architecture

Virtual architecture enables us not only to make advanced designs for the future, it also offers new ways of understanding our architectural heritage. Buildings that have been demolished long ago can now be digitally reconstructed and visualised. The virtual reconstruction of Eileen Gray's building demonstrates what possibilities a digital rendering of a demolished building can offer. This chapter sets out to clarify the consequences of such a virtual reconstruction.

A peculiarity and a decisive aspect of a virtual reconstruction of a historic building is that work is being done independently from the object itself. A lost, no longer existing situation can be virtually re-created. In this way, a real-life reconstruction can be prepared up to the smallest details. The computer gives us a precise and comprehensive image of the building. Its design can always and everywhere be virtually experienced. The ETH Zurich[2] in cooperation with the Delft University of Technology[3] were among the first research institutes to introduce the virtual reconstruction of historic buildings. With the help of a computer, Eileen Gray's Maison en Bord de Mer was virtually re-created.

Figure 19.1. *Salle* (large room) *Maison en bord de mer*, original state 1929
Source: Eileen Gray Archive, V&A, London.

Figure 19.2. Salle, virtual reconstruction of original state
Source: Hecker and Müller, 1993.

The fate of Eileen Gray's Villa E-1027

Like so many architectural monuments, fate was against the Villa en bord de mer. After moving to another house Eileen Gray built a few kilometres away, Badovici moved into the house E-1027 in the mid-1930s. His friend Le Corbusier often stayed in the house, and during some of his visits in 1938 and 1939 he painted large murals on what he considered not the best walls of the villa, but on the contrary, 'they burst out from dull sad walls "where nothing is happening". The result – meaningful paintings on indifferent walls and all the fine walls preserved.'[4]

After Badovici's death in the late 1950s the house was bought by a Swiss, and changed ownership again about twenty years later. The new owner had very limited interest in maintaining the building. In 1991 he put a unique set of twenty-eight pieces of furniture up for auction at Sotheby's in Monaco. We immediately initiated a campaign to have the sale cancelled, or at least to preserve the set as an entity. DOCOMOMO International became alarmed by the situation a few days before the sale was scheduled. In just three days an international campaign which they launched was unable to prevent the furniture being dispersed.[5] We had no choice but to document the interiors taking measurements and photographs. The story of this villa became even more grotesque when, in August 1996, the owner was murdered in the house. He must have lived in very strange and sad circumstances in the house for his last days. Today only parts of the building and its furnishings remain, albeit in very poor condition. The future of the house is now more uncertain than ever.

Digital model

The composition of a digital model of the house required several steps. First, all salvaged parts of the building that were still available, and relevant information on the building, were collected, arranged and processed. The actual reconstruction consisted of joining these individual elements together into a three-dimensional, archeological puzzle. The first stage was to re-build, step by step each of the available parts and to insert them into a digital model. Components that were insufficiently documented were compared with the adjoining parts and completed on this basis. It was to prove an advantage that the virtual reconstruction did not have to follow the same process as real-life construction. During the second stage the quality of every surface area had to be examined and defined. The final result is an extremely extensive, detailed model of the house and its furnishings.

A computer program for visualising enables viewers to, as it were, enter the digital model and move through it interactively. Pre-programmed animations and readily available bird's-eye views serve as orientation. Yet, at the same time, the model serves as a data bank. This means that when a certain surface area of the digital model is being 'clicked', background information on the chosen part of the house, or its furnishings, will appear. In this way, original photographs, maps, sketches and descriptions are easily accessible. Finally, the virtual model also allows for an analytical representation of the object. The building's spatial composition as well as, for instance, the construction process can be studied by specifically highlighting certain elements of the building that are isolated in one of the layers of the model, or by compositing specific overlays. The interactive circuit of the virtual model not only provides an impression of a real home, but also the didactic and analytical possibilities of such a representation are highly versatile.

Artifact versus fiction

When the results of the effort are being interpreted, it must be kept clearly in mind that digital work is always an abstraction to represent the real materials involved. The question remains to what extent an abstraction approaches reality. But what exactly *is* the relationship between fiction and the artifact? On the one hand the fictitious object serves as a tool, but on the other hand it is equally a form of documentation. The computer helps us to compose the individual parts into a complete whole as well as rendering the project totally accessible. In this way the method replaces and completes for documentary purposes, the original reality. Certain rules must be followed in order to distinguish the virtual model from the building itself, otherwise there might be a risk that the significance and relevance of the original are taken over by the virtual or, in the worst scenario, replaced by it. Thus, the virtual transformation must always make its reference to the original manifest. The public must be allowed to form their own impressions. In the case of Eileen Gray's villa this has been made possible by including period photographs, descriptions by the architect and indications to distinguish hypothetical parts of the reconstruction, all of which are included in the computer model. Should such indications and references be omitted, the original would, in effect, be betrayed by its virtual equivalent.

A preservationist's dilemma

The potential of virtual reality has consequences for our perceptions of conservation. Taking the case of the Maison en Bord de Mer as an example, there are two very different causes which explain why there is nothing remaining of the original character of the building. At a stroke the original furniture was

Figure 19.3 View towards the guest's balcony and main terrace, original state 1929
Source: Eileen Gray Archive, V&A, London

Figure 19.4 View towards the main terrace, virtual reconstruction
Source: Hecker and Müller, 1993

removed and other fittings destroyed. Moreover, the empty rooms were later dramatically altered by the Le Corbusier murals which were added to the interior without the agreement of the original architect. If the only concern had been the conservation of the house, the National Trust would have been able to reach an easy decision. It is quite clear that the Eileen Gray interiors and Le Corbusier's murals are not compatible. Moreover no authentic work of art by Eileen Gray had been preserved, either in the house or elsewhere. These might be seen as sufficient cause to remove the Le Corbusier paintings and reconstruct the original interiors. However, Le Corbusier's reputation would have made this course of action very risky, if not impossible under French law, due to the classification as a 'Monument Historique'. In addition the setting of these paintings provides interesting insights into his personality, reason enough to preserve the paintings in their locations. A way out of this dilemma can be provided by virtual technologies. The National Trust can search for solutions to restore Eileen Gray's house without removing these traces of its history. At the same time, the original state can be re-created with the help of the computer.

Virtual Disneyland

This example demonstrates that virtual reality provides new options in architectural conservation. The now widely-held view that a historic building should display the various stages of its history and not one random moment in time is reinforced by this technology. The virtual model provides the opportunity to show one or more stages in the history of a building. This task of the National Trust will not, however, be made any easier. Their aim should be to make distinct and important elements which represent the various stages of a building's existence perceptible, and to fulfil this task creatively. Simultaneously assurance is required that virtual reconstructions and presentations do justice to the building and meet scientific criteria. Without such assurance there is the risk that a virtual Disneyland is presented in place of the original reality. Could virtual reality provide the alibi for demolition or disfigurement of an historical building? For example, before the restoration of an archeological excavation, a virtual model could be constructed and certified as an adequate record; this possibility exists, and such incidents do occur. The National Trust has the responsibility of preventing this from happening.

The question whether only second-hand documentation will do adequate justice to the artefact in every respect is certainly justified and must be raised. The answer to the problem can only be given by the object itself and will never depend upon the nature of a visual rendering, however produced. Virtual rendering can contribute to the forming of an opinion. The sense, and nonsense, of an intervention can be examined and debated without affecting the building in question. For each individual object the best possible solution can be determined. It is to be expected that virtual reality will increase understanding, interest and sensitivity with respect to the artefact. With this in mind we return to the issue mentioned above, that the virtual rendering of a historic building allows for a differentiated approach in professional terms. At the same time, a lively representation by a virtual model will advance the cause of opening up our architectural heritage to a wider spectrum of society.

Notes and references

1   Eileen Gray and Jean Badovici, 'E-1027; Maison en Bord de Mer' in *Architecture Vivante*, Paris 11-1929.
2   Professorship for architecture and CAAD, Prof. Dr. Gerhard Schmitt and the Institute for the Preservation of Historical Monuments and Sites, Prof. Dr. Goerg Mörsch.
3   Professorship for Technical Design and Computer Science, Prof. Dr Ir. Sevil Sariyildiz.
4   'Le Corbusier' Oeuvre Complète 1938–1946 (W. Boesinger, Zürich 1946).
5   See *DOCOMOMO International Newsletter* No 6, November 1991, pp. 9–10.

Appendices

APPENDIX A

1. DOCOMOMO

DOCOMOMO is the acronym for the DOcumentation, COnservation of buildings, sites and neighbourhoods of the MOdern MOvement. It is a voluntary organisation, and was founded in 1990 at a conference in Eindhoven, the Netherlands.

The following, known as the Eindhoven Statement, is its manifesto:

- Bring the significance of the Modern Movement to the attention of the public, the authorities, the professions and the educational community concerned with the built environment.
- Identify and promote the recording of the works of the Modern Movement, which will include a register, photographs, archives and other documents.
- Foster the development of appropriate techniques and methods of conservation and disseminate knowledge of these throughout the profession.
- Oppose the destruction and disfigurement of significant works.
- Identify and attract funding for documentation and conservation.
- Explore and develop the knowledge of the Modern Movement.

DOCOMOMO is an interdisciplinary network involving architects, conservation officers, architecture historians, urban and landscape architects, teachers and students, and has active working parties in 36 countries. It has formed International Specialist Committees (ISCs) on Registers, Urbanism and Landscape, Technology, Education, and Publications.

2. DOCOMOMO conferences and symposia

- First International DOCOMOMO Conference *September 12–15, 1990: Eindhoven, the Netherlands* (*Newsletter 3*, pp. 18–24: *Newsletter 8*, pp. 10–12)
- First DOCOMOMO UK Symposium *February 29 – March 1, 1992: London, UK* (*Newsletter 5*, p. 20: *Newsletter 7*, pp. 12–13 and 25)
- First DOCOMOMO NL Seminar *Modern Movement Restored Today July 1, 1992 – The Hague, the Netherlands* (*Newsletter 7*, p. 26: *Newsletter 8*, p. 30)
- Second International DOCOMOMO Conference *September 16–19, 1992: Dessau, Germany* (*Newsletter 5*, pp. 14–16: *Newsletter 6*, pp. 25–26: *Newsletter 8*, pp. 8-11)
- Inaugurating Conference DOCOMOMO Scotland *Visions Revisited* October 10, 1992: Glasgow, Scotland (*Newsletter 8*, pp. 14–16: *Journal 11*, p. 33: *Journal 18*, p. 27)
- Conference – *How to Protect our Modern Movement Architecture* October 15–16, 1992: Stockholm, Sweden (*Newsletter 7*, p. 27: *Newsletter 8*, p. 32: *Journal 10*, p. 35)
- Second DOCOMOMO UK Symposium *March 27, 1993: London, UK* (*Newsletter 8*, p. 33: *Journal 9*, p. 11)
- First DOCOMOMO Italia Symposium *April 27, 1993: Rome, Italy* (*Journal 9*, pp. 12–14 and 26–27)

- First DOCOMOMO Estonia Symposium *May, 1993: Tallinn, Estonia* (*Journal 10*, p. 30)
- Debate on *Preservation of 20th Century Architectural Monuments* May, 1993: Talliin, Estonia (*Journal 10*, p. 30)
- First DOCOMOMO Argentina presentation *May 12–19, 1993: Buenos Aires, Argentina* (*Journal 9*, p. 24: *Journal 10*, p. 29)
- Second DOCOMOMO NL Sympoium – *Postwar Social Housing in the Netherlands 1945–65* July 1, 1993: Rotterdam, the Netherlands (*Journal 10*, pp. 18–19)
- Third International DOCOMOMO Conference *September 14–17, 1994: Barcelona, Spain* (*Journal 10*, pp. 9–11: *Journal 11*, pp. 23–24: *Journal 12*, pp. 8–10 and 12–13)
- First Brazilian DOCOMOMO Seminar *June 12–14, 1995: Salvador, Brazil* (*Journal 13*, pp. 36–37: *Journal 14*, pp. 27 and 31)
- Conference *Swedish Modern Movement Buildings from the 1950s* October 13–14: Stockholm, Sweden (*Journal 13*, p. 58: *Journal 15*, p. 20)
- International Seminar – *Curtain Wall Refurbishment* January 25, 1996: Eindhoven, the Netherlands (*Journal 14*, p. 6: *Journal 15*, p. 4: *Journal 16*, p. 5)
- Fourth International DOCOMOMO Conference *September 18–20: Bratislava/Sliac, Slovakia* (*Journal 13*, p. 9: *Journal 14*, pp. 7–8: *Journal 16*, pp. 6–13)
- International Seminar *Concrete Repair* April 8, 1997: Eindhoven, the Netherlands (*Journal 17*, p. 4)
- Second Brazilian DOCOMOMO Seminar *September 10–12, 1997: Salvador, Brazil* (*Journal 17*, p. 26: *Journal 18*, pp. 32–33)
- First Iberian DOCOMOMO Seminar *November 13–15, 1997: Zaragoza, Spain*
- Workshop – *Preserving 20th Century: Curtain Walls* December 5, 1997: Vancouver B.C., Canada (*Journal 18*, p. 34)
- First Italian DOCOMOMO Conference *January 21–24, 1998: Rome, Italy*
- Four Lectures – *Conservation of Modern Architecture* February 20, March 13, April 3 and May 8, 1998, Leuven, Belgium (*Journal 18*, p. 35)
- International Seminar *Preserving Modern Windows* May 20, 1998: Copenhagen,

Denmark (*Journal 17*, pp. 23–24: *Journal 18*, p. 12)
- Fifth International DOCOMOMO Conference *September 15–19, 1998: Stockholm, Sweden* (*Journal 13*, p. 10: *Journal 15*, pp. 8–9: *Journal 16*, pp. 14–15: *Journal 17*, pp. 6–9: *Journal 18*, pp. 8–9)
- Sixth International DOCOMOMO Conference *September 19–22, 2000: Brasilia, Brazil* (*Journal 16*, p. 15: *Journal 17*, p. 26: *Journal 18*, pp. 32–33)

3. Conferences and symposia supported by DOCOMOMO

- Colloquy on Modern Movement Architecture *April 22–27, 1991: Wroclaw, Poland* (*Newsletter 4*, p. 22)
- International Symposium on *Modern Architecture in Slovakia October 21–26, 1991: Pietany, Czechoslovakia* (*Newsletter 6*, pp. 19–20 and 30)
- Conference on *Modern Movement Architecture of 1920–1930* January 23–24, 1992: Leningrad, Russia (*Newsletter 7*, p. 41)
- Symposium on *Vytautis Landsbergis, Architect* March 10, 1993: Vilnius, Lithuania (*Newsletter 8*, p. 30: *Journal 8*, p. 18)
- Russo-Finnish Seminar on *Viipuri Library* May 21–22, 1993: St Petersburg, Russia and Vyborg, Finland (*Journal 10*, p. 14)
- *International Style Architecture in Tel Aviv May 22–28, 1994: Tel Aviv, Israel* (*Journal 10*, pp. 24 and 32: *Journal 12*, pp. 16–18)
- *Preserving the Recent Past March 30 – April 1: Chicago, USA* (*Journal 10*, p. 13: *Journal 11*, p. 24: *Journal 13*, pp. 15–18: *Journal 14*, p. 4)

4. DOCOMOMO campaigns

- Dr. de Beir House, Belgium (*Newsletter 3*, p. 4: *Newsletter 5*, p. 18: *Newsletter 6*, pp. 44–47) Huub Hoste
- Alexander Fleming House, London, UK (*Newsletter 4*, p. 18: *Newsletter 5* p. 20: *Newsletter 11*, p. 8: *Proceedings 1990*, pp. 296–299) Erno Goldfinger
- Lawn Road Flats, London UK (*Newsletter 4*, p. 18: *Newsletter, 5* p. 20: *Newsletter 8*, p. 30: *Journal 11*, p.35: *Proceedings 1992*, pp. 188–

190) Wells Coates

- Weissenhofsiedlung, Stuttgart, Germany (*Newsletter 4*, p. 21 and pp. 29–32: *Newsletter 5*, p. 20 and others) Mies Van der Rohe
- Technical School, Leuven, Belgium (*Newsletter 5*, p. 17) Henry van de Velde
- Céramique Plant, Maasricht, the Netherlands (*Newsletter 4*, p. 22: *Newsletter 5*, p. 23: *Newsletter 6*, p. 33: *Newsletter 7*, p. 30: *Proceedings 1990* pp. 291–293) Jan Wiebenga
- Dwellings at Wasserwerkstrasse, Zurich, Switzerland (*Newsletter 5*, p. 25 and pp. 30–32: *Proceedings 1990*, pp. 273–275) Max Ernst Haefeli
- Air Terminal, Copenhagen, Denmark (*Newsletter 6*, pp. 8–9 and 30) Vilhelm Laurentzen
- Furniture in Villa E-1027, Roquebrune, France (*Newsletter 6*, pp. 9–10: *Newsletter 7*, p. 5: *Newsletter 14*, pp. 61–64) Eileen Gray
- Narkomfin Flats, Moscow, Russia (*Newsletter 6*, pp. 60–67: *Newsletter 8*, p. 27: *Proceedings 1992*, pp. 275–276: *Journal 14*, p. 10) Moisei Ginzburg
- Bergpolder Flats, Rotterdam, the Netherlands (*Newsletter 7*, p. 26 and pp. 46–49: *Newsletter 8*, p. 30: *Journal 13*, pp. 6–7: *Proceedings 1990*, pp. 80–83; *Proceedings 1992*, pp. 198–203) Willem van Tijen
- Feniks Building, Kraków, Poland (*Newsletter 7*, pp. 26–27: *Journal 10*, p. 40) Adolf Szyszko-Bohusz
- Sveaplan School, Stockholm, Sweden (*Journal 9*, p. 32: *Journal 11*, pp. 34–35: *Journal 15*, p. 17: *Journal 17*, p. 8) Ahbom and Zimdahl
- Cohen House, London, UK (*Journal 9*, pp. 38–40) Eric Mendelsohn
- Gorbals Flats, Glasgow, Scotland (*Journal 9*, p. 33: *Journal 10*, pp. 6–7 and 31) Basil Spence
- Zonnestraal Sanatorium, Hilversum, the Netherlands (*Proceedings 1990*, p. 50: *Proceedings 1994*, pp. 140–142: *Journal 11*, pp. 6–7 and 33: *Journal 13*, p. 36: *Journal 14*, p. 10) Jan Duiker
- Boatstations and Rowing Club buildings, Danube Banks, Slovakia (*Journal 11*, p. 12) Emil Bellus
- Keeling House Flats, London, UK (*Journal 11*, p. 35) Denys Lasdun
- British Rail Road Vehicle Depot, London UK (*Journal 11*, p. 35) Bicknell & Hamilton

5. DOCOMOMO register and documentation of the Modern Movement

The Modern Movement comprises, perhaps, the most significant product of architecture, urbanism and cultural landscape in the 20th Century, and is distinguished by the value systems established in its name. Since 1992 the working parties and the DOCOMOMO International Specialist Committee on Registers have been engaged in documenting modern buildings and sites on two levels. At the first, local, level each working party,* is requested to compile and maintain a *National* or *Regional Register*, an open file recording the local 20th Century heritage and maintaining an on-going survey of modern development by succesive register campaigns.

The second, international, level is the *International Selection*. This is developed from the earlier *International Register*, presented at the Barcelona Conference in 1994 by 15 working parties which reported over 500 buildings and sites. These submissions are stored in the DOCOMOMO Registers archive at the École d'Architecture de Belleville, Paris. A publication will be based on the archive which will form a representative catalogue, a result of the collaborative work of DOCOMOMO International through the working parties.

Criteria for local documentation in National Registers are determined by the respective working parties but are based upon the guidelines established by the Specialist Committee. The guidlines require that selected buildings and sites should be shown to be innovative – technically, socially and aesthetically – and that their historical significance has been evaluated. For buildings and sites of more than local importance these evaluations, with basic factual information, are recorded in standardised format in the *International Selection* fiches. The *IS* criteria for technical, social and aesthetic innovation have provided a valuable qualitative test of 'modernity' which has assisted the Specialist Committee in preparing the tentative list of modern buildings and sites for the World Heritage List.

Modern architecture is essentially seen as innovative (socially, technically and aesthetically) and the *IS* fiche calls for separate assessments under each of these three heads, a brief discussion of the building's historical significance and, where appropriate, evidence of canonic status, that is, the building as a radical prototype for architectural change at national or international level. Selection is not restricted to the 'canonic' but includes the 'ordinary', which exhibit manifestations of national or regional modernity, illustrating the diversity of modern architecture.

About 350 cultural monuments are now inscribed on the World Heritage List, and together they represent a building history of thousands of years. In the twentieth century building production has increased significantly in comparison with previous ages, so that a considered balance is required between 'older' and more recent heritage. The twentieth century heritage, consequently, demands a very selective approach regarding the World Heritage List, recognising the Modern Movement's continuing and vital role in meeting social need.

The agreement between ICOMOS and DOCOMOMO required submission of a world-wide selection of modern buildings and sites of 'outstanding universal value' which might be proposed for the World Heritage List. In the course of conducting this survey it became clear that priority must be given to proper evaluation and application of selection criteria, to distinguish the 'important' from the 'merely famous'. DOCOMOMO has therefore submitted a tentative list, suggesting modern buildings and sites judged to be of World Heritage List significance and quality (see Appendix B Items 4.1 and 4.2; see also 'The Modern Movement Heritage and the World Heritage List' *published November 1997 by DOCOMOMO International*).

* DOCOMOMO Preliminary Registers of Modern Movement Architecture have been composed for:

- Argentina, Belgium, Brazil, Bulgaria, Estonia, Finland, France, Germany, Greece, Hungary, Iberia, italy, Latvia, Lithuania, the Netherlands, Norway, Ontario (Canada), Poland, Québec (Canada), Scotland, Slovakia, Sweden, United Kingdom.

6. Campaigns supported by DOCOMOMO

- Rijksverzekeringsbank, Amsterdam, the Netherlands (*Newsletter 4*, p. 21) D.

Rosenburg
- Library, Viipuri, Russia (*Newsletter 6*, p. 31: *Newsletter 8*, pp. 52–57: *Newsletter 10*, pp. 14–15: *Journal 12*, pp. 5 and 37: *Journal 14*, p. 23: *Journal 16*, p. 23) Alvar Aalto
- Primary School, Badhoevedorp, the Netherlands (*Newsletter 7*, p. 35) Gerrit Rietveld
- Modernist Park, São Paulo, Brazil (*Newsletter 7*, p. 6) Burle Marx
- Bundesschule, Bernau, Germany (*Newsletter 7*, pp. 8–9: *Journal 9*, p. 26: *Proceedings 1992*, pp. 111–116 and 290) Hannes Meyer
- Olympic Stadium, Amsterdam, the Netherlands (*Newsletter 7*, p. 26: *News;etter 8*, p. 30: *Journal 9*, p. 29) Jan Wils
- Hat Factory, Luckenwalde, Germany (*Newsletter 8*, p. 5: *Journal 9*, p/26: *Journal; 17*, p. 5) Eric Mendelsohn
- Villa Muggia, Italy (*Newsletter 8*, pp. 61–63: *Journal 9*, p. 7: *Journal 11*, p. 31: *Journal 13*, p. 7) Piero Bottoni and Mario Pucci
- Villa Müller, Prague, Czech Republic (*Journal 13*, p. 5: *Journal 17*, p. 35) Adolph Loos
- Cineac, Amsterdam, the Netherlands (*Journal 13*, p. 5: *Journal 17*, p. 25) Jen Duiker
- Allen Parkway Village, Houston, Texas, USA (*Journal 13*, p. 8: *Journal 14*, pp. 24–26) MacKie & Kamrath
- Garage des Nations, Geneva, Switzerland (*Journal 14*, p. 4) Braillard Maurice and Pierre and Robert Maillar
- Pastelaria Mexicana, Lisbon, Portugal (*Proceedings 1994*, pp. 174–176) Jorg Chaves
- Schocken Library, Jerusalem, Israel (*Journal 9*, pp. 36–37: *Journal 15*, pp. 9 and 12: *Journal 17*, pp. 5 and 14–15) Eric Mendelsohn

7. Watchdog projects

- Rijnlands Lyceum, Wassenaar, the Netherlands (*Newsletter 4*, p. 21: *Newsletter 8*, pp. 58–60) Jan Piet Kloos
- The WUWA Estate, Wroclaw, Poland (Newsletter 4, pp. 2 and 37–39)) Herrman Wahlich and Paul Heim
- Bata Colony, Möhlin, Switzerland (*Newsletter 6*, p. 35)

- French-Japanese house, Tokyo, Japan (*Newsletter 7*, p. 27) Yoshizika Takamasa
- Dairy Farm, Plauen, Germany (*Journal 9*, p. 26)
- Swimming Pool, Haarlem, the Netherlands (*Journal 9*, p. 29) J.B. Van Langhem
- Södra Ängby, Stockholm, Sweden (*Journal 9*, p. 32: *Journal 17*, p. 8)
- Concert Hall, Helsingborg, Sweden (*Journal 9*, p. 32) Sven Markelius
- Bethnal Green Housing, London, UK (*Journal 9*, p. 33: *Journal 18*, p. 31) Denys Lasdun
- Klingsberg Cinema, Oslo, Norway (*Journal 10*, p. 33: *Journal 18*, p. 33) Blakstad & Eliassen Vestkantbadet
- Country House 't Kôrnegoar, Enschede, the Netherlands (*Journal 11*, p. 33:*Journal 12*, p. 38) J.B. Van Loghem
- Van Nelle Factories, Rotterdam, the Netherlands (*Journal 13*, p. 38: *Journal 16*, p. 24: *Journal 17*, p. 27) Brinkman and van der Vlugt
- Hvalstrand Bath, Oslofjord, Norway (*Journal 18*, p. 34) Schistad and Moestue
- Hvalstrand Public Bath, Oslo, Norway (*Journal 18*, p. 34) A. Peters

8. Exhibitions

- Modern Architecture Restored *July 20 – August, 1992 – Cambridge, UK*. This exhibition later travelled to Dessau, Breda, Switzerland and Canada (*Newsletter 7*, pp. 18–19 and 25: *Newsletter 8*, p. 33: *Journal 10*, p. 31: *Journal 11*, p. 35: *Proceedings 1992*, p. 286)
- Moisei Ginzburg *March 1993 – Moscow, Russia, under the auspices of DOCOMOMO* (*Journal 9*, p. 18)
- Scotland and the Brave new World: Postwar Architecture in Scotland *August 16, 1993 – Edinburgh, Scotland* (*Journal 9*, pp. 20 and 35)
- Gabo and the Soviet Palace *October 15–19, 1993 – Moscow, Russia, under the auspices of DOCOMOMO* (*Journal 10*, pp. 20 and 35)
- A + PS: Alison and Peter Smithson *January 20 – February 19, 1994 – London, UK*. This exhibition later travelled to Newcastle, Edinburgh, Aberdeen, Bath and Spain (*Journal 10*, p. 31: *Journal 11*, p. 35)
- Avantgarde Soviet Architecture 1924–1937

March 13 – May 15, 1994 – Rotterdam, the Netherlands, under DOCOMOMO auspices. The exhibition later travelled to St. Gallen, Switzerland (*Journal 11*, p. 22)
- Instruments of Modernity: Armstrong, Frey, Neutra, *September 7 – 30, 1994 – Barcelona, Spain, co-ordinated by DOCOMOMO* (*Journal 11*, p. 35)
- Connel, Ward & Lucas *September 2 – 24, 1994, London, UK* (*Journal 12*, p. 27)
- Tallinn Arts hall 1934 *February 1995, – Tallinn, Estonia* (*Journal 14*, pp. 28–29)
- Old Town and Modern Buildings *June – September, 1995 – Tallinn, Estonia* (*Journal 14*, pp. 14–15 and 29)
- Windows to the Netherlands: Van Loghem and Wiebenga *May 1998 – Moscow, Russia, under the auspices of DOCOMOMO* (*Journal 18*, pp. 19–19)
- Rimanóczy Gyula (1903–1958) *September 1998 – Bratislava, Slovakia, prepared by DOCOMOMO Hungary* (*Proceedings 1996*, p. 260: *Journal 16*, p. 11)

9. DOCOMOMO publications

- DOCOMOMO Newsletter 1 – *August, 1989 – International*
- DOCOMOMO Newsletter 2 – *January, 1990 – International*
- DOCOMOMO Newsletter 3 – *June, 1990 – International*
- DOCOMOMO Newsletter 4 – *March,1991 – International*
- Conference proceedings – First international DOCOMOMO Conference, Sept. 12–15, 1990 *March, 1991 – Eindhoven, the Netherlands*
- DOCOMOMO Newsletter 5 – *June, 1991 – International*
- DOCOMOMO Newsletter 6 – *November, 1991 – International*
- DOCOMOMO Newsletter 7 – *June, 1992 – International*
- 'Take Care of our Functionalist Inheritance!' – *October, 1992 – Stockholm, Sweden* (*Newsletter 7*, p. 27: *Newsletter 8*, p. 32)
- DOCOMOMO Newsletter 8 – *January, 1993 – International*
- DOCOMOMO Journal 9 – Special Edition:

Technology – *July, 1993 – International*
- DOCOMOMO Journal 10 – *November, 1993 – International*
- Conference Proceedings – Second International DOCOMOMO Conference, Sept.16–19,1992 – *November, 1993 – Dessau, Germany*
- DOCOMOMO Journal – Special Edition: North America – *June, 1994 – International*
- Top Register – Slovakia, 1st Proposal – *June, 1994 – International*
- DOCOMOMO Journal 12 – Special Edition: Metal - *November, 1994 – International*
- DOCOMOMO Journal 13 – Special Edition: Latin America – *June, 1995 – International*
- Conference Proceedings – Third International DOCOMOMO Conference, Sept. 14–17, 1994 *November, 1995 - Barcelona, Spain*
- DOCOMOMO Journal 14 – Special Edition: The Image of Modernity – *November, 1995*
- DOCOMOMO Journal 15 – Special Edition: Curtain Wall Refurbishment – *July, 1996 International*
- Technology Expertise Database – *August, 1996 – International*
- Top Register – Czech Republic, 1st proposal – *September, 1996 – Brno, Czech Republic*
- Curtain Wall Refurbishment: a Challenge to Manage – Preservation Technology Dossier 1, Seminar Proceedings, January 25, 1996 – *March, 1997 – International*
- DOCOMOMO Journal 16 – Special Edition: Urbanism, Gardens & Landscape – *March 1997 – International*
- DOCOMOMO Journal 17 – Special Edition: Exposed Concrete – *September, 1997 – International*
- The Modern Movement and the World Heritage List – advisory report to ICOMOS composed by DOCOMOMO International Specialist Committee on Registers – *November 1997 – International*
- Conference Proceedings – Fourth International DOCOMOMO Conference, Sept. 18–20 1996 *September, 1997 – Bratislava. Slovakia*
- DOCOMOMO Journal 18 – *February, 1998 – International*
- The Fair face of Concrete: Conservation and Repair of Exposed Concrete – Preservation Technology Dossier 2, Seminar proceedings, April 8, 1997 – *April, 1998 – International*

APPENDIX B

1. International agencies include:

ICOMOS: the International Council on Monuments and Sites is a non-governmental body composed of specialists drawn from over 50 nations professionally concerned with conservation.

Its aims are to pioneer conservation by establishing a philosophically consistent approach internationally as the basis for a working framework for evaluation and grant aiding.

Its membership consists of appointed representatives of participating countries. Its activities include:
- establishing a series of Charters e.g. the Venice Charter (1964), the Burra Charter (Australian Branch 1979);
- drawing up a list of buildings considered worthy of inclusion by the World Heritage Council to which DOCOMOMO International is submitting a list within its own member countries.

THE COUNCIL OF EUROPE: in 1988, under the auspices of the Council of Europe Steering Committee for the Integrated Conservation of Historic Heritage, the first meeting took place in Strasbourg and three areas of work were identified:
- preparation of inventories and selection criteria;
- problems of legal protection;
- physical conservation and dissemination of information for education of political decision-makers and the public.

2. Council of Europe Proposal 1991

At a meeting in Barcelona in 1990 a committee of the Council of Europe agreed an outline for a policy on the protection of the twentieth-century architectural inheritance in Europe. In 1991 their proposal was adopted by the Committee of Ministers to member states of the Council, resulting in a recommendation for the:
- identification of significant items;
- management and training in modern conservation;
- the promotion of awareness and European co-operation.

3. The World Heritage List criteria

The *Operational Guidelines* (UNESCO) state the current criteria in article 24 as follows: 'A monument, group of buildings or site – as defined above – which is nominated for inclusion in the World Heritage List will be considered to be of outstanding value for the purpose of the Convention when the Committee finds that it meets one or more of the following criteria and the test of authenticity. Each property nominated should therefore:

   (a) (i) represent a masterpiece of human creative genius; or

      (ii) exhibit an important interchange of human values, over a span of time or within a cultural area of the world, on developments in architecture or technology, monumental arts or town planning and landscape design; or

      (iii) bear a unique or at least exceptional testimony to a cultural tradition or to a civilisation which is living or which has disappeared; or

      (iv) be an outstanding example of a type of building or architectural or technological ensemble or landscape which illustrates (a) significant stage(s) in human history; or

      (v) be an outstanding example of a traditional human settlement or land-use which is representative of a culture (or cultures), especially when it has become vulnerable under the impact of irreversible change; or

      (vi) be directly or tangibly associated with events or living traditions, with ideas, or with beliefs, with artistic and literary works of outstanding universal significance (the Committee considers that this criterion should justify inclusion in the List only in exceptional circumstances or in conjunction with other criteria cultural or natural); and

   (b) (i) meet the test of authenticity in design, materials, workmanship or setting and in the case of cultural landscapes their distinctive character and components (the Committee stresses that reconstruction is only acceptable if it is carried out on the basis of complete and detailed documentation on the original and to no extent on conjecture);

      (ii) have adequate legal and / or traditional protection and management mechanisms to ensure conservation of the cultural property or cultural landscapes. The existence of protective legislation at the national, provincial or municipal level or well-established traditional protection and / or adequate management mechanisms is therefore essential and must be stated clearly on the nomination form. Assurances of the effective implementation of these laws and / or management mechanisms are also expected. Furthermore, in order to preserve the integrity of cultural sites, particularly those open to large numbers of visitors, the State Party concerned should be able to provide evidence of suitable administrative arrangements to cover the management of the property, its conservation and its accessibility to the public.

During the preparation of this report the World Heritage Committee reconsidered the guidelines and made some revisions, while the WPS continued to use the amended version of December 1994. So, when the tests were running, the term *technology* had not yet entered the two later revised criteria (a), (ii) and (iv). This extension reflects a more positive additude towards both industrial and recent heritage and might also favour modern architecture which focuses on appropriate use of industrial resources.

4. World Heritage List

As an illustration of the DOCOMOMO contribution to compiling the World Heritage List, the following are examples of two recommendations made to enhance the range of entries – for a full record see *The Modern Movement and the World Heritage List – advisory report to ICOMOS composed by DOCOMOMO's International Specialist Committee on Registers* – 30 November 1997.

4.1 The World Heritage List (December 1996) inscribed the following: .

Country	City	Site	Architect	Year
BRAZIL	Brasilia	Lay-out / public buildings	Lucio Costa/Oscar Niemeyer	1957–60
GERMANY	Dessau/Weimar	Bauhaus and its sites	Walter Gropius	1925–26
			Henry van der Velde	1904–06
			Georg Muche	1923
SWEDEN	Stockholm	Woodlands Cemetery	Asplund and Lewerentz	1918–40

4.2 DOCOMOMO International has recommended the *oeuvres* of the following architects should be considered of outstanding universal value:

Alvar Aalto (1898–1976) – Paimio Sanatorium: Villa Maireia: Sunila – Factory and Housing: Säynatsälo Town Hall.

Le Corbusier (1887–1965) – Villa Savoye, Poissy: Weekend House, St Cloud: Unité d'Habitation, Marseilles: Notre-Dame du Haut, Ronchamp: Chandigarh, layout and public buildings, Punjab.

Ludwig Mies van der Rohe (1886–1969) – Tugendhat House, Brno, Czech Republic: lake Shore Drive Apartments, Chicago: Crown Hall, Illinois Institute of Technology, Chicago: Seagram Building, New York.

Frank Lloyd Wright – Unity Chapel, Chicago: Robie House, Chicago: Falling Water, Bear Run: Johnson Wax Factory, Racine: Usonian Houses: Guggenheim Museum, New York.

DOCOMOMO International has further recommended consideration of the following buildings and sites as of outstanding universal value:

Country	City	Site	Architect	Year
BRAZIL	Belo Horizonte	Pampulha complex	Oscar Niemeyer	1943
		Garden	Roberto Burle Marx	1943
CANADA	Montreal	Habitat '67	Moshe Safdie	1964–67
CZECH REP.	Prague	Müller House	Adolph Loos	1930
	Zlín	Bat'a Company Town	K.L. Gahura, V. Karfíc *et al*	1920–50
DENMARK	Århus	Town Hall	Arne Jacobsen + E. Moller	1937–41
FRANCE	Villejuif- Paris	Karl Marx Schools	André Lurçat	1929
	Le Havre	Reconstructed City	Auguste Perret *et al*	1945–60
GERMANY	Frankfurt/Main	Housing estates	Ernst May *et al*	1927–28
	Löbau	Schminke House	Hans Scharoun	1933
	Potsdam	Einstein Tower	Eric Mendelsohn	1920–24
	Stuttgart	Weissenhof Estate	Ludwig Mies van der Rohe	1927
			Peter Behrens/J.J.P. Oud	
			Victor Bourgeois/	
			A.G. Schneck	
			Le Corbusier/J. Frank	
			Mart Stam/Hans Scharoun	
ITALY	Como	Casa del Fascio	Giuseppe Terragni	1928–36
	Turin	Exhibition Pavilion	Pier Luigi Nervi	1947–48 and 1953
JAPAN	Tokyo	Nagakin Capsule Tower	Kisho Kurokawa	1971
	Tokyo	Olympic Halls	Kenzo Tange	1961–64

NETHERLANDS	Amsterdam	Orphanage	Aldo van Eyck	1955
	Rotterdam	Van Nelle Factories	J.A. Brinkman/	
			L.C. van der Vlugt	1928–31
	Utrecht	Schröder House	Gerrit Th Rietveld	1924
RUSSIA	Moscow	Narkomfin Collective Housing	Moisei Ginsburg	1932
	Moscow	Russakov Club	Konstantin `Melnikov	1927–29
SWITZERLAND	Zürich	Dolderthal Apartment buildings	A. & E. Roth/ Marcel Breuer	1933
UK	Bexhill-on-sea	De La Warr Pavilion	Eric Mendelsohn/ Serge Chermayeff	1934
	London	Highpoint I and II	Berthold Lubetkin & Tecton	1934–38
USA	New York	Lever House	SOM/Gordon Bunshaft	1952
	Pacific Palisades	Case Study House no. 8	Charles and Ray Eames	1947–49
	Philadelphia	Philadelphia Savings Fund Bank	George Howe/William Lescaze	1932
	Philadelphia	Richards Medical Research Building	Louis Kahn	1957–65

Index